The Whole Kitty CATalog

The Whole Kitty CATalog

More than 800 Terrific
Toys, Treats, and True Cat Facts—
for You and Your Kitty!

by John Avalon Reed

Crown Trade Paperbacks   New York

Dedicated to the belief that all life is precious and that this day—this one fleeting moment in the series of moments that make up our lives—is a gift.

Published by Crown Trade Paperbacks, 201 East 50th Street, New York, New York 10022. Member of the Crown Publishing Group.

Random House, Inc. New York, Toronto, London, Sydney, Auckland

http://www.randomhouse.com/

Crown Trade Paperbacks and colophon are trademarks of Crown Publishers, Inc.

Design by Barbara Balch

Printed in the United States of America

Library of Congress Cataloging-in-Publication Data is available upon request.

ISBN 0-517-88689-8

10 9 8 7 6 5 4 3 2 1

First Edition

Acknowledgments

A special thanks to the hundreds of individuals and companies that lent their enthusiastic support to the creation of this book. From big to small, they all, in their own ways, show their love of cats with the creations you see in this book. Special thanks to the two resident cat geniuses of the house, Rollo and Bella; to my agent, Felicia Eth, a cat lover who has the uncanny ability to laugh, and believe, at the same time; and to Wendy Hubbert, a "cat person" and my editor at Crown, who had the fortitude to take a big dream and urge it gently along to reality. Serious thanks to Mary Jo, who accepted my baffling writing schedule; my dear son, Addison, and his teenage enthusiasm for life; Mike, Abbie, and Lisa for their easy, warm support; the many animal behaviorists on the forefront of a new acceptance for life in all its forms; and to the beautiful state of California, where anything still seems possible . . . and is.

Contents

Introduction: The First-Ever
Whole Kitty CATalog

Welcome to an amazing collection of quality products, books, and services for cat owners. In this catalog, you'll find incredible one-of-a-kind products from all over the world, celebrating cats and their owners. Though I call them products, most are truly works of art—lovingly produced crafts and inspirations that mean as much to their creators as they do to you. Many are made by small to tiny companies that have put their hearts in their work. They love cats. They care deeply about what they make, often starting their business as a hobby, believing fully in the precept "Do what you like, and the money will follow."

She had given me much pleasure over the years. But things had gotten out of hand, out of control.

I'd thought about this conversation for a long time. It would be hard. But it had to be.

Looking back, I suppose it was my fault. After all, she did like to live well, and who could blame her? I loved to see her happy, but something needed to be done. This constant spending and spending, running up the credit cards, writing checks left and right . . . it had to stop. Burning up the phone lines with purchases on 800-numbers. Faxes. Stamps and letters and order forms. Endless. Did she think I was made of money?

First it was a new house. Then jewelry. Catered food began to arrive almost daily, along with endless baubles (toys, really). It didn't stop there. Last week a commissioned, framed oil painting arrived, of—who else?—Her Majesty. There it was, in a gorgeous gold frame, a beautiful likeness, right over the fireplace. Could we afford this? It was as though she had never spent money before, never truly lived life, as though she had been turned loose with a vaultful of cash to have fun without a care in the world. Each day as the FedEx and UPS trucks left the driveway, I heard squeals of delight as she strewed packages and wrapping about the house. I began to worry that the torrent of modest purchases would turn into a customized red Ferrari, or a new five-level luxury home. We had to talk.

I caught her at a good time. Drowsy in the warmth of a sunny afternoon, she reclined on her brand-new cushioned sofa. As I drew close, before I could get out a single word, she gave me a look that melted all my resolve. I was putty in her paws.

"Meow," she said, purring as she resumed her nap. I picked up her well-worn copy of *The Whole Kitty CATalog*. She did have a birthday coming soon, after all, and she'd certainly need a reward after her next trip to the veterinarian . . .

The shopping, I realized, had just begun.

If you've picked up this book, chances are you understand and share their passion. We cat lovers are a dedicated bunch, and we want only the best for our kitties. I put this book together because I just couldn't buy enough stuff for my two beautiful Himalayans, Rollo and Bella. So in these pages you'll find more than 600 fabulous toys, treats, and health-and-grooming products; more than 125 terrific fiction and nonfiction cat books for adults and children; and 100 True Cat Facts—intriguing and useful cat trivia and all-natural tips for the care and well-being of your cat.

You'll notice that for all these products, I've provided specific addresses and phone numbers for contacting the makers and/or distributors. Here are some ordering guidelines.

1. In general, check your local pet or specialty store for those items I've marked with a . This means you're likely to find the item sold at retail. If you're unable to find a product at retail, call or write the manufacturer to learn where you can find it or if you can order it directly from them. Most of the books I've reviewed here are available through bookstores, but you can contact the publisher to order if you'd prefer.

2. If there's no by a product, contact the manufacturer to discuss your purchase. You may find the item at retail, but the manufacturer will help you direct-order, if you'd like.

3. If I've provided detailed shipping-and-handling information for a product, it means you're not likely to find the item at retail, and the manufacturer is set up to take your order through the mail or over the telephone. Call or write to place your order.

Finally, since I've selected only a few of the best products from each manufacturer, you should be sure to ask about a catalog of their other products if you're interested. They will almost all send you a free catalog if you ask, so within *The Whole Kitty CATalog* I've singled out only those catalogs for which you'll have to pay a dollar or two.

Cats are utterly unique. The dog hunts and retrieves. The horse is used for transportation and labor; the donkey and mule have a tedious monotony to their workday world. The caged bird, the fish in a bowl, the hamster in a cage . . . these are our pets, the "domesticated" creatures that serve man in one way or another.

But the beauty of the cat is that it serves no one. It chooses whom it loves, and what it does, and how it lives. Cats are the last free animals in our daily life, and that's a big reason why we love them. I hope you'll enjoy this world of expression—celebrations of our love of cats, and their freedom.

The Whole Kitty CATalog

Chapter One

The Best Kitty Toys

The Bag "Sound Machine" ®

Cats love the crinkle of paper bags. This clever polyethylene toy sack produces a crinkle sound that entertains cats for hours. In and out, rolling around . . . cats crawl, play, even *sleep* inside it. Measuring 19″ × 13″, it's specially made of high-density polyethylene sewn between two poly-cotton layers. Machine-washable, with attractive eyelet lace sewn around the opening. You'll be able to hear Kitty playing for hours. Lots of laughs and fun.

Kitty Krinkle Sack, $15.99

Flexi-Mat Corporation
2244 S. Western Ave.
Chicago, IL 60608
(312) 376-5500

Chasin' Round the House!

The Motorized "Krazy" Ball just keeps going and going as an action toy and exerciser. It rolls and swivels, indoors or out, over and under almost everything. Endless fun for your cat! It requires a single AA battery (not included) to operate.

Motorized "Krazy" Ball, $7.99 + $5.99 S&H (Wis. res. add 5% sales tax)

Drs. Foster & Smith
P.O. Box 100
Rhinelander, WI 54501
(800) 562-7169

Cat Astrology: The Complete Guide to Feline Horoscopes

Astrology for cats? There just might be some unexplained reason for the chemistry between you and your furry friend. This pretty hardcover book is just the way for you to explore the "heavenly" bond you both share. Nicely illustrated with rambunctious full-color drawings that capture fun cat personalities.

By Michael Zullo, 1993, 82 pp., $14.95

3361 Flagler Ave.
Key West, FL 33040
(305) 292-1068

Mr. Mouser's Catch-of-the-Day

I love things made one at a time by hand. In this crazy, busy world of fast food and fast everything, it's nice to find this carefully hand-sewn cat toy by Jeanine Corbin. Very lifelike and cute as can be; you pull it around with the attached string as you play with your cat. Great toy for your mouser!

Meggie Mouse, $4 + 50¢ S&H (Calif. res. add 31¢ sales tax)

Silver Dollar Sheep Station
5020 Winding Way
Sacramento, CA 95841
(916) 489-8742

Rockin' & Rollin' with the Domino ®

Kitty's bouncing and grabbing for that glitter ball again . . . rockin' all day long. Sticks his paws in the hole while the whole contraption seesaws up and down. Interactive; engages bored brains. Mini roller-coaster action; big fun!

Cats Domino, $6.96

Information:
Designer Products, Inc.
P.O. Box 201177
Arlington, TX 76006
(817) 469-9416

Stinky Snake, Rabbit Racer, & Kiddy Puff with Feathers

Blastoff! Instant insanity for cats! Unroll the rawhide on the smooth wand and the action starts. Fabulous slides and acrobatics! I can't recommend these wands too highly for all-out, intensive playtime. All I have to do is get one out and my previously disinterested cats race across the floor, leaping in the air, eager to sink their teeth and claws into these wonderful playthings. Stinky Snake comes with the added attraction of catnip. These are great, great toys and, if you ask me, priced way too cheaply. Good exercise for the kitties; amusing, mindless escape for you. I like them best on a slick wood floor or on linoleum. Highest recommendation for Kiddy Kompany, a small family-run business that makes beautiful and lasting toys.

Stinky Snake, $5.95
Rabbit Racer, $5.95
Kiddy Puff with Feathers, $5.95
Each play wand, $5.95; all three for $16.95
Orders shipped COD + S&H

Kiddy Kompany
P.O. Box 1211
Pleasanton, CA 94566
(800) 724-2287

Entertainment for Cats

I don't know what they think about it, but my cats watch TV. I try to get them involved when a good nature show is on, preferably something with birds or lions —something they can relate to. They sit on the bed and follow the action like spectators at a tennis match. *Video Catnip* is especially interesting for house cats, who can only wish for and dream about all the action on the screen. It features birds, squirrels, and chipmunks professionally videotaped in a backyard setting and designed for cats to watch. Get this: more than 100,000 copies sold. Highly recommended.

Video Catnip, 25 minutes, VHS, $19.95

PetAvision, Inc.
P.O. Box 102
Morgantown, WV 26507
(800) 521-7898

The Story of Blue Rat

God bless her; here comes Judith McCullough from Hatboro, Pennsylvania, on a mission to create maximum fun and havoc for America's cats. She stuffs all her toys with premium organic catnip, which she hand-picks for that *wild* cat-attracting scent. At this very moment, thousands of cats everywhere are delirious with rapture, sniffing, chewing, and rolling around with the Cat Carrot, Le Mouse, Heart on a String (for the kitty who's close to your heart), and Magic Catnip Stick, making fools out of themselves. Blue Rat is especially cool. Colorful, handmade, superpotent catnip toys.

Cat Carrot, $4.99
Magic Catnip Stick, $3.99
The Nip, $1.99
Heart on a String, $3.99
The Best Catnip on Earth, (2″ × 2″ bag), $1.99; (large, 3″ × 4″ bag), $3.99 (add $1 S&H for each item)

Blue Rat
229 Green Lane Terrace
Hatboro, PA 19040
(215) 443-8681

Scratch Me Every Day

Finally, hanging scratch toys that look nice. More important, cats really do use them. Heavily weighted to provide stability while kitty scratches away, they're attractive and, at this price, they're a bargain. Inside the mouse with red ears there's a hollow compartment with rattles for extra fun. And each one has a bell attached for added interest. Simple pleasures.

Hanging Fish Scratcher (16″ l), $9.99 + $5.99 S&H
Hanging Mouse Scratcher (13″ l), $9.99 + $5.99 S&H (Wis. res. add 5% sales tax)

Drs. Foster & Smith
P.O. Box 100
Rhinelander, WI 54501
(800) 562-7169

Fun With Mrs. Thumb

Mrs. Thumb, a genteel wooden doll, lived happily in her pretty dollhouse until a kitty came along and decided to poke his paws through every window. It's fun for the cat, but for Mrs. Thumb . . . well, you and your child can decide.

Delightful illustrations by Nicola Bayley; this hardcover is for young children.

By Jan Mark, 1993, 30 pp., $9.95

Candlewick Press
2067 Massachusetts Ave.
Cambridge, MA 02140
(617) 661-3330

Hanukcats ®

Twenty traditional Jewish songs have been rewritten in this hardcover from a cat's point of view. Join in the fun and sing along. "Hava Nagila" becomes "Have a Burrito" and "Kemah, Kemah" becomes "K mart, K mart." Oy! Year-round giggles, big emphasis on food and fun. So where's the chopped liver?

By Laurie Laughlin, 1995, 48 pp., $6.95

Chronicle Books
275 Fifth St.
San Francisco, CA 94103
(800) 722-6657

Scratching the Itch

Do what you will, cats will scratch. They have to. Some scratch while all stretched-out on the carpet. Some like to stand on what they scratch and shred it to bits. This catnip-laced goody is perfect for your little angel to tear into, instead of your curtains. Measures 9″ × 11″. Your cat (and you) will feel much better after a good "scratch out."

Cat Scratch, $6.10

Designer Products, Inc.
P.O. Box 201177
Arlington, TX 76006
(817) 469-9416

Stop, Then Go, Lizard Action

Bella, my Himalayan, fell asleep (horrors!) watching this cat entertainment tape. But these things happen, and there's no accounting for taste with cats anyway. The soundtrack's not bad—outdoor sounds, including birds —but the action consists of a few brilliant moments— lizards dashing off with their peculiar wiggling movement, then long pauses as the lizards contemplate what to do next. Some cats will love it, others will give you that blank "Huh?" stare. Let them choose.

The Adventures of Larry Lizard, 30 minutes, VHS, $19.95 (includes S&H)

PetAvision, Inc.
P.O. Box 102
Morgantown, WV 26507
(800) 521-7898

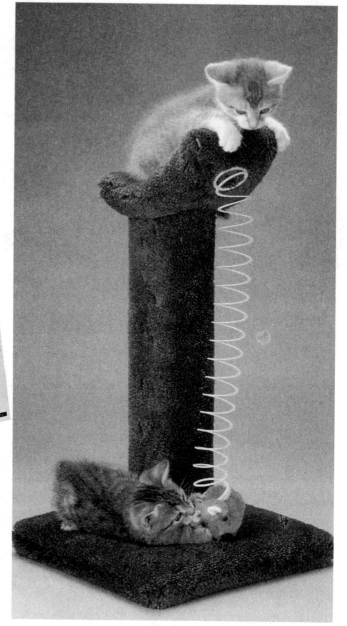

Young Claws

Many people think you can stop your cat from ripping up your furniture if you train him early, as a kitten, with a scratching post. This clever little piece of furniture keeps kitties amused and gives them a nice, safe place to scratch and claw . . . away from your sofa! It has a carpeted base and a mouse toy attached to the top.

Action Post, $34.99 + $6.29 S&H (N.Y. res. add 8.5% sales tax)

Pedigrees
1989 Transit Way
Brockport, NY 14420
(800) 548-4786

C'mon, We Need Some New Toys!

That's the constant complaint I get every day from Rollo and Bella, my two Himalayan companions. Enjoy the latest handmade toys and beds by Cat Action Toys, a lovely little company in Petaluma, California, former chicken capital of the West.

Jute, Catnip Toys with Feathers, $4.95 + $3.50 S&H
Shearling and Leather Catnip Mice, $3.95 + $3.50 S&H
Cotton Cat Beds, $19.95 + $3.50 S&H
(Calif. res. add 7.5% sales tax)

Cat Action Toys
3034 Skillman La.
Petaluma, CA 94952
(800) 647-8777

Fast and Loose Cat Dictionary: Improbable Definitions

CATatonic: *knockout gin drink for a wild cat party*

CATapult: *falling movement off a fence by wailing tomcat as a bottle misses his head*

CATastrophe: *cat-show award for best cat derriere*

CATegory: *violent, scary Stephen King book for kittens*

CATch: *hopeless game played with a tennis ball and cat's mouth*

CATechism: *oral exchange of affection with lips*

CATsup: *that fishy stuff in the cat dish every evening*

CATalyst: *cat with speech impediment*

CATalog: *written record of a seasick sailing cat*

CATty: *formal wear for cats on a hot date*

CATwalk: *yearly fashion event hosted by Yves St. Laurent in Paris and New York*

CATtle: *the propensity for cats to confess when under pressure*

CATerpillar: *semiprofessional, always-gloved man who gives pills to cats*

It's a Bird Attack!

Here's how it happened. The FedEx guy showed up. Ho hum, another package. Opened it up. Wow! Got so excited I went into the living room and woke up Rollo. Buzzed this beautiful red bird around his head. His eyes popped open—instant interest. He started swatting at it. This went on for half an hour. As you play with the toy (a gorgeous bird on a wire, attached to a clear plastic wand), the wings flap up and down. Lifelike birds—6″ long with an 8½″ wingspan—are made of brilliantly colored fabric with wonderful feather detail. One of the best. Demand this toy!

Audubon's Birds, $11.50 + COD/UPS shipping (Calif. res. add 7.75% sales tax)

Metropolitan Pet
354 Oaktree Dr.
Mountain View, CA 94040
(800) 966-1819

Old Possum's Book of Practical Cats ®

Kept in print since its first publication in 1939, this outlandish book of cat rhymes by T. S. Eliot, with illustrations by Edward Gorey, is a classic. Amusing for adults, and a wonderful rhyming book to read to young children. Words twist and turn, turning back upon one another. Every manner of cat personality is explored.

By T. S. Eliot, 1967, 56 pp., $5.95

Harcourt Brace & Company
6277 Sea Harbor Dr.
Orlando, FL 32887
(407) 345-2000

Joy in a Can ®

This is different . . . a pure catnip extract you can spray on toys or an old scratching post to perk up Kitty on slow days. Not a good thing to spray on your houseplants!

Four Paws Super Catnip Spray, $5.49

Information:
Four Paws Products, Ltd.
50 Wireless Blvd.
Hauppauge, NY 11788
(516) 434-1100

TRUE CAT FACT

Cat Hearing

Cats, dogs, and people hear just about the same when it comes to low-pitched sounds. On the higher end, most people in good health can hear sounds up to 18,000 cycles per second. Dogs top out around 35,000 cycles per second, while cats (ta da!) can hear nearly 100,000 cycles per second. That makes sense, since hearing and hunting go together. Higher pitches resonate well with cats because much of their prey—such as mice—emit high-pitched sounds.

A Riot of Wiggles

Cats love these toys. Flexible wands that wiggle back and forth; topped with peacock feathers that flutter in the wind. No small threads to swallow accidentally. Named 1993 Product of the Year by *Cat Fancy* magazine. Each 3'-long toy contains tiny beads that rattle mischievously when you wiggle the lure. Big-kitty-fun made by nice folks who really love cats.

The Purrfect Cat Toy, $9 + $2 S&H

Vee Enterprises
1066 S. Ogden Dr.
Los Angeles, CA 90019
(800) 733-1903

House Scooters

Cats love little round things they can knock around and chase . . . down the stairs, through rooms, rolling all over the place. Scooters are densely folded Mylar batting toys for cats who love the sound of things that *crunch*. Brilliantly colored, nontoxic, waterproof, and very durable. Each is a handmade original, packed with festive curling ribbon. Just a tad bigger than 1″ in diameter. Give Kitty a new one each week.

Scooters (package of 4), $5 + COD/UPS shipping (Calif. res. add 7.75% sales tax)

Metropolitan Pet
354 Oaktree Dr.
Mountain View, CA 94040
(800) 966-1819

Zen for Cats: Teachings of the Zen Cat Masters ®

It's a perfect fit—Zen and cats. It's like a natural recipe: Mix generous portions of this ancient Buddhist philosophy of clean, spare dogma with the inscrutability of cats, and the result is a humorous hardcover book, lovingly illustrated with pithy Zen sayings that explain the Cat Mind. "What is the sound of one can opening?"

By Alfred Birnbaum and Riku Kanmei, 1993, 90 pp., $9.95

Weatherhill, Inc.
420 Madison Ave.
15th Floor
New York, NY 10017
(800) 437-7840

Bucketafun!

Here's fun in a bucket . . . three ounces of rarin'-to-go organic catnip. After you open it once, your cat will be staring at you every day, saying, "Where's the bucket, where'd you put the bucket?"

Natural Animal Organic Catnip, $5.95 + $3.50 S&H (Fla. res. add 6% sales tax)

Natural Animal
7000 U.S. 1, N.
St. Augustine, FL 32095
(800) 274-7387

Tail Talk

Cats have lots of ways to tell you, and other animals, what they're thinking. Tail movement, for example, is a good indicator of what's about to happen. See if you agree:

Tail swishing from side to side: *angry cat, seriously thinking about an attack.*

Tail curving down and up at the tip: *mellow cat, at peace with the world.*

Tail straight up, stiff tip: *a big hello greeting that says, "It's great to see you!"*

Tail tucked between hind legs: *depressed cat with so-so self-esteem. Can be fixed, however. Consult your nearest animal behaviorist.*

Tail straight up and bristled: *a sign of near-maximum anger. Fight or flight is next. A soothing word would be nice.*

Okay, Who Turned on the TV?

It's 3 A.M. and there's a racket downstairs. Down the steps you go and there they are—again—endlessly viewing that crazy cat-safari video, wildly meowing, batting at the TV in that "hunting-frenzy" mode. Video features close-up views of busy birds, mice, squirrels, and more. Hide the remote.

Kitty Safari: A Video Adventure for Cats, $19.95 + $3.95 S&H

Creative Department
P.O. Box 69552
Portland, OR 97201
(800) 557-3378

World's Oldest Cat Toy

The Egyptians, way back in the time of the pyramids, probably amused their cats with ibis feathers. They're still among the simplest and most fun kitty toys. But these are *huge* feathers—16″–18″-long catnip-scented ostrich feathers, shipped in a tube—that will get any cat up and moving. You can also buy a cool cat collar (not shown) with 15 Austrian crystals that produce a rainbow spectrum of color under sunlight. Just ask for it.

Tickle Feathers (3 feathers), $6.95 + $2 S&H

Tickle Feathers
P.O. Box 386
Pt. Arena, CA 95468

When's the Party Start?

I once heard a true story about a kitten that grew up with three little girls. Once a week they'd put the kitten in little dresses and hats and booties and have a tea party. The girls grew up, and so did the cat, who went on to become a famous Holly-wood cat model. You could dress the cat up in *anything* and it was okay. No kidding. Good cat models are hard to find: Most get nervous with strange people, lights, cameras. Not this guy. After all those years of tea parties, he figured every modeling gig was another party about to start.

"Kitty's dress-up kit lets every cat put on a real show! The steamer-style trunk contains a wardrobe complete with fashion accessories. Set includes a cowboy hat, straw hat adorned with a bird, sunglasses, tutu, bandanna, and more. A 'how-to' book is included for creative playtime ideas."

Kitty's Dress-Up Kit, $29.95 + $4.95 S&H (Calif. res. add sales tax)

Rabbit Foot, Inc.
23247 Oxnard St.
Woodland Hills, CA 91367
(800) 228-6902

Big Fun Hand Puppet!

Slip on this hand puppet to roust the cats when they need a thrill. Your hand has become a monster. Big fun! The fabric tongue holds catnip, and the lamb "fur" body extends almost to your elbow.

"We've tested this on our worst rowdies and hooligans, and teeth and claws can't penetrate."

Harum-Scarum, $16 + COD/ UPS shipping (Minn. res. add sales tax)

Rom Designs, Inc.
1717 Van Buren
St. Paul, MN 55104
(612) 644-0433

The Fat-Cats at Sea ®

Sit back with your children and join the captain of *The Frisky Dog* as his fat feline crew sails the seven seas in search of Buns, found only on the remote island of Sticky-Goo. Actually, these kitty sailors aren't that tough. They get homesick, battle a shipload of poodles with taffy torpedoes and marshmallow harpoons, pick buckets of sticky buns off trees, and encounter many more adventures in this charmingly illustrated hardcover for young children. Lots of laughs.

By J. Patrick Lewis, 1994, 36 pp., $15

Random House
Apple Soup Books
400 Hahn Rd.
Westminster, MD 21157
(800) 733-3000

Big Kitten Fun!

If you love the antics of kittens—racing around, chasing their tails, knocking one another over, wrestling and chasing—you will love this video. My family laughed through the whole thing. Nicely produced with scads of kittens—there were eight playing around in one scene. It's an ideal gift for adults and children. Cleverly filmed, many different settings, nonstop action, good soundtrack. Cute hoot!

Non-Stop Kittens, 30 minutes, VHS, $19.98 (includes S&H)

PetAvision, Inc.
P.O. Box 102
Morgantown, WV 26507
(800) 521-7898

Crispy, Cracklin' Crinkle Puffs ®

Cats love a noisy toy; listen as they dive headfirst into a paper bag. This fun toy makes a cool crackling sound as it's batted around. Made of a soft material. Comes in three bright colors.

Crinkle Puffs (package of 4), $4.60

Information:
Classic Products
1451 Vanguard Dr.
Oxnard, CA 93033
(805) 487-6227

Feather Fight!

Brightly colored feathers twist and turn as Kitty plays. She stuffs the feathers in her mouth, and walks off with her prize. 5″ tall.

Feather Cat Toys (set of 3), $11.99 + $5.29 S&H (N.Y. res. add 8.5% sales tax)

Pedigrees
1989 Transit Way
Brockport, NY 14420
(800) 548-4786

Catnip, Cellophane, Crinkle Mania

This cat toy is just right for jumping on, rolling over, grabbing with the teeth, holding on to with the front paws and really digging into with those back claws. A shredding-and-ripping festival for cats who need to act out their hunting urge. Cool toy; noisy fleece exterior filled with potent catnip and crinkly cellophane. Two shapes: cat and fish.

Paw & Claw Playtoy for Cats, $3.50 + $3.80 S&H (Ariz. res. add 7% sales tax)

Pet Affairs, Inc.
691 E. 20th St.
Tucson, AZ 85719

Menopaws: The Silent Meow ®

Life is constantly changing. Every minute. Every day. The changes of life for women as they approach menopause are well-documented; and here's a paperback that takes a lighter approach to this time of transition. We need to laugh it up once in a while. Explore the dilemmas—and solutions—of a "menopawsal" cat. Hilarious illustrations.

By Martha Sacks, illustrations by Jack E. Davis, 1995, 64 pp., $9.95

Ten Speed Press
P.O. Box 7123
Berkeley, CA 94707
(800) 841-2665

Crazy About California (or Florida)

Love California? Does your cat want a souvenir of his visit? Former teacher Suzanne Simmons makes this California-shaped catnip toy, in bright yellow with a red heart sewn over San Francisco, and a star over L.A.

When Kitty walks around with this in his mouth, you'll think of beautiful California. And you don't even have to visit to get one. Suzanne also makes a catnip alligator for folks who like Florida.

Purr-Fect California Catnip Toy, $5 + $1.50 S&H (Calif. res. add 8.25% sales tax)

Purr-Fect Growlings
P.O. Box 90275
Los Angeles, CA 90009
(213) 751-3613

Is Your Cat Crazy? ®

How much more can you take? You've changed brands of litter twice and tried three different litter boxes in four different rooms. You've shut the cat in the bathroom all day, and she *still* prefers to pee on top of the piano. Is she nuts?

Probably not. This book has plenty of suggestions for the bewildered cat owner dealing with weird problems, including the two biggest: litter-box issues and aggressive behavior. Some cat problems seem so strange that you probably think your cat's brain is wired wrong. Here's salvation in one simple, smart book. Don't give up till you've read these solutions from the casebook of a cat therapist.

By John C. Wright, 1994, 228 pp., $18

Macmillan Publishing Company
201 W. 103d St.
Indianapolis, IN 46290
(800) 428-5331

Flying Fishing Flies!

Great toy idea. Take actual fishing flies—the kind people use for casting—make them bigger, add ears and eyes and tails, attach them to a clear cord and an acrylic handle. Ultimo toy. Whip it around in the air and see how high your cat can jump. Tickle noses.

Provoke your hunter. Keep Kitty busy!

Fly! $11.50 + COD/UPS shipping (Calif. res. add 7.75% sales tax)

Metropolitan Pet
354 Oaktree Dr.
Mountain View, CA 94040
(800) 966-1819

Twisted Kitty Toy ®

This slippery little toy keeps moving around the house. A basic toy made of curled plastic, cats can move it around easily whenever they want to play.

"Kookie Kitty Kurls have a mind of their own, not unlike our feline friends. Kitty will roll it, slide it, or send it flying, never knowing where the Kurl will land or if it will bounce, slide, or roll."

Kookie Kitty Kurls, $1.79 to $2.50

Omega Products, Inc.
292 Old Dover Rd.
Rochester, NH 03867
(800) 258-7148

Cats in Flight

Both Rollo and Bella, my Himalayans, had a fairly serious interest in this recreational film. Tape is all birds—mostly seagulls and ravens—with birdsong soundtrack. Cats like lots of sudden movement on the TV, and will remain glued to the screen as they follow the walking and flying motion of the birds.

The Adventures of Betty Bird, 30 minutes, VHS, $19.95 (includes S&H)

PetAvision, Inc.
P.O. Box 102
Morgantown, WV 26507
(800) 521-7898

A Catland Companion ®

In the 19th century, many people in England took to keeping cats to control exploding rat and mouse populations in their cities. When Queen Victoria declared her love of cats, a wild Victorian Age feline romance began that lasted for 40 years around the world. Nothing remotely like it has happened since.

Books, calendars, postcards, and paintings were produced by the millions. Cats were depicted by the finest artists of the age, doing everything people did: ice skating, vacationing at the beach, enjoying the opera, dancing, dressing in haute "cature" fashion, playing golf, riding bikes—you

name it. The best part of this great fantasy was that cats were depicted with respect for their personalities, as if, indeed, they were the nicest of people.

This extraordinary paperback chronicles the Victorian period's incredible (obsessive?) love of cats, reproducing remarkable artwork in hundreds of pictures and paintings. It's not only interesting, it's lots of fun. You and the kids could spend hours looking at the pictures . . . exclaiming with "oohs" and "aahs" as you turn each page.

By John Silverster and Anne Mobbs, 1994, 96 pp., $12.99

Random House Value Publishing
Crescent Books
40 Engelhard Ave.
Avenel, NJ
07001
(800) 733-3000

Show Biz Kats

Funny, you don't have to convince your kids to watch television, but the cat takes some coaxing. Plunk your kitty down in front of the TV, pop in this tape, and simultaneously pet Kitty while tapping on the screen until something exciting happens. This video stars many cats walking, running around, playing. I thought it would be a dud. It had a slow start, and too many shots of lions and tigers. My cats were losing interest fast, when all of a sudden things picked up. Rollo and Bella were definitely glued to the screen. In fact, Rollo gave it his highest rating by jumping on top of the TV and trying to climb into it.

All cat action with a birdsong soundtrack.

The Adventures of Krazy Kats, 30 minutes, VHS, $19.98 (includes S&H)

PetAvision, Inc.
P.O. Box 102
Morgantown, WV 26507
(800) 521-7898

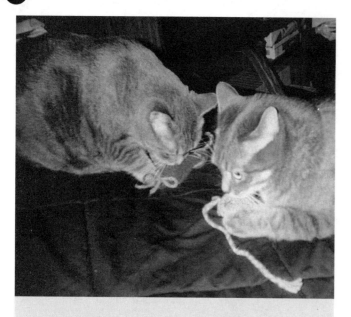

Nibbling Micey Heads

Joan Blanchard's been making little goodies— stuffed organic-catnip mice for her Persians— for years. Lucky them. Now she's got a small business selling her mice for a very reasonable price. Each is 3″ long with a 12″ tail, in assorted colors. Order a bunch, and surprise Kitty with a new one every few weeks.

"Four large Persian cats love these little mousies—they will not leave them alone! They are so cute! Kittens again—all four of them!"

Homemade, Catnip-Stuffed Mice, $3 each + 21¢ Fla. sales tax

Kitten Soft Creations
2913 Swifton Dr.
Sarasota, FL 34231
(941) 923-9313

The Official Cat Codependents Handbook

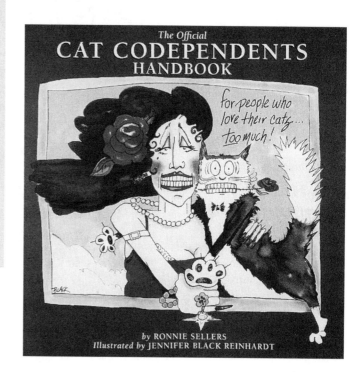

Smooth Moves Felt Mouse ®

Linda Bagne has made her love of cats into Country Catnip Toys. Below is a drawing of her organic-catnip-stuffed felt Patchwork Mouse. She also makes sheepskin mice, sheepskin rabbits, a pillow toy, puff balls, and other goodies.

"Cats love felt. It breathes, allowing cats to enjoy the catnip. And your cats *can really get their claws into the durable fabric."*

Patchwork Mouse, $4.99; catalog, $1

Country Catnip Toys
P.O. Box 232
Roswell, GA 30077
(800) 396-6126

This wacky paperback just goes on and on with crazy— but oddly realistic— thoughts about cats and cat "owners." Every aspect of cat caring/love/obsession is explored in words and illustrations. Thousands of readers have written the author, sharing how much they love their cats. If you're a "cat nut," go ahead, get a copy. You know you want to.

Wallow in the joy of cat-dependency.

By Ronnie Sellers, 1995, 112 pp., $9.95

Ronnie Sellers Productions
P.O. Box 71
Kennebunk, MA 04043
(800) MAKE-FUN

Fish and Bones (Bones?) for Kitty ®

Dr. Daniels', the oldest catnip manufacturer in America, has been making catnip toys since 1878. This venerable company now makes a cute fabric bone in tan or blue, packed with 100 percent pure catnip. Also, there's a Catnip Fish Value Pak that includes three toy fish in red, blue, and green. Good catnip products made by Massachusetts Yankees.

Information:
Dr. A. C. Daniels', Inc.
109 Worcester Rd.
Webster, MA 01570
(508) 943-5563

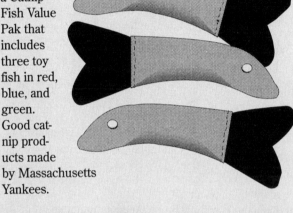

**Dr. Daniels'
Catnip Bone,**
$2.10
Catnip Fish
(Value Pak), $4.75

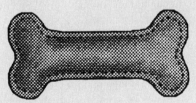

Round 'n' Round It Goes

Watch Kitty chase this ball round and round for hours. The track is lined with evenly spaced openings to provide windows of opportunity to paw at the spinning ball. Made of break-resistant plastic; includes a lightweight ball. Clean with a mild cleanser and soft cloth. Great entertainment.

Cat Track, $8.99 + $5.99 S&H
(Wis. res. add 5% sales tax)

Drs. Foster & Smith
P.O. Box 100
Rhinelander, WI 54501
(800) 562-7169

TRUE CAT FACT

Why Do Cats Like Warmth?

The small body mass and higher body temperature (around 101°) of cats require more energy to sustain than larger animals, so cats have no problem finding a warm spot and using it. Besides, cats enjoy life's comforts. If they get too hot, they have sweat glands in their paws, and they'll sweat, pant, and lick their fur to keep cooled off. P.S.: Cats that lie in the sun secrete from their skin a chemical called cholecalciferol. Sunlight converts this to vitamin D. Cats then lick their fur and get their vitamin D, sorta like kids getting vitamin D from milk.

Endless Mouse Chase ®

Your cat will never catch this mouse, but she won't stop trying. Lil' Jake, a fake fur mouse, hides inside this big chunk of bright yellow fabric-covered fake Swiss cheese. Stuffed inside of Jake is a nice handful of fresh catnip, and he's attached to a clever spring-action system that makes him very tough to catch. Cats love to try!

I Know He's In There!

**Cat 'n' Mouse Cheese
Chase,** $13

Clawtuff Corporation
13602-12th St.
Chino, CA 91710
(800) 252-9883

Simple

The deceptively simple Kitty Go Round can be an endless source of play-pleasure. Cats—especially indoor cats—need entertainment and physical exercise. Spin it like a top to get your cat interested, and it will keep spinning. This toy is really for solo cat fun. Place it on a hard, flat surface or on shallow carpeting and let your cat go to it. Cats love to knock the device around. If the wire gets bent from heavy play, you can straighten it by hand, or replace it with a new wire available from the company. Sometimes the simplest is the best. Patented design.

Kitty Go Round, $6.95 + $1.25 S&H (Mich. res. add 6% sales tax)

M&M Enterprises
P.O. Box 2354
Livonia, MI 48151
(313) 525-2680

My God! What's That Hanging Off the Door? ®

You're headed into the bathroom, late at night. You reach for the door handle and put your hand on a weird furry thing. You freak out! It's understandable—but this crazy-looking monster is actually sort of cute in the daylight, and your cat'll love it. Eight-legged furry octopus attaches to a door frame or other flat surface with a suction cup, and the accordionlike cable dangles and jiggles as your cat bats it around. Up and down, up and down, flying all over the place. Big fun!

Leapin Legs Octopus, $3.12

Information:
Classic Products
1451 Vanguard Dr.
Oxnard, CA 93033
(805) 487-6227

Round & Round For Hours

The catnip-filled ball races around as Kitty bats it with her paw. Just put it on the floor, get the attention of your cat, then give the ball a push with your finger. Cats enjoy sticking their mischievous paws into things.

The Feline Challenger, $10.59
(N.Y. res. add 8.25% sales tax)

Real Animal Friends
101 Albany Ave.
Freeport, NY 11520
(800) 654-PETS

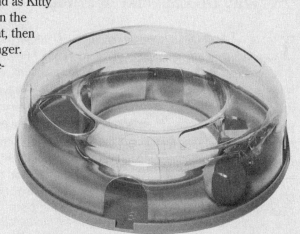

The Calvin and Hobbes Tenth Anniversary Book ®

In November 1985, the magic of *Calvin and Hobbes*—a six-year-old boy and his tiger—first appeared on the funny pages. Unfortunately for the strip's zillions of fans, it officially came to an end 10 years later. This great paperback collection from over the years includes insight into

the world of C&H creator, Bill Watterson. A must-have collectible for fans.

By Bill Watterson, 1995, 208 pp., $14.95

Andrews and McMeel
4520 Main St.
Kansas City, MO 64112
(816) 932-6700
(800) 826-4216

TRUE CAT FACT

The First Cat Show in America

As reported by *The New York Times* on Sunday, March 6, 1881, "Manager Bunnell stood in the center of his museum on Broadway, his hands in his hair, utterly perplexed, late last night. He was surrounded by cats in cages, cats in wooden boxes, cats in bandboxes, cats in bags, half of them yelling, spitting and scratching, as mad as cats can be in uncomfortable quarters and in a strange place. A deep scratch on his nose and three fingers tied up in oil and rags told how inexperienced he was in the way of cats. As fast as the cages were completed and the cats were placed in little sections, each one alone, they settled down for the night, and silence reigned."

Talk about a rough beginning!

Electric Fun!

When I unwrapped my Mouse Chase and plugged it in, my cats were chasing it around within minutes. With a variable-speed motor (which automatically reverses the direction of the toy mouse on the end of the string) and a grate on top that makes the mouse bump and jump as it turns around, this toy will keep your cat busy for a long, long time. Carpeted post doubles as a scratching post, and it's safe—shuts off automatically if the cat knocks it over. Wooden base is 10″ dia. × 17″ h.; cord comes with wand/mouse attachment. No supervision needed!

Mouse Chase, $39.99 + $6.99 S&H (Wis. res. add 5% sales tax)

Drs. Foster & Smith
P.O. Box 100
Rhinelander, WI 54501
(800) 562-7169

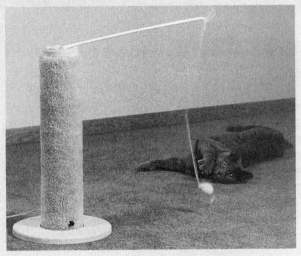

Fish Dinner Dreams

Cats have been watching fish—and thinking *Oh, boy, fresh seafood*—for thousands of years. Here's a video feast for Kitty, with hundreds of different fish floating, bobbing, swimming around. My cats liked it. Plenty of action—from aquarium shots to pools of carp—with a bubbling-air-pump soundtrack. Sure it's goofy, but they like it.

The Adventures of Freddy Fish, 30 minutes, VHS, $19.95 (includes S&H)

PetAvision, Inc.
P.O. Box 102
Morgantown, WV 26507
(800) 521-7898

How to Get a Cat to Sit in Your Lap

D. Michael Denny is not your typical cat author. He's a kind of tough guy from the ad-agency world who's written a crazy illustrated book of true-life anecdotes, behavioral reports, historical analysis, and assorted masculine musings on cats. Like Thurber, he's a ruminator, always observing, getting his feelings involved. Nothing dry and boring in this paperback. Light on the hearts and flowers. Highly recommended for cat lovers and people who ought to be cat lovers but don't know how: Tough Female Executives with no kids who want a pet, and insensitive men who wear T-shirts. There's also a funny poster and T-shirt you can order from the publisher.

By D. Michael Denny, 1995, 72 pp., $14.95 + $3.50 S&H

Andiron Press
P.O. Box 303
E. Hanover, NJ 07936

Three-Way Batting Practice for Cats

Cats like this three-in-one toy. You can use the pompom and toy to play with the cat, or mount the wand into the solid base for spring action when Kitty plays alone. Add more fun by turning the base upside down, so it rocks and rolls as Kitty knocks it around.

A bored cat is not living up to her potential!

Slap Happy Cat Toy, $5.99

Information:
Flexi-Mat Corporation
2244 S. Western Ave.
Chicago, IL 60608
(312) 376-5500

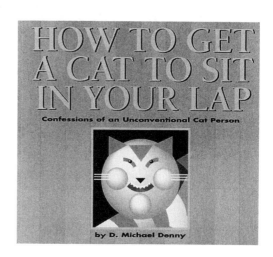

There's Something Fishy About This

Can you believe it? Anchovy-scented cat toys! All of your cat's wishes are now fulfilled! Actually, studies have shown that not all cats relate to catnip . . . but all cats love the light anchovy scent of these toys in bright neon colors. Something new for the fisherman in every cat.

Fish 'n Fun Green Ferret, $2.99
Fish 'n Fun Small Mouse (3½″), $2.19
Fish 'n Fun Large Mouse (4½″), $2.69
Fish 'n Fun Small Ferret, $2.59

Information:
Ethical Products
216 First Ave.
Newark, NJ 07107
(201) 484-1000

Kitty Pong!

Cats love sticking their paws into things and batting stuff around. Kitty Pong, measuring 6″ × 6″ × 11″, is a fun toy for cats, made of hand-crafted natural pine that combines an exercise toy with a carpet top to encourage scratching. Inside Kitty Pong is a Ping-Pong ball that can be batted around forever, but never caught. It's virtual reality for cats, always just out of reach.

Kitty Pong, $18.95 + $4.75 S&H (Ohio res. add 6% sales tax)

Pet Warehouse
P.O. Box 310
Xenia, OH 45385
(800) 443-1160

Time for a Good Scratch

Is this cat enjoying this, or what? Look at the pleasure on her face. This could be your cat! The Fantasy Brush is naturally attractive to cats. Its shape allows cats to groom themselves easily, using their natural tendency to brush against the curved structure as their weight holds the base in place. The brush traps and holds cat hair, reducing matting, while the catnip-enhanced base (refillable) serves as a scratching pad. Entertaining, wildly practical, veterinarian approved, patented!

Feline Fantasy Brush, $24.95 + $5 S&H (Mich. res. add 6% sales tax)

M&M Enterprises
P.O. Box 2354
Livonia, MI 48151
(313) 525-2680

Why It Works, I Don't Know

We get a lot of cat toys. This one arrived; I yawned and put it aside. My son picked it up and the cats were flying through the air two minutes later. They *love* this toy, and I don't know why. It's like a little fishing pole, 38″ long with a bow tie of denim on the end of a clear string, and it must remind them of butterflies, or birds, or something. I don't know why it works. I've asked them, and they're not telling. All I know is my best toy critics—the cats— won't leave it alone, and that's good enough for me. This is one of the best cat toys you will ever buy.

Kitty Tease Cat Toy, $5.95 + $4 S&H

The Galkie Company
P.O. Box 20
Harrogate, TN 37752
(423) 869-8138

TRUE CAT FACT

Sounds Like Cats to Me

If it sounds like a cat, but doesn't look or walk like a cat, well, it could be a lot of things. It might be an instrument. Here are some that sound like cats, or were inspired by cats, from around the world.

Musical Saw. *Weird noises emanate if a lumber handsaw is bent and played with a violin bow. Sounds like a cattery at full moon. Try it late at night. Certain to drive your neighbors crazy.*

Javanese Saron. *This bronze chime makes plaintive meowing sounds when banged like a gong. Use your imagination.*

Sistrum. *The Egyptians literally worshiped cats. This ancient instrument consisted of a metal frame with metal parts that were shaken to chime together.*

Samisen. *A favorite of Japanese geisha (hostesses), this three-stringed instrument makes long, drawn-out tones that mimic a cat in heat.*

Your Voice. *Practice opera in the shower.*

Purring in the Light: Near-Death Experiences of Cats ®

Americans have a fascination with near-death experiences. Here's the first cat book with stories—straight from the cats' mouths—of what they experienced on the edge of life. Feline other-world phenomena include: "The Paper Bag Tunnel," "Purrgatory and Purradise," "The Nine Lives Review," "Transfurmations," and let's not forget "Cat Angels," "Meowing Muses," "The Celestial Warming Room," and "The Great Sofa in the Sky." Mostly whimsy, part mysticism, each highly imaginative story is accompanied by drawings that make each story almost believable. Cats don't lie.

By Stefanie Samek, 1995, 134 pp., $7.95

Plume Paperbacks
375 Hudson St.
New York, NY 10014
(212) 366-2000

Morris Is Actually Living with Elvis

Remember Morris? In his day, he was probably the most famous cat in America. (We're not counting cartoon cats like Garfield.) Originally found by his owner at an animal shelter, Morris went on to become a star. He appeared regularly on TV as the spokescat for all sorts of products. He lived in Chicago, getting tons of mail each week, which his owner dutifully answered.

Contrary to popular belief at the time, Morris wasn't on drugs. He was just so mellow by nature that he routinely fell asleep on live TV.

Pleasure Sticks

You know about catnip. What about honeysuckle? Are you ready to watch your cat sniff, lick, drool, flop on, roll around, hug, rub, and jealously protect a piece of wood? Cats are crazy about this natural treat, which most people have never heard of. Not for chewing, just licking and hugging. Two packages (give one to a friend with a kitty) include four ounces of Honeysuckle Slices, and you can always get more. Two-package minimum assures a nice, lengthy supply of irresistible treats. You'll be amazed.

Honeysuckle Slices (2 packages), $8 + $5 S&H

The Cat House
110 Crowchild Trail, N.W.
Calgary, Alberta T2N 4R9
Canada
(800) MEOW-CAT

A Cat's Little Instruction Book ®

Two hundred and one warm, wise, amusing bits of advice for cats to live a happy and contented life. Upbeat, insightful, short quotes (from a cat's perspective) and line drawings of cats in many poses. The author, Leigh Rutledge, lives in Colorado, where he shares his home with 28 house cats. He's been known to save cats from storm sewers, unscrupulous pet stores, abusive owners, and busy interstate highways. Cute advice that both cats and people can take to heart.

By Leigh W. Rutledge, 1993, 104 pp., $10

Dutton
375 Hudson St.
New York, NY 10014
(212) 366-2000

Light-as-Air Balls ®

Pick up a pack of these playballs sometime. They weigh almost nothing. A cat gives them a good swat and they go flying. Big, too . . . about 3″ in diameter. Bright red, yellow, and blue colors, three to a pack. Great chasing fun!

Kitty Caper Exercise Playballs (package of 3), $3.44

Information:
Lixit
P.O. Box 2580
Napa, CA 94558
(707) 252-1622

LIXIT

Kitty Caper ™

"Feather-Light"™ EXERCISE PLAYBALLS

Dancing and Playing ®

There's a certain amount of subtlety involved in playing with a cat. All the moves: planning, crouching, sizing things up, attacking. We've had a ball with this toy—or rather, the cats have had a ball. Little cardboard twisties on the end of an undulating 3′, 20-gauge spring steel wand always get the cats interested. Nice price, too.

Cat Dancer, $2.50

Information:
Cat Dancer Products
2448 Industrial Dr.
Neenah, WI 54956
(414) 725-3706

"Get Even" Kitty Activation Toys

There's a certain satisfaction both you and Kitty will experience as he chews up the vet (Vet the Victim, 7″ tall), the annoying dog down the block (Revenge Rover, 4″ × 4½″), and that impossible neighbor kid (Nasty Neighbor Kid, 6″ tall). Well, not really, but these are absolutely fabulous, hilarious catnip toys with just the right personalities and expressions. Great presents!

Kitty Activation Toys, $5.99 each (3 or more, $5.50 each) + $2 S&H

Kitty Hoots
73 Troy Ave.
Colchester, VT 05446
(800) 799-MEOW
E-mail: kittyhoots@aol.com

TRUE CAT FACT

Cat Bods

How come cats don't come in as many shapes and sizes as dogs? Mostly because of breeding. Dogs have been bred for thousands of years, while cats have been bred for less than 200. It's possible, even likely, that there will be totally new breeds of cats in the year 2500.

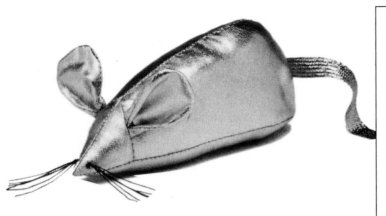

I'll Take the Gold Toy, Please

There are lots and lots of cat toys, but nothing quite like this. The catnip-filled gold lamé Le Mouse flashes as Kitty chases it about your condo, glistening as she rounds the corner with it in her mouth. In fact, it's so beautiful you might want to keep one just for appear ances. Generous ears and body, perky black whiskers, amusing gold tail. A perfect gift for the discriminating cat fancier.

Le Mouse, $10 + $3.50 S&H

L. Coffey Ltd.
4244 Linden Hills Blvd.
Minneapolis, MN 55410
(800) 448-4PET

Cat Feathers ®

Amusing little feather toys for your kitties. Catnip-filled and brightly colored, they come in a wide variety of styles, including pom-pom face, furry mouse, and a great interactive wand with a cute bird.

Kitty Toys, $3.99

Information:
Ethical Products
216 First Ave.
Newark, NJ 07107
(201) 484-1000

I've spent a lot of time checking out cat products. It's been a relentless pursuit to find the coolest stuff for cats. So, how'd I pick what you see in this book?

I'm a firm believer in the CAT (Completely Amateurish Testing) method of product evaluation.

Here's how it works. The mail arrives. I open it. I leave it spread out on the carpet near my desk while I bang away on the computer. I yell, "Mail's here." Bella and Rollo, brother and sister Himalayan cats, come in and check out the mail. They sniff and probe, batting things around, sticking their heads into envelopes. They do this on schedule each day. They expect to check the mail each and every day. They drag out the cool stuff, like catnip toys and playthings. At any given time there are toys in the bathroom, in the kitchen, on stairs, all over the place.

One time I got this great big envelope full of cute, brightly colored, stuffed catnip toys from Blue Rat. Maybe ten or fifteen catnip toys sewn in brightly color fabrics. Screaming pinks, fluorescent yellows, brilliant turquoise. Bright.

I left it on the carpet for the daily mail call.

Later that day, I went out the front door to take a walk. All over the front lawn I saw little bright patches—stuffed mice, catnip carrots, catnip hearts, in the driveway, in the street, under bushes, you name it. It was like some wild, drunken cat fraternity party with empty beer bottles all over. A neighborhood cat was fleeing the scene with a bright souvenir in his mouth.

Everything was gone by the next day. Cats all over the neighborhood took their toys home, as if Christmas had come early and Santa and his reindeer had randomly dropped gifts from the sky.

So, I don't test the products in this book. The cats test the products. If they don't like them, I don't like them. Simple.

P.S. Sundays are a problem. No mail. Disappointed faces. I tell them, "No mail on Sunday." They don't believe me.

Where the Toys Live

Sooner or later you'll have to buy one of these because your cat-toy collection will be all over the place. Stuffed inside the lid and inside covering of this toy box for cat toys are fresh catnip buds to liven up the toys that are visiting. Most cats immediately turn it into a bed. They either sleep on top—it's nice and soft—or inside, lying on top of the toys. Either way—when the toys are about to make their appearance, or when Kitty is conking out for a nap—you just press the heart on the lid and the soothing strains of Brahms's *Lullaby* drift up from the music box. Measures about $1' \times 1\frac{1}{2}'$, and about 5" deep. How can you live without this?

Lullaby Joy Box, $28.98 + $4.95 S&H (Calif. res. add 8.25% sales tax)

Allie Cats
c/o Pacific Fulfillment
P.O. Box 2474
Martinez, CA 94553
(800) 444-5917

Fishy Doorknob

Start the fun with these bright cotton fabric fish, filled with batting and catnip. Each 3½" fish dangles on an elastic cord with a bell at the bottom. The middle fish moves up and down on the string. Hang it in place, peek around the corner, and watch your kitty having fun.

School of Fish, $6 + $1 S&H (Calif. res. add 44¢ sales tax)

Small Town Ideas, Inc.
P.O. Box 1905
Lower Lake, CA 95457
(707) 994-0552

Connoisseur Catnip

There's catnip, and then there's Mountain Lion Catnip. These folks have been raising super-premium catnip for nearly 10 years now, and they've got it down. Your catnip buds arrive in a sealed black-and-gold clear plastic tube, perfectly presented, hand-tied with a colorful green ribbon. Pure buds, the pick of the litter, the top 1 percent of their catnip crop. Potent, all-natural, no pesticides. Just a pinch will get even the laziest cat moving. Great gift!

Black Tie Mountain Lion Catnip, $5.50 + $2 S&H (W.Va. res. add 6% sales tax)

Mountain Lion
P.O. Box 120
Forest Hill, WV 24935
(304) 466-1437

Feline Française

These delightful cosmic catnip-filled boy and girl kitties, in blue and white fabrics, are sure to please any feline with their stylish design. The boy reclines comfortably wearing his beret, the girl's arms are outstretched with French exuberance. Simply beautiful.

Le Fleurettes Catnip Toy, Boy or **Girl**, $10 each + $3.50 S&H

L. Coffey Ltd.
4244 Linden Hills Blvd.
Minneapolis, MN 55410
(800) 448-4PET

Cat Nips Feline Cuisine ®

Humorous illustrations accompany a wild collection of recipes, and who would believe cats eat this stuff? Plenty of great recipes for Kitty in this colorful paperback, including Potato Fritters with Anchovies (yum!), Seafood Fajitas, Octopussy Salad, Mackerel Munchie, String-Bean-and-Beet Medley, Shoestring Potatoes with Sole, Cantaloupe Cocktail (cantaloupe?), Clams Allegro, Tomato-and-Turkey Jerky, Cheesy Chewies, Banana Cakes, and lots more crazy, fun, delicious recipes for Mr. or Ms. Fuzzy. Remember: The way to your cat's heart is through her stomach. Whipping up one of these meals will automatically earn you big points with Kitty.

By Rick and Martha Reynolds, 1992, 96 pp., $8.95

Berkley Books
200 Madison Ave.
New York, NY 10016
(212) 951-8800

Knock-Around Catnip Toys ®

These are cool. Catnip-filled natural sisal toys with feathers, in the shape of a round mouse, a plump pig, or a spool that Kitty can toss around and chew on to her heart's content.

Paw Pleasers, $2.49

Information:
Ethical Products
216 First Ave.
Newark, NJ 07107
(201) 484-1000

TRUE CAT FACT

A Cat in Any Other Language

Cats were a big part of early Egyptian culture, nearly 4,000 years ago. They were identified with the goddess of maternity and fertility, named Bast, or Pasht, which might be where we get the word *puss*. The Spanish for *cat* is *gato;* French, *chat;* German, *katze;* Latin, *catus;* Yiddish, *kats;* Arabic, *quttah;* Dutch, *kat;* Swedish, *katt;* Greek, *gata*. Sound familiar?

Doorknob Batter

Hang this adorable face off your doorknob and wait for the cats to find it. Instant fun as fresh catnip aroma drifts through the house, luring your kitties to play. Stretch elastic allows the toy to bounce all around as your cat gives it a workout. Pretty face, too!

Batty Cat, $4.49 + $4.95 S&H (Calif. res. add 8.25% sales tax)

Allie Cats
P.O. Box 2474
Martinez, CA 94553
(800) 444-5917

Friendly House Spider

Cats love this crazy toy. The leather legs of the spider fly through the air as Kitty grabs for the soft, catnip-filled body. It's also the right color for a spider—pink, with red and green legs.

Along Came a Spider, $4.49 + $4.95 S&H (Calif. res. add 8.25% sales tax)

Allie Cats
P.O. Box 2474
Martinez, CA 94553
(800) 444-5917

Video Fun

It's a quiet, rainy night—time for you and Kitty to share some fun. Turn on the VCR, pop in *Cat TV,* and see how excited Kitty will get watching squirrels racing around, mice dashing about, fluttering wild birds, and darting fish, all with realistic outdoor sounds. It'll give you a nice break from a hectic day, and all that action is sure to engage your cat.

Cat TV, 30 minutes, VHS, $14.95 + $3.50 S&H

Media West Home Video
P.O. Box 1563
Lake Grove, OR 97035
(800) 888-TAPE
E-mail: Globalhv@aol.com

Kong Lives

The wacky Kitty Kong toy includes mouse and whisker replacements. There's a full quarter pound of microencapsulated catnip coated on each mouse—scratch-and-sniff style. Big rolling-fun toy.

Kitty Kong, $5.59 (Colo. res. add 7% sales tax)

The Kong Company
11111 W. 8th Ave.
Lakewood, CO 80215
(303) 233-9262
E-mail: jawrobics@aol.com

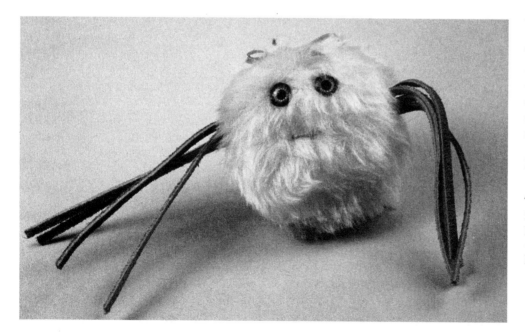

Flying Kites

Doorknobs are a great place to hang toys. The Kite Doorknob is a 3½″ cotton fabric kite, complete with tails and a bell, on elastic. Slightly stuffed with batting and catnip. Available in beautiful cotton prints. Sometimes the best cat fun is also the simplest.

Kite Doorknob Toy, $4.50 + $1 S&H (Calif. res. add 33¢ sales tax)

Small Town Ideas, Inc.
P.O. Box 1905
Lower Lake, CA 95457
(707) 994-0552

Tough as the Australian Outback ®

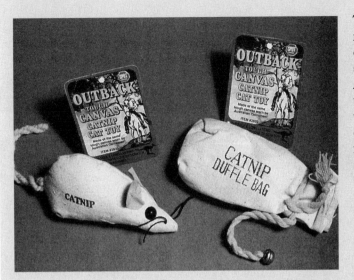

These toys are cute—made of canvas, like an ole-time cat toy, the same canvas used by Australian cattlemen in the outback—and they're packed with catnip for extra kitty fun. Canvas is safe and nontoxic. Outback Canvas Kitty goes with the rough, tough Catnip Duffle Bag (full of catnip); perfect for Kitty when he decides to take a hike and wants to bring his fun along.

Outback Canvas Catnip Mouse, $2.29
Outback Canvas Catnip Duffle Bag, $2.29

Information:
Ethical Products
216 First Ave.
Newark, NJ 07107
(201) 484-1000

Big Fun Play Wand

Some toys excite cats, others elicit that "ho-hum" look. My cats have a blast with this one. They never seem to get enough of it, but when I've had enough play, I wedge it between cushions on the sofa, so it hangs near the floor. Then I go downstairs. Every morning, it's lying on the floor. *Aha,* I think, *they've been playing at night again.* Soft, rubberized tassle-tip on a long, flexible wire with a solid wooden handle. Fun toy that will give you both exercise.

Cat-Aerobics, $6.99 + $1 S&H (Calif. res. add 8% sales tax)

SunRae Products
P.O. Box 84
Redwood City, CA 94064
(415) 365-8919

Mittens for Paws

You'll never fit these mittens on Kitty's feet. They're stuffed with catnip! Each toy includes two, 2½″ cotton fabric mittens, connected to each other with a gold cord and a bell. Available in assorted prints. Affordable fun!

Kittens Mittens, $3.25 + $1.00 S&H (Calif. res. add 24¢ sales tax)

Small Town Ideas, Inc. P.O. Box 1905 Lower Lake, CA 95457 (707) 994-0552

Cats Vanish Slowly ®

Lavish color illustrations accompany 12 poems recounting the lives of the countless cats on Grandmother's farm. They hide in the shade of the porch, prowl through the grass, doze in comfortable laps, and vanish as they please in the shadows. You feel a real sense of the country in this beautiful hardcover— a different time and place where things move more slowly, and people take the time to see the succession of moments that make up our lives. A wonderful book to read with your child, and relax with after a busy day.

By Ruth Tiller, illustrations by Laura L. Seeley, 1995, 32 pp., $16.95

Peachtree Publishers 494 Armour Circle, NE Atlanta, GA 30324 (404) 876-8761

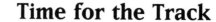

Time for the Track

Well, no, it's not jogging for cats. The Booda Track 'n Scratch includes a ball-and-track chase game in the base, catnip for the two sisal scratching posts, and let's not forget that hanging toy for swatting around when the spirit moves Kitty. Indoor home-entertainment center.

Booda Track 'n Scratch, $31.95 + UPS shipping (N.J. res. add 6% sales tax)

J-B Wholesale Pet Supplies, Inc. 5 Raritan Rd. Oakland, NJ 07436 (800) 526-0388

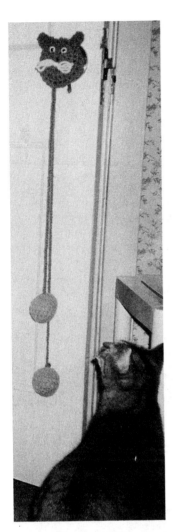

Hang It Up or Lay It Flat ®

Your cat will love digging her claws into this big 18″ scratcher. The little ball is refillable with catnip and hangs on a flexible cord so when you hang it, it bounces all around as Kitty digs in. Big fun for felines!

Big Mouse Cat Scratcher, $21.99

Information:
Ethical Products
216 First Ave.
Newark, NJ 07107
(201) 484-1000

Crochet Fun Time!

Hang these cuties off your doorknobs and watch the action begin. The colorful crocheted cat is attached to two dangling crocheted balls and a bell. The face fits right over your doorknob for easy installation. A clever, amusing creation, handmade by Jeanne Adlon of Cat Cottage, who also does cat calls/-sitting in Manhattan.

Cat Door Knob Toy, $6.50
(N.Y. res. add 8.25% sales tax)

Cat Cottage
133 Lafayette Ave.
Holbrook, NY 11741
(516) 981-6685

Hot Catnip Links

Full Circle Herb Co. is a cottage industry nestled in the foothills of the Oregon Cascades. They grow catnip, and produce a product meant to drive cats wild. What you get with their Single Hot Cat is a sausage-shaped cloth "link," packed with red-hot organic catnip. Cheaper in quantity. Tell me the guy on the left doesn't like it.

Single Hot Cat Catnip Link,
$4.50 + $3 S&H

Full Circle Herb Co.
39582 Mohawk Loop
Marcola, OR 97454
(541) 933-2151

Feather Fun ®

Most cats like feather toys.
Perhaps it reminds them of
bird hunting. This kitty is
obviously very busy with his
Kittybird; the bright, almost
neon turkey feathers are
colored with nontoxic dyes,
and the base is weighted
with sawdust. When
attached to a 36″ fiberglass
wand with a stretchy elastic
cord, this same toy is called
the Kitty Flirt. Toy is easily
removed from wand. Great
hunting!

Kittybird, $3 to $4
Kitty Flirt, $6 to $6.50

Kittybird, Inc.
3601 N. Dixie Hwy., Suite 2
Boca Raton, FL 33431
(516) 393-3775

Rolling Kitty Balls ®

The pink ball rolling inside
the translucent Cat-A-Ball
provides lots of fun when
Kitty tries to push it around.
Openings are perfect for
inquiring paws and noses.

Cat-A-Ball, $4.95

Information:
Doskocil Mfg. Co., Inc.
4209 Barnett
Arlington, TX 76017
(817) 467-5116

Maze of Delights

Entertain your cat for
hours with the Amazin
Kitty Maze, a clear acrylic
toy with a catnip-filled ball
on a string. Kitty reaches
through the openings and
bats the ball around. It's
refillable, to keep things
interesting. Like all cat
toys, it's good to use for a
while, then put away and
bring back out in a week
or so.

**Amazin Kitty
Maze,** $8.99
(N.Y. res. add 8.25%
sales tax)

Real Animal
Friends
101 Albany Ave.
Freeport, NY 11520
(800) 654-PETS

The Hunt for Lil' Jake ®

Lil' Jake is
a stuffed catnip mouse
tethered to a spring and hidden in this fiendish toy.
Kitty will root around with
her paws, whacking at Jake,
sticking her nose in the play
holes, doing her best to
stuff Jake in her mouth.
Assorted colors; interactive
exercise for the best cat in
the world—yours.

Catsino, $13

Information:
Clawtuff Corporation
13602-12th St.
Chino, CA 91710
(800) 252-9883

Fun for Your Little Tiger

A larger version of this cool toy is used by zoos to entertain their Bengal tigers. Just a slight touch of your cat's paw sets everything in motion. Adjusts easily to hang almost anywhere; hanging hooks included. A toy mobile for cats.

Tiger Toy, $19.95 + $3.25 S&H (Fla. res. add 6% sales tax)

Pet Doors USA, Inc.
4523 30th St., W.
Bradenton, FL 34207
(800) 749-9609

The Tao of Meow: Life's Little Instruction Book fur Cats ®

Charming minibook, illustrated with color drawings. Many of the things we always suspected cats know are presented in this paperback in a series of witty epigrams. Brief, clever contemplations of cat life and behavior.

By Margaret Gee, 1993, 96 pp., $7.95

Ten Speed Press
P.O. Box 7123
Berkeley, CA 94707
(510) 559-1600

Incidentally, There's a Rat in Your Mailbox ®

A rat you'll like! Le Rat comes stuffed into a little mailing tube. You open it up, pull him out, and say, "Wow!" Stuffed with catnip and fiberfill, this rat sports a velvet tail, safety eyes, and felt ears for nibbling. Big! Measures 6″ × 3″. Krinkle Rat, with stripes, has catnip and a hidden layer of cellophane, which makes a crinkly sound cats love.

Le Rat in a Tube, $6.99
Krinkle Rat, $7.99 + S&H (Calif. res. add 8.25% sales tax)

Information or to order:
Maggie Mae's Gourmet Pet Products, Inc.
P.O. Box 4245
Mountain View, CA 94040
(415) 967-9492

Montana Cats

From the heart of Livingston, Montana, come Pet Pals cat toys. Each is made of strong, high-quality sheepskin fabric, with aqua and pink leather laces for legs and tail. Bright colors, stuffed with organic catnip, all nontoxic materials. White Spider is 4″ in diameter, pink Caterpillar is 13½″ long with 8 leather feet, cute gray Mouse is 5½″ long with 6″ leather tail, Catnip Ball is 2½″ in diameter. All except for Catnip Ball have a jingly bell sewn inside.

Spider, Caterpillar, Mouse, $5 each
Catnip Ball, $3

Pet Pals, Inc.
107 Sun Ave.
Livingston, MT 59047
(800) 999-5366

Giant White Fish ®

This is beautiful. Giant white all-natural sisal hanging fish measures a big 21″ from tip of his nose to bottom of his broomlike tail. Long hanging cord with bell makes it the perfect scratch toy for hanging on your doorknob. Watch where you hang it, or your cat might use it to wake you up in the morning.

Paw Pleasers Natural Sisal Hanging Fish Scratcher, $19.99

Information:
Ethical Products
216 First Ave.
Newark, NJ 07107
(201) 484-1000

The Indoor Cat ®

What a nice idea: a book for indoor kitties who never go outside. They live in high-rise apartment buildings, or on the plains of Kansas— inside, safe, and secure. But how do you keep them healthy and happy, and prevent boredom? Indoor cats are different, often suffering from "confinement stress," and this paperback provides plenty of helpful solutions and tips on whether your cat needs a buddy; kitten adolescence and growth; diet for the "lounge lizard" or the "gymnast"; routine upkeep; the "high-rise" syndrome and other hazards; general health information; behavior problems and bad habits; and keeping your cat happy and loving. Written in an easy, entertaining style, it's the perfect book for anyone who keeps a cat totally indoors . . . where it belongs.

Oh. About that "kitty buddy" stuff. My advice: If you're going to buy a cat and it will live totally

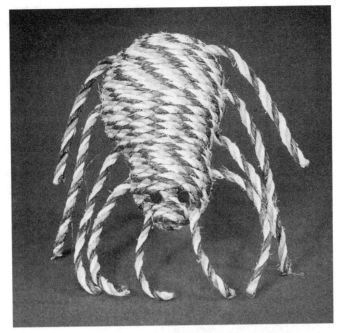

indoors, buy or adopt *two* kitties from the same litter if at all possible. They will have each other to play with, they'll have each other for love and companionship when you're not there, and they'll never be lonely.

By Patricia Curtis, 1981, 174 pp., $9.95

Berkley Books
200 Madison Ave.
New York, NY 10016
(800) 223-0510

Scratch & Chew! ®

The nice thing about this 6″ Sisal Spider is that it's both a chew toy, scented with catnip, and a scratching toy. Bright pink, blue, and white. Its precarious balance makes it lots of fun to roll around.

Paw Pleasers Sisal Spider, $2.59

Information:
Ethical Products
216 First Ave.
Newark, NJ 07107
(201)484-1000

House Mouse & Soft Sachets

UltraMouse, available in eight colors and prints, is made of UltraSuede, a man-made washable fabric, and stuffed with premium catnip. The Kitty Sachet is a catnip toy with all the wonderful features of the UltraMouse in a simpler design. Christmas Kitty Stocking is filled with catnip and fiberfill. Heart Kitty Sachet is a heart-shaped catnip-filled sachet suspended on a clear elastic cord.

UltraMouse, $9.50
Kitty Sachet, $6
Christmas Kitty Stocking, $6.50
Heart Kitty Sachet, $7.50

UltraMouse, Ltd.
123 Assembly Ct.
Cary, NC 27511
(800) 573-8869

Cowboy Fun

Sometimes I'll stick one of my cats' wand toys under a pillow so they feel challenged to drag it out and play with it alone. Cowboy Dave perfects that concept —a toy a cat can play with at will. The birdie on the end is stuffed with high-quality cultivated catnip. The 26″ flexible steel rod allows the toy to fly in any direction; just moisten the two suction cups on the end of the rod, apply it to a flat, hard surface (windows, doorjamb, appliances), and the toy is out there for Kitty to play with at her leisure.

Cowboy Dave, $6.95 + $3.50 S&H

Vision Products
9034 W. National Ave.
West Allis, WI 53227
(414) 321-5999

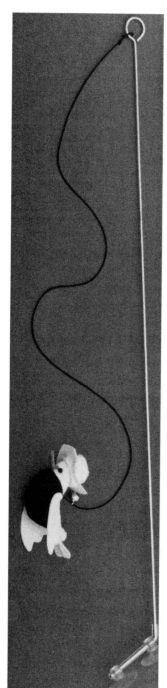

Rolling Fun

The 7″-diameter Cat-O-Sphere is made of three colorful rings that form a ball. Inside is a refillable catnip sphere. Fun for cats to roll around. Check out UPCO's excellent free catalog for more products.

Cat-O-Sphere, $10.95 + $3.75 S&H (Mo. res. add 76¢ sales tax)

UPCO
3705 Pear St.
St. Joseph, MO 64502
(800) 254-UPCO (8726)

Trail Fun in Your House ℝ

The Cat-a-Trail is an amazing expandable cat tunnel that can go from room to room, or up the stairs of your house—in any length—for big cat fun! Connect two or more of the colorful nylon tunnels (available in red, blue, or teal) with attached drawstrings. Lined with plush sheepskin, includes catnip-filled toys sewn inside, and features convenient drawstring storage.

Cat-a-Trail, $20 each

Information:
Dogloo, Inc.
1241 Old Temescal
Corona, CA 91719
(909) 279-9500
E-mail: dogloo1@aol.com

Sheepskin-Catnip Combos! ℝ

Cats like the texture of sheepskin. The Sheepskin Rabbit Toy, with lovely pink-and-white ears and pink nose, dangles from a cord for batting around. The Sheepskin Streamer Toy, with a white body, blue ears, and pink, green, and yellow tassels, is perfect for the cat that likes to swat at things with his paws. The Sheepskin Spider Toy is a fluffy, *pretty* monster with a puffy white body and orange legs. The Sheepskin Mouse Toy has a soft white body with pretty red ears, and you can hang him up for aerial battles. All come filled with catnip.

Sheepskin Rabbit Toy, $2.49
Sheepskin Streamer Toy, $3.59
Sheepskin Spider Toy, $2.89
Sheepskin Mouse Toy, $1.99

Information:
Ethical Products
216 First Ave.
Newark, NJ 07107
(201) 484-1000

Chapter Two

The Finest Feline Furniture and Furnishings

Now We're Living!

What's this? A lovely love seat for leprechauns? Not a chance. Finally, your cat gets her very own sofa to bunk on, instead of yours. Stylish, bright floral pattern, elegant design: 33″ w. × 16″ dia. × 18″ h., machine-washable cover, 100 percent foam cushions. Folds flat. I'd like to see a whole room of this stuff—little tables and chairs and TVs (for watching cat videos) and lights . . . a whole room set aside for your cat's entertainment. You know your cat deserves this.

Kitty's Love Seat, $49.99 + $6.99 S&H (N.Y. res. add 8.25% sales tax)

Pedigrees
1989 Transit Way
Brockport, NY 14420
(800) 548-4786

Illustrated Catwatching ®

Desmond Morris is probably the world's most popular author on the behavior of cats. This hardcover book consists primarily of questions and answers from his many readers over the years—why cats purr, how they manage to fall on their feet, how they use their whiskers, how their sociability varies, etc. Morris has a nice, dry wit that makes cat trivia amusing, as well as fascinating. Superb photography.

By Desmond Morris, 1994, 144 pp., $17.99

Random House Value Publishing
Crescent Books
40 Engelhard Ave.
Avenel, NJ 07001
(800) 733-3000

Deluxe Accommodations

Wow! Completely covered in carpet, this extra-large Cat Clubhouse has entrances in the front, rear, and through the removable roof. There's also easy access between floors, and two trees for perching. Base measures 30″ w. × 22″ dia., and the house itself is 25″ w. × 19″ dia. × 33″ h. (includes the roof). Height of tree is approximately 36″. Available in assorted colors. The site of your next cat party!

Extra-Large Cat Clubhouse, $299.99 + $9.99 S&H (Wis. res. add 5% sales tax)

Drs. Foster & Smith
P.O. Box 100
Rhinelander, WI 54501
(800) 562-7169

Stone Cats

Nagata Yoshimi is a Japanese artist who makes wonderful, expressive, curious cats out of pebbles and rocks. Though primarily a full-color picture paperback of his many fabulous creations, *Stone Cats* includes complete instructions for you to explore this craft as well. Step-by-step, you'll learn how to make your own stone cats carefully and meticulously. Extraordinary stuff—beautiful folk art if you're in the mind to make gifts for cat-loving friends.

By Nagata Yoshimi, 1993, 48 pp., $14.95

Weatherhill, Inc.
420 Madison Ave.
15th Floor
New York, NY 10017
(800) 437-7840

Nice, Fluffy Cat Beds

My cats love to nestle into sofa cushions or anything deep and comfy. After all, who doesn't want to be cozy for his nap? Sweet Dreams makes beautiful, thick cat beds with your choice of floral, paisley, modern, or plaid designs. They will also custom-make a cat bed for you when you provide the material. Just send them fabric: 2 yd. (small), 3 yd. (medium), 4 yd. (large), or 5 yd. (extra-large). Nice service, especially when you want to match your cat's furniture to yours. These are handmade, washable, very attractive, and comfortable beds. Kitty will be on his in 10 seconds flat!

Sweet Dream Cat Beds, $39.99 (sm.), $49.99 (med.), $59.99 (lg.), $69.99 (xl.)

Moniban, Inc.
43825 Paulita Rd.
Temecula, CA 92592
(800) 242-9966

World Headquarters

Caesar the Housecat Commander peeks out his submarine porthole, in complete control of the situation from world headquarters.

Pet Cradle, $29.95 + $3.95 S&H (Ark. res. add 6.5% sales tax)

Cat Claws, Inc.
1004 Broadway
Morrilton, AR 72110
(800) 783-0977

Immediate Occupancy: Two-Story, Split-Level CatHome with Deck

Given the price of houses these days, it's nice to see a high-quality all-cedar home you can finally afford. It'll be a bit snug for you, but perfect for a cat or two. These great-looking, solid (will support a 200-pound man on the roof) cat homes are lovingly made by a small specialty company. Cats like having their own space, and with the two-story model shown, Kitty can hang out on the bottom floor, on the top floor, or catch some rays on the deck. Though designed for outside use, your cat would love to curl up for a catnap in his house in *your* house. Three design options. What cat wouldn't want his own pad?

Two-Story CatHome with Deck, $276 including shipping (10% discount for altered pets)

Kitty Comforts
P.O. Box 2972
El Cajon, CA 92021

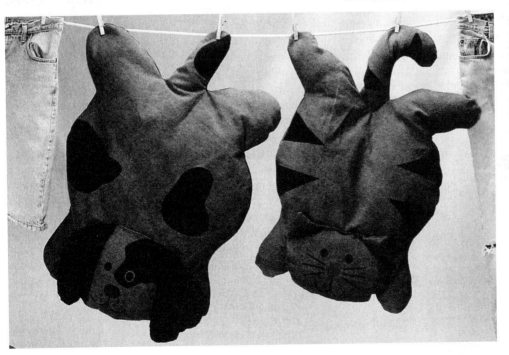

A Cat for Kitty ®

This unusual 220-tall carpeted cat scratching post has eyes, a mouth, whiskers, and a bow, and he just waits there, every day, hoping to be scratched. Plunk it down and let the cat go to work.

Nashville Cat, $69

Information:
American Cat Emporium
103 Oakdale Rd.
Camp Douglas, WI 54618
(608) 427-6875

Chubby Kitty Bed

A kitty squashed by gravity? This fabulous cat-shaped bed is gray and white with pink ears, nose, and tongue. Measures 20″ × 16″, just right for stretching out. Comfy stuffing makes it warm as well as cute. Totally machine-washable, perfect for reclining by a window and watching the world go by.

Denim Cat-Shaped Bed, (blue, white, & pink) $26.95 + $4.95 S&H (Wash. res. add 8.25% sales tax)

Keller Design, Inc.
P.O. Box 3854
Seattle, WA 98124
(800) 683-1227

Rainy-Day Funhouse

Dreary, rainy day? No birds to watch? Liven things up with the Playhouse, a 27″ "hot spot" with lots of fun openings, places to hide, and walls to scale. Catnip-treated carpeted scratching post and lively ostrich feather with 16½″ flexible handle. Affordable, sturdy, and durable. Let's start playing!

Cat Playhouse, $18.30

Designer Products, Inc.
P.O. Box 201177
Arlington, TX 76006
(817) 469-9416

Biggest Cat House in the Neighborhood

This is incredible. The ultimate activity center for multiple cats or for one incredibly pampered cat, custom-created of all-natural materials. Six levels include cushioned sleeping lodge and multiple landings. All-cedar construction, unfinished or stained to the finish of your choice. Nontoxic water-based finish available for allergic cats. Oak tree limbs for scratching and climbing, hemp-rope scratching pads (manila or sisal). Hand-washable lounging cushions in choice of heavy-duty leather suede or 100-count cotton denim or duck canvas. Suspended batting and spinning toys provide fun and exercise for your pampered kitty. Personalized laser-engraved plaque with your cat's name. Six rollers (which may be locked in place) for moving around. Large (1-qt.) removable stainless-steel food and water bowls for convenient filling and cleaning, with Plexiglas splash guard for messy cats. Environment may be constructed in dimensions to fit any space, and prices will vary according to complexity. Ask for a free estimate. They also build world-class cat-friendly patio and outdoor enclosures.

Large Environment
Indoor/Covered Patio $4,000
Outdoor/Covered/Enclosed $5,500
(Tex. res. add 6.75% sales tax)
Price includes free home delivery and setup within the U.S., except Alaska and Hawaii.
Wt.: approx. 200 lbs.

House of Cats International
25011 Bell Mountain Dr.
San Antonio, TX 78255
(800) 889-7402

Luxury Cat Climbing Furniture

The Pussicat Corporation's catalog may very well be the only cat brochure in six languages (as if language makes any difference to a cat climbing around on this high-quality, European-designed modular furniture). You can purchase and assemble a rudimentary climbing arrangement, and add to it in time. Or, go with the top-of-the-line model shown above, the Himalaja. This is very clever cat furniture—like a giant Tinkertoy set with essentially unlimited configurations. Prices start at $46.

Himalaja, Model 55, $304
+ UPS

Pussicat/Interwood
Corporation
P.O. Box 4981
Spartanburg, SC 29305
(800) 817-1936

TRUE CAT FACT

Do Indoor Cats Miss Out on the Action?

You bet. Here's a partial list of what your cat misses by staying indoors:

- Fights with other cats
- Attacks by free-roaming dogs and raccoons
- Infections from puncture wounds
- Fleas, ticks, and worms
- Poisoning (pesticides, herbicides, etc.)
- Exposure to Feline Immunodeficiency Virus
- Exposure to Feline leukemia
- Being stolen
- Being hit by a car
- Getting lost
- Getting caught in a steel-jaw trap
- Encountering sick or rabid raccoons and skunks

The average life span of an indoor cat is about 15 years. It's less than half that for outdoor pets. Keep 'em in, keep 'em safe!

The Complete Book of Cats ®

This hardcover encompasses almost everything you'll ever need to know about cat history, anatomy, and life cycle; how to choose and care for your cat; the healthy cat; plus details on all kinds of cats—shorthaired, Siamese and Burmese, long-haired, and curious. Big, beautiful color cat photos throughout. This is the U.S. edition of a funny British book—you'll see that English cats look just like American cats! One big world of cats.

The complete book of **CATS**
YVONNE REES

A colorful look at the world of cats, from their history to the latest show variety

By Yvonne Rees, 1993, 124 pp., $12.99

Random House Value Publishing
Crescent Books
40 Engelhard Ave.
Avenel, NJ 07001
(800) 733-3000

House "Jungle" Hammock ®

Cradle your cat in comfort with this great hammock that's especially useful in front of floor-to-ceiling windows. Kitty can recline while watching the action outside the window. Paw-print design, available as a single- or double-level hammock. Machine-washable and -dryable plush covers attach with hook-and-loop fasteners. Simple assembly, light and easy to move around. Just right to settle in for a day of observation after a good breakfast!

Cat Napper Hammock, $71.99 (single), $99.99 (double)

Information:
Flexi-Mat Corporation
2244 S. Western Ave.
Chicago, IL 60608
(312) 376-5500

"I'll take a wing chair, and one of those, and . . ." ℝ

"Well, of course I deserve furniture!" said Bella as she settled onto her first real piece—a luxurious flower-print Flip Chair. "What's wrong with luxury?" she meowed. Measuring 33½" l. × 18½" h. × 16" dia., the chair is just the right size for one reclining cat or two scrunched together. Cushion flips out for overnight parties. For the two-cat (or more) household, the Flip Couch is a must, measuring a comfortable 50" l.

× 18½" h. × 29" dia. Removable zippered cover. Variety of patterns to choose from. A nice warm spot above the cruel, cold floor.

Flip Wing Chair, $96.99 + S&H
Flip Couch, $118.99 + S&H

Information:
Flexi-Mat Corporation
2244 S. Western Ave.
Chicago, IL 60608
(312) 376-5500

Extra-Stable Hanging Scratcher ℝ

Cats are like people, and we'd never expect all people to like the same flavor ice cream. There'd be nothing but vanilla! Same with scratching posts. There are hundreds of different kinds to suit hundreds of different cats. This three-sided Sisal Scratcher stands 18" tall, and its big, flat back is perfect for the cat that wants a secure scratching surface. Just hang it on a doorknob or hook, and it won't move all over the place when your cat uses it. Some cats (Democats?) like their scratcher to fly all over the place. Others are skeptical and prefer no sudden movements. Think of this as a scratch pad for Republicats.

Paw Pleasers Three-Sided Sisal Scratcher, $16.99

Information:
Ethical Products
216 First Ave.
Newark, NJ 07107
(201) 484-1000

Cat and Rat: The Legend of the Chinese Zodiac ℝ

According to legend, the animals in the Chinese Zodiac were selected when the emperor held a great contest to see which 12 animals would be first across a finish line. The Chinese lunar calendar (which follows a 12-year cycle) is the contemporary result, with years named after these animals. There is no better interpretation than this strikingly illustrated hardcover tale of the Jade Emperor of Heaven: how, 5,000 years ago, the rat and the cat became eternal enemies— and how the rat earned its place in the Chinese Zodiac.

By Ed Young,
1995, 32 pp., $15.95

Henry Holt & Company
115 W. 18th St.
New York, NY 10011
(800) 488-5233

Room with a View ®

Cats love to look out windows and to be warm and off the ground. This combination window perch/cat bed meets all their needs. CatNapper adjusts to fit any window with a sill, so your cat can contemplate the world—both outside and inside—and you can move it from window to window for a change of scene.

Comfortable hammock design will hold up to 35 lbs. Washable fleece cover is warm in winter, cool in summer.

CatNapper, $42.99

Information:
Flexi-Mat Corporation
2244 S. Western Ave.
Chicago, IL 60608
(312) 376-5500

Home Exercise Center

Your complete scratching-and-grooming gym! The Sisal Post (sisal is a ropelike natural material that cats love for scratching) with suspended toy is 20″ h., including a secure 12″ dia. base and a 3″ dia. post. After a good scratching, your kitty will love to rub against the arched Sisal Groomer, 9″ h. × 8″ w. Personal fitness for Kitty.

Sisal Post w/Toy, $19.99
Sisal Groomer, $16.99
Add $6.99 S&H for both (Wis. res. add 5% sales tax)

Drs. Foster & Smith
P.O. Box 100
Rhinelander, WI 54501
(800) 562-7169

Best Cat Stories ®

Graceful and intuitive, independent yet endearing—cats are all of these. But the best word to describe them may be *enigmatic*. Much of their charm lies in their silent mystery, penetrating eyes, and irresistibly soft fur. In this paperback, 27 of the world's best authors attest to the awesome appeal of cats. From silly to serious to sublime, *Best Cat*

Stories presents promising insights into the true nature of cats.

Compiled by Lesley O'Mara, 1992, 256 pp., $8.99

Random House Value Publishing
Wings Books
40 Engelhard Ave.
Avenel, NJ 07001
(800) 733-3000

TRUE CAT FACT

Let's Get a Room, Kitty

It had to happen. People traveling with pets are now welcome at many hotels and motels across the U.S. The newest and brightest is American Pet Motels of Prairie View, Illinois. Their $1.25-million lobby—complete with a 6,500 sq. ft. "O'Hair Port" for pet grooming—includes an $80,000 video wall that continuously runs "animal-friendly" movies and cartoons to entertain children; human-sized stuffed animals that carry on interactive conversations; a gift shop for both people and pets; and a variety of pet supplies. Ray Kroc, former McDonald's chairman, provided financial backing.

Cadillac Cat on the Go

The litter box. You've got to cover it up—somehow! What a cool solution. Kitty does her business in a pink Cadillac frame (other designs include a beach scene, the office, and Halloween) that fits most standard litter boxes. Easy to assemble, die-cut from sturdy corrugated cardboard to support Kitty's weight. Wipeable varnished surface and super-high-quality color printing. Three sizes: small, medium, or large/jumbo. Does not include actual litter box, just the artwork to go around it.

Glitter Box, $9.95 + $3.60 UPS shipping (Vir. res. add 45¢ per unit)

ZetaMax
2200-102 Wilson Blvd., Suite 129
Arlington, VA 22201
(703) 522-2000
E-mail: Bobbylev@aol.com

Cat Tales: Lessons in Love from Guideposts ®

This collection of cat stories is steeped in the religious inspiration of *Guideposts,* as published by the United Methodist Publishing House. Contributors of all ages share their experiences with the cats they have loved, along with lessons they have learned from their feline friends—about friendship, forgiveness, acceptance, nurturing, trust, loving, and grieving. The lessons provide perspective on how people should help one another during times of tragedy, what it means to trust and accept one another unconditionally, and the responsibilities of parenthood.

This paperback is meant to provide everyday inspiration, and perhaps the strength you may need if difficulty arrives at your door.

Foreword by Marjorie Holmes, 1995, 96 pp., $7

Dimensions for Living
P.O. Box 801
Nashville, TN 37202
(800) 251-3320

Is This a Bed or a Litter Box?

Well, that depends on you. If you picture Kitty snoozing away in this cat-shaped pan, just add the optional machine-washable pillow with a 100% cotton cover and polyester fill. Already have a kitty bed? Order the cat-shaped plastic pan and use it as an upbeat, modern, one-piece, watertight litter box.

Cat-Shaped Pan, $18.95 + $3.95 S&H
Cat Pillow with Leopard Print, $14.95 + $3.95 S&H (Wash. res. add sales tax)

Keller Design, Inc.
P.O. Box 3854
Seattle, WA 98124
(800) 683-1227

Getting from Here to There

Other than jumping, bridges are the smart way for your cat to move from Point A to Point C—without stepping on Point B. Incredible cat bridges await you—a swinging suspension bridge, a stepladder, a barn-style ladder—each with or without guardrails, in the finish of your choice. The Straight Bridge is designed for use independently, and may also be used in conjunction with entertainment centers. The OverBridge with Guardrails (pictured here, adaptable for outdoor use) would look exceptional over a reflecting pool or pond. All-cedar construction. Nontoxic water-base finish available for allergic cats.

Bridges may be used for spanning large or small spaces on the floor or in the air. Also ask about Catwalks, designed to be installed along interior walls, a foot or two below the ceiling. Catwalks can completely surround a room—they look incredible.

The cubist Kitty Elevator (bookcase style) is custom built to fit your house. And when it comes to feline shelter, the Kitty Luxury Apartment, standing 6′6″ tall and including a hemp-rope scratch pad, an enclosed triangular sleeping loft, and a jumbo litter box on the bottom, is just about as good as it gets.

OverBridge with Guardrails,
8″ width, $36 linear ft.; 10″ width, $40 linear ft. (above)
Geometric Elevator, prices are based upon custom design
Kitty Luxury Apartment,
$1,200 (right)
Straight Bridge, custom 8″ width, $15 linear ft.; 10″ width, $20 linear ft. (guardrails available)
Price includes free home delivery within the U.S., except Alaska and Hawaii.
(Tex. res. add 6.75% sales tax)

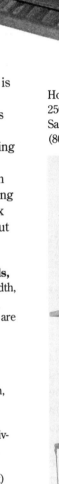

House of Cats International
25011 Bell Mountain Dr.
San Antonio, TX 78255
(800) 889-7402

TRUE CAT FACT

Whisker News

Because cats are basically farsighted, they don't see things well that are very close to their faces. So kitty whiskers have evolved as a hunting and protective mechanism. Whiskers are extremely sensitive to air currents and are connected to a mass of nerve endings deep in a cat's upper lips. A cat with her eyes closed could detect the passage of a nearby mouse or bird just from the movement of the air on her whiskers. Whiskers also serve as antennae to tell a cat about objects very near her head and front feet. And they help tell her whether an opening is wide enough to squeeze through.

Sky's the Limit Condos ®

The nicest thing about these condos is that they stack and lock together with a special Catnector nut that keeps them from falling apart with even the roughest cat play. Your cats can use the condo for a cat-nap or observation—excellent by a window so Kitty can watch birds and the outside world. Carpeted, with an optional 20″ × 20″ Action Base, which includes a spring mouse toy. Stack as high as your cats desire.

Two-Suite Clawtuff Condos, $79.90
Additional stackable Condo Suites, $39.95 each

Information:
Clawtuff Corporation
13602-12th St.
Chino, CA 91710
(800) 252-9883

Papa Piccolo ®

In their world of cowboys, soldiers, Power Rangers, and Ninja Turtles, little boys may not learn as much about nurturing as their sisters do. Piccolo, the Venetian tomcat hero of this book, teaches girls *and* boys about taking care of those who are smaller, younger, or weaker, and shows them that it can be an exciting, rewarding adventure. Perfect for ages 5 to 9. Nicely illustrated hardcover; gives a meaningful message to children about learning and responsibility.

By Carol Talley, 1992, 32 pp. $16.95

Information:
MarshMedia
P.O. Box 8082
Shawnee Mission, KS 66208
(800) 821-3303

Tunnel of Love

Picture your cat tunneling through this! The interior is lined with denim, the outside is made of ⅜″ manila or sisal (ideal for scratching and climbing) over a core of cardboard (for indoor use) or PVC pipe (for outdoor use or for spanning large interior or exterior spaces). The tunnel moves within triangle braces when the cat climbs on it. Braces are 15″ h. × 29″ w. Rope tunnel has 10½″ dia., available in your choice of length. Sold by the linear foot, so your tunnel can be as long as you want.

Rope Tunnel (Indoor/Cardboard Core), $50 ft.
Rope Tunnel (Indoor-Outdoor/PVC Core), $60 ft.
Triangle Braces (Cedar), $30 each
Price includes free home delivery within the U.S., except Alaska and Hawaii. (Tex. res. add 6.75% sales tax)

House of Cats International
25011 Bell Mountain Dr.
San Antonio, TX 78255
(800) 889-7402

Indoor Jungle Gym

Do you demand the best for your cat? If so, take a close look at this ultimate kitty activity center. Sturdy handmade construction of sanded cedar with ramps and a real tree limb, ideal for scratching and climbing. Includes hemp-rope scratching pad and corner scratching pad with matching lounging cushion in choice of heavy-duty suede, 100% cotton denim, or duck canvas. Designed by a sculptor; will fit anywhere in your house. It's 5½' tall, includes batting and spinning toys. Place it near a window for your cat's viewing enjoyment, and it becomes a clever refuge from other pets and children. Removable stainless-steel bowls for food and water. Personalized wooden plaque for your kitty's name. Quality materials and craftsmanship; unconditional money-back guarantee. Other custom options. Extraordinary quality—this is the Cadillac of play centers.

The Standard Environment
Partially assembled, $500
Preassembled, $675
(Tex. res. add 6.75% sales tax)
Price includes free home delivery. Ask about setup within the U.S. Wt.: approx. 200 lbs.

House of Cats International
25011 Bell Mountain Dr.
San Antonio, TX 78255
(800) 889-7402

Continental Condos

This is where America's cats prefer to stay . . . and play. These ingenious kitty "hotels" offer a place to hide and seek. Also great as scratching posts, or for napping and observation. Extra fun for your cat when placed by a window!

Three-Story Resort, $59.99 + $7.99 S&H
Two-Story Suite, $39.99 + $6.99 S&H
(Wis. res. add 5% sales tax)

Drs. Foster & Smith
P.O. Box 100
Rhinelander, WI 54501
(800) 562-7169

King of the Kastle

The Kitty Kastle allows your king or queen to rule with dignity in his or her very own house, made of the best-quality carpet treated with fresh catnip. Kastle is 33″ h. with 13″ dia., and includes two 12″ × 12″ platforms. Choose blue, mauve, beige or gray.

Kitty Kastle, $39.99 + $6.99 S&H (Wis. res. add 5% sales tax)

Drs. Foster & Smith
P.O. Box 100
Rhinelander, WI 54501
(800) 562-7169

TRUE CAT FACT

Purrfect Purr

It's hard to get two people to agree on anything. For example, people still can't agree on how a cat purrs. Some think it results from the pressure of a cat's blood as it passes through his chest. Others think it's the cat's voice box, which vibrates even though his mouth isn't open. You decide.

Cat Scratch Fever!

Cats love to get on this tilted wooden frame and just go at it! Scratching away, ripping it up, getting all that aggression out of their systems. Wooden frame in a light-color stain firmly holds two easily replaceable scratching pads. Be sure to request at least two scratching pads to fit into the frame.

Double Climb 'N' Claw Tray, $18.95 + $3.95 S&H
Scratching Pads, (2–5) $6.75 each, (6–11) $6 each + S&H (Ark. res. add 6.5% sales tax)

Cat Claws, Inc.
1004 Broadway
Morrilton, AR
72110
(800) 783-0977

Furniture or Litter Box?

It's both. Let's face it: There's no getting around the fact that litter boxes are unsightly. They smell, and no matter what, litter sticks to cats' paws and gets tracked all over the place. Toddlers think the litter box is a sandbox, and dogs root around in it for a "kitty cookie." But here's some help—an attractive, practical product that looks good enough to put just about anywhere. Inside is a compartment for the litter box, and an upper compartment that the cat uses as entrance and exit. Considering the option—you know, that ugly plastic thing you've hidden in the laundry room—this looks like a winner to me.

Purr-Fect Privy (light oak or white melamine laminate), $129 + $15 UPS (N.J. res. add $7.80 sales tax)

Baillie Corporation
P.O. Box 462
Lakehurst, NJ 08733
(800) 434-1919

High-Tech Floor-to-Ceiling Playground

Modular assembly, unlimited building possibilities, high-strength carpeted beams, and space-age design make this a very attractive cat playground. Easy to assemble, the Deluxe Starter Kit includes plenty of components, such as three Plush Fur Hammocks for lounging and a Spring Action Cat Toy for fooling around. Just snap everything together. You can build any size unit—no tools needed!—straight up to the ceiling, if that's what you want, which offers you some interesting design possibilities for the room of your choice. Standard and automatic waterers and feeders available separately. They'll fit anywhere on the platforms. This is a great, intelligently thought-out product.

Catnex Deluxe Starter Kit, $69.95

Information:
Clawtuff Corporation
13602-12th St.
Chino, CA 91710
(800) 252-9883

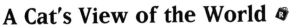

Cats in the Sun

Cats live wild amid the whitewashed buildings on the Greek islands of Mykonos, Milos, and Naxos, rarely entering homes. Though some have owners and get regular meals, most make their living off the streets—catching a mouse or rat here and there, snatching a fish off a boat, living a splendid, free life in sight of the shimmering ocean that fades into the horizon. Here, the only "rat race" happens when there's a cat in hot pursuit. This paperback of fabulous photos by Hans Silvester—his fifteenth— would make many people (not to mention cats) envious of life in the sun-drenched islands. Pack your bags!

By Hans Silvester, 1995, 144 pp., $18.95

Chronicle Books
275 Fifth St.
San Francisco,
CA 94103
(800) 722-6657

A Cat's View of the World

Keep kitties busy and happy with this window perch/cat bed in a paw-print design. The hammock cradles cats in total comfort, holding up to 35 lbs. Cats love to observe the world, and here's a way for Kitty to stay off your furniture and still keep an eye on what's going on. Sturdy black plastic frame will adjust to fit any window with a sill.

Paw Print Catnapper, $45.99

Information:
Flexi-Mat Corporation
2244 S. Western Ave.
Chicago, IL 60608
(312) 376-5500

Adopting Cats and Kittens

Everybody knows there are far too many cats without homes. Animal shelters are full of them. Many come from unplanned litters, others are strays, lost or abandoned by their owners. All shelters house potentially great pets, but the question is, how do you choose an adopted animal? Is it the cutest, the most outgoing, the youngest, the shyest, the one that says "meow" and looks you straight in the eye? This paperback gives you practical advice to consider in addition to trusting your emotional instincts. Here is vital information on how to adopt a cat or kitten, what to look for, what to avoid, and how to take care

of your newfound friend. The average cat lives about 15 years, and that's a long time to be committed to a pet. Make sure you're making a wise decision.

By Connie Jankowski, 1993, 112 pp., $8

Information:
Macmillan Publishing U.S.A.
201 W. 103d St.
Indianapolis, IN 46290
(800) 662-3058

TRUE CAT FACT

Domestication of the Cat

Egyptian art from the time of the pyramids shows that cats were both domesticated and worshiped at least 4,000 years ago. In fact, evidence points to cats having been domesticated in Mediterranean civilizations as many as 6,000 to 8,000 years ago. This is due, in part, to the need to control mice and rats in order to protect harvested crops stored in clay containers and early buildings.

Jungle Igloo World

If your cat had hands and could build a neat little shelter, hiding place, and hunting blind out in the woods, it would probably look like this. Cats love the design because it affords maximum privacy, safety, and a great view. Comfy cushion inside, too! 17″ w. × 14″ dia. × 13″ h.

Cat Wicker Hutch, $44.99 + $7.29 S&H (N.Y. res. add 8.25% sales tax)

Pedigrees
1989 Transit Way
Brockport, NY 14420
(800) 548-4786

The Cat's Easy-Access Ramp

Your cat might find it hard to get around if he's put on a few years, has arthritis, or has suffered an injury. This ramp is made just for that: cats who want to get to their favorite resting spots but need a little help. The adjustable ramp is American-made, crafted in pine or oak, and covered with stain-resistant almond-colored carpeting. What a thoughtful product.

PawsWay
Small, $55 + $10 S&H
Medium, $75 + $15 S&H
Super Utility, $110 + $20 S&H
(Ill. res. add 7.75% sales tax)

Pet Care With Love, Inc.
P.O. Box 764
Glenview, IL 60025
(800) 441-1765

TRUE CAT FACT

The Wrong Way to Remove a Tick

Use of tweezers, fingers, or any other means of removal that puts pressure on the tick's body, or use of alcohol, solvents, butter or oils, burning, or anything that risks killing the tick, can cause it to excrete its body fluids, which immediately increases the risk of tick-borne infections. Removing it without the head also increases the risk of infections.

Scratch for Joy!

Save your furniture and drapes and provide entertainment for your favorite feline with this big scratching pad you can hang on the wall or use on the floor. The Big Mouse Scratcher has heavy-duty surfaces to keep Kitty's nails healthy. The refillable catnip ball bobs on a flexible elastic cord to attract your cat and hold her interest. You can also hang it on a doorknob.

Big Mouse Scratcher, $9.99 + $5.99 S&H (Wis. res. add 5% sales tax)

Drs. Foster & Smith
P.O. Box 100
Rhinelander, WI 54501
(800) 562-7169

Georgian Cat Furniture

Three years ago, The Cat Kingdom began making furniture for three new kittens who needed some personal space in a household that contained two very large dogs. They now make several designs of fine furniture for felines. Each has been "cat tested" by those same three cats. All are custom creations, made with the wood and stain of your choice. Mystic's Castle is made of white pine, stands 7' tall, and is stained and polyurethaned for easy cleaning, long life, and cat enjoyment. Eggard's Sleeping Slings are easily removed, washed, and reinstalled. Mustache's #2 PlayHouse combines a ramp, play area, sleeping sling, and playhouse interior, where you could easily place a cozy cushion for nap time.

Mystic's Castle, starting at $1,520
Mustache's #2 PlayHouse, starting at $530

The Cat Kingdom
LA 1005
Waleska, GA 30183
(770) 720-7771

Futon for Kitty Guests

This contemporary futon-style couch is made of solid oak, with a strong Cordura nylon seat support. Cotton covers available in floral, beige, plaid, southwestern patterns, or denim. Great for overnight kitty guests or catnaps.

Contemporary Kitty Futon, $79 + $15 S&H (Calif. res. add 7.75% sales tax)

Critter Couch Company
13315 Simon La.
Los Altos, CA 94022
(800) PET-BEDS

Rest on My Bottom

These are hilarious. Catnip Cat Cushions are made of denim shorts, spiced with fresh organic catnip. You can load them up with new catnip *through the zipper.* Each features a different kitty photo on the back pocket. Nutty cushion fun! You might also want a Catnip Cat Mat to place in the bottom of your pet carrier. Loaded with catnip, various designer patterns, 13″ × 17″.

Denim Catnip Cat Cushions, $12.95 + $4.95 S&H (Fla. res. add 91¢ sales tax)
Catnip Cat Mat, $8.95 + $3.95 S&H (Fla. res. add 63¢ sales tax)

Cathy's Cat Country
P.O. Box 86181
Madeira Beach, FL 33738
(800) 814-6811

Floor-to-Ceiling Abode

Straight up, from the floor to the ceiling! Enclosed 20″ dia. penthouse, plus two 19″ sq. perches and a solid 19″ sq. base. There are 4″ dia. sisal posts everywhere to satisfy scratching needs, plus two 10″ dia. hoops just for fun. Adjusts from 90″ to 100″ in height to secure at the ceiling. Covered post will hold securely for even the rowdiest cat parties! Your choice of blue, beige, mauve, or gray. Imagine the looks on their furry faces when they first see it.

The Khartoum, $299.99 + $9.99 S&H (Wis. res. add 5% sales tax)

Drs. Foster & Smith
P.O. Box 100
Rhinelander, WI 54501
(800) 562-7169

I'm Not Sharing My Scratching Pad!

Cats love this product. Take it out of the box and tap it a few times to settle the catnip back down into the cardboard. Put it on the floor. Call the kitty. And the scratching begins. I've had more than one of these completely shredded by my cats.

Scratch 'n' Sniff Cat Scratching Pad, $7.95

HappyCo., Ltd.
P.O. Box 514
Newport, RI
02840
(401) 849-6337

Shack or Mansion?

The choice is yours. Either the White House or the Catty Shack will fit snugly over Kitty's litter box. Both help keep litter in the box— where it belongs—and both are soil- and wear-resistant. A 7½″ round opening gives your cat plenty of room for entrance and exit. Lift off the roof for easy cleaning. Simple assembly; no tools or glue required. White House is 18″ h., Catty Shack is 25½″ h. Designed to fit most sizes of litter pans. They look great!

White House or **Catty Shack,** $19.95 each + $4.50 S&H

E. J. Jordan Company
11400 Jordan Rd.
Ocean Springs, MS 39565
(601) 392-5157

Paw Prints on My Bed ®

A snug bed with paw prints makes a cozy spot for late-afternoon catnaps. Solid plush or poly-lambswool interior. Washable, with a comfy foam core. Assorted colors.

Paw Print Plus Kitty Kup, $27.99

Information:
Flexi-Mat Corporation
2244 S. Western Ave.
Chicago, IL 60608
(312) 376-5500

Deluxe Kitty-Climbing Aerie

Close to the ultimate in cat furniture! Standing 83″ tall, this playground for the affluent kitty is manufactured with nontoxic materials, including Masonite and soft plywood. Plastic sheeting under semiplush carpet allows for easy cleaning, solid pine-rope posts, five-year written warranty. Shipping weight: 300 lbs. Call for assembly options. A spectacular climbing treat for these six lucky kitties, all of whom were adopted by their "mom," Peggy Odick, from the Montgomery County Humane Society in Maryland.

Super Deluxe MO-21 Feline Flat, $1,250 + shipping
(Md. res. add 5% sales tax)

The Company Cat House, Inc.
5916 Griffith Rd.
Laytonsville, MD 20882
(800) 238-2287

Toasty Bed ®

It's one of those chilly nights when the wind is doing its best to get into the house. Snug under your covers, you doze off with a smile on your face, knowing your kitty is as warm as you. The Thermo-Bed is great, especially for older cats. Plug it in and the double-sealed heating element directs heat upward. Soft, plush filling, available in small, medium, and large, and three colors— red, blue, and tan. Incredibly, it draws no more power than a 10-watt lightbulb. Your cat will need no coaxing!

Thermo-Bed, $35 (small), $42 (medium), $53 (large)

Information:
Pet Heating Products
P.O. Box 1674
Loveland, CO 80539
(970) 667-8492

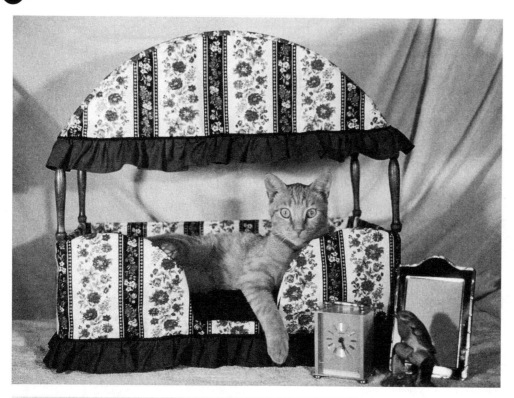

A Bed for Your Princess

There was a brief, cryptic message on my answering machine: "This woman, Stella Mitson of Santee, California, makes these incredible cat beds and somehow you have to track her down and get some pictures and put it in your book." I picked up the phone, and now you see it. These are some of the most elaborate, detailed, wondrous wooden-poster beds you will ever find. Each bed includes a two-piece wire frame, four dark-wood posts, a plush pillow, and a three-piece cotton cover set (canopy cover, pillowcase, and base cover). You can order additional cover sets separately, in a nice range of colorful fabric choices. Just beautiful.

Princess Pet Bed, $104.95 + S&H (HI, AK, PR additional shipping) (Calif. res. add 7% sales tax)

Stella's Princess Pet Beds
P.O. Box 712454
Santee, CA 92072
(619) 258-9078

Pets' Names of the Rich and Famous ®

Here's your chance to fulfill a secret longing. You've always wanted to know the names of famous people's pets, from Rum Rum Tugger (T. S. Eliot) to Pissed Off (Bo Derek) to Sophocles (Ray Bradbury) to Thunder (Olivia Newton-John) to Weeney (Martha Stewart); they're all in this paperback!

Thousands of pet names, and the stories of why those names were chosen. Cute stories, and you'll get great ideas for the name of your next cat!

By Robert Davenport, 1995, 192 pp., $5.95

General Publishing Group
2701 Ocean Park Blvd.
Suite 140
Santa Monica, CA 90405
(310) 314-4000

Launching Pad

This guy looks like he's about to take off! My cats love this scratching ramp, and its wide design provides more stability than other scratching pads. When your cat is done shredding one side, turn it over for additional thrills. You can also order replacement pads when necessary.

Max's Purr-Fect Cat Scratching Ramp with catnip, $9.95 + $3.50 S&H (Colo. res. add 38¢ sales tax)

The Cat Doctor
1710 S. Buckley Rd.
Aurora, CO 80017
(800) CAT-LUVR
E-mail: PETPROD
@aol.com

Cat's Dream Room

I'm not suggesting you purchase one of each, but would your cat complain if you did? You may, however, order this cat furniture one at a time from this company's attractive color brochure. Huge variety. One is sure to please your kitty.

The Company Cat House, Inc.
5916 Griffith Rd.
Laytonsville, MD 20882
(800) 238-2287

To Dream in a French Chateau

The French-country look of contrasting blue-and-white checks and stripes makes this an especially pleasing, comfy cat bed for Kitty. A trapunto French boy cat and girl cat trim the border. Oval in shape, measures 20″ × 16″ × 4″. Would look wonderful in a sunlit room with pastel decor.

"Le Chat" Oval Cat Bed in blue and white,
$65.50 + $6.50 S&H

L. Coffey Ltd.
4244 Linden Hills Blvd.
Minneapolis, MN 55410
(800) 448-4PET

TRUE CAT FACT

Saintly Cats

The image of cats has shifted dramatically over the centuries. The Egyptians worshiped cats. Colonial New England condemned cats as agents of the devil. And back in the Middle Ages, cats were often associated with saints. St. Agatha was called, among other things, St. Gato (Italian for *cat*); St. Gertrude of Nivelles, France, was considered the patroness of cats. St. Yves, the patron saint of lawyers (lawyers and saints? Give me a break!), was represented by a cat, which was meant to symbolize all the evil qualities of lawyers.

Teach Your Cat to Read ®

I love this crazy book. It comes in a small, flat box. Open the box and pour some kitty food (or milk) in the attached bowl. The book has large words such as *mouse, milk, cushion, bird* printed on each page, and when you prop it up, your cat starts learning to read . . . instantly! What a goof. Includes *Advanced Cat's Reader* (with bigger words, like *exercising*) and nutty suggestions for future reading. Kit includes one feeding dish with decorative embossed alphabet, two books, and built-in book stand. Kitty literacy guaranteed!

By Jean Bedford and Linda Funnell, 1994, 16 pp. each, $12.95 for kit

Chronicle Books
275 Fifth St.
San Francisco, CA 94103
(800) 722-6657

Warm Dreams

Snuggling on this sheepskin Kitty Komfort Mat will seem like a good idea to any cat. Heated bed stays 20° warmer than the surrounding area, so it's never too hot or cold. Machine-washable, soft sheepskin cover measures 12″ × 19″.

Kitty Komfort Mat, $56.95 + $6.95 S&H (Ark. res. add 6.5% sales tax)

Cat Claws, Inc.
1004 W. Broadway
Morrilton, AR 72110
(800) 783-0977

Feline Cat Tree

Your cat's ancestors lived throughout the world, and spent a sizable portion of their lives in trees—observing a potential meal and resting high in the branches after chasing it down. This tree for modern-day indoor cats has solid hardwood construction, two scratching surfaces (tree bark and carpet), a virtually untippable design, and four carpet weaves and colors to match any decor. Shown below is one of the most popular designs, featuring a perch and a tunnel for hiding and playing. Stands 34″ tall; comes fully assembled. Nontoxic silk leaves are also available for decoration (extra charge, but think about it, they look great). You can also send a swatch of your own carpet and they will match it as closely as possible.

Small Cat Tree, $99 + UPS shipping (Fla. res. add 6% sales tax)

The Jellicle Cat Company
9311 NW 26 Pl.
Sunrise, FL 33322
(954) 748-0698

Expecting?

When you're about to hear the pitter-patter of little kitty paws, you can do a couple of things. Build a comfortable, warm nest in a closet, or think about this nursery/playpen from PurrPLE Kat Pet Designs. Put it together, place it in a quiet spot, and both you and Kitty are ready for the big day. Unique three-section design offers a roomy, private den for the pregnant or nursing mother, plus there's a separate feeding area for weaned kitties and another room for the litter box. It can also serve as a den for recuperating small animals. Instant shelter and privacy. Comes folded, only 3″ h. × 36″ l.

Opened, it's 36″ l. × 36″ w. × 24″ h. Plastic (shown) or cardboard. Also makes a convenient traveling home.

Nursery/Playpen
Plastic, $79 + $15 S&H (Calif. res. add $5.53 sales tax)
Cardboard, $49 + $15 S&H (Calif. res. add $2.73 sales tax)

PurrPLE Kat Pet Designs
P.O. Box 262151
San Diego, CA 92196
(619) 689-6412

Designer Pet Houses

Please. There is absolutely no reason to stare at that old, plain plastic litter box on the bathroom floor any longer. Style, practicality, and exciting designs make these houses a sure hit with any cat owner. All can be used as either a litter box, cat bed, or pet house, and each comes equipped with a litter tray. Made from durable, lightweight 100% polypropylene, they'll handle all types of litters, will help control odors, and you can hose 'em down if necessary. Shipped folded flat; easy to assemble. And I love the designs. The gray Outhouse has a crescent moon and skylight over the hinged door, the red-and-white Barn has swinging doors, and the Pyramid . . .

the Pyramid is *great,* available with metallic gold Egyptian designs. Do yourself and the cat a big favor—take a step into the 21st century, recycle your old litter box and never look back to that tedious "tub with crud."

The Outhouse, The Barn, or **The Pyramid,** $24.95 each + $5 S&H (Calif. res. add 7.25% sales tax)

PetHouse Products
5060 Shoreham Pl., #200
San Diego, CA 92122
(800) 807-7040
www.netusa.com/
pethouse.html

My Foot's Asleep

Who's the wiseguy sticking a slipper in a cat book? Plus, where's the other one? Who's gonna buy one slipper? *You* might. This is actually a very cool, comfy, big (24″ × 14″) Musical Slipper Bed that plays Brahms's *Lullaby* when you press on the heart. Cats love its soft texture, and some snuggle in under the strap for extra warmth. Washable, too. Allie, the owner of Allie Cats, soaked one underwater for a week, and the music box still worked. Far-out and cute.

Musical Slipper Bed, $27 + $4.95 S&H (Calif. res. add 7.25% sales tax)

Allie Cats
P.O. Box 2474
Martinez, CA 94553
(800) 444-5917

TRUE CAT FACT

Where the Cat Never Goes

Let's say you don't want the cat on the kitchen counter, or the antique upholstered chair. Cats, as you know, require your approach to this problem to be pretty subtle and smart. Your cat probably isn't interested in cooperating with you. The harder you try to control him, the more he wants to be right *there,* right *now.*

Here are a few options. Try a product like the Scat Mat (page 130), which delivers a mild shock to the cat when he jumps up where you don't want him. It only takes once or twice before he gets the message. Another approach is using aerosol cat sprays that smell bad to cats. They may also smell bad to people, cost as much as $7 per can, and sometimes they work, sometimes they don't. Do a test spray to check out the smell before you buy.

Finally, here are two effective natural approaches. Cut a white onion in half and rub it lightly on the counter or furniture. Cats hate the smell. Even when you can't smell it, they can. Vinegar is the ultimate cat deterrent. It's cheap, invisible, and the sharp odor is deeply offensive to Kitty's nose. If you have an old bottle of white wine around that's been open for some time, you might want to try using that (wine turns to vinegar over time). If you ask me, I'd say the natural approach is the best approach.

Dear Tabby: Feline Advice on Love, Life, and the Pursuit of Mice ®

Letters from cats to Tabby, asking advice à la the *Dear Abby* column we humans turn to every day in newspapers, reveal that cats have lots of questions. Serious questions. Here's what they're asking about in this hardcover: romance, parental anxiety, behavior protocol, grooming problems, curiosity . . . it's endless and very funny. Much more interesting than human problems.

By Leigh W. Rutledge, 1995, 104 pp., $10.95

Dutton
375 Hudson St.
New York, NY
10014
(212) 366-2000

First-Class Exhibitor's Cage

For those of you with a fancy for formally showing your beautiful kitties, consider the catSafe Exhibitor's Security Cage. If you're new to cat shows, start out by visiting a few, talking to folks, reading some books, and getting information from the many cat-breeder associations. When you're ready, this clever cage will be great for housing your kitties at a show. Folds down to just 4″ wide for traveling, provides quality protection against theft (heavens!), poisoning (gasp!), bacterial problems, mites, and other bugs floating around cat shows. Hidden air holes, exhaust fan displaces 13 cu. ft. of air per minute, acrylic sliding doors with cabinet-type lock, kitty sleeping shelf, includes battery charger. It just plain looks good, too. Only the best for your precious kitties.

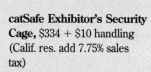

catSafe Exhibitor's Security Cage, $334 + $10 handling (Calif. res. add 7.75% sales tax)

CD&E Enterprises
5933 Sea Lion Pl.
Suite 101
Carlsbad, CA 92008
(800) 528-2243

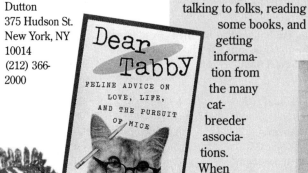

Making an Entrance

The leopard-print Hollywood Pet House is so elegant it puts most other cat houses to shame. Comfy inside for naps and observation (measures 13″ h. × 17″ dia.). Place a plant on top, add the matching Hollywood Catnip Ball, and you get the picture.

Hollywood Pet House, $139.50 + $10.50 S&H
Hollywood Catnip Ball, $12 + $3.50 S&H

L. Coffey Ltd.
4244 Linden Hills Blvd.
Minneapolis, MN 55410
(800) 448-4PET

TRUE CAT FACT

Lyme Disease and Ticks

Lyme disease has been described as "a year-long case of the flu." Humans affected by the disease typically experience low energy, arthritislike symptoms, a concentric-circle rash, neurological disorders, and heart problems. Pet symptoms include lethargy, lameness, and potential heart problems. Lyme disease in both humans and pets is treatable with antibiotics, and it's more common than most people realize. Most researchers agree that it's transmitted by the bite of infected ticks, but new evidence suggests that it might also be passed through the saliva, blood, or urine of an infected animal. So keep your eyes open for ticks, and keep them off your cats!

Large Cat Tree with Pagoda

One of the best things about The Jellicle Cat Company is that they'll custom-make the cat tree of your very own design. The S2/G2 model has room for three or more cats to have a place way up high, perched on the roof of the pagoda. Add in the tunnel and viewing/napping cubbies, and you have a towering 75"-tall masterpiece of solid hardwood and plush or Berber carpet. Want more? What you see is just one possibility. Custom-design your perch, using Jellicle's catalog. Tree-trunk posts can be waterproofed for outdoor use.

Large Cat Tree with Pagoda, (Model S2/G2), $429 + freight (Fla. res. add 6% sales tax)

The Jellicle Cat Company
9311 NW 26 Pl.
Sunrise, FL 33322
(954) 748-0698

Custom Triplex for Your Kitty Family!

Don't you just love this? The triplex roof is pitched stylishly on an angle, making plenty of room for sunbathing. Three side-by-side living spaces, with nice doorways and stained trim. Indoor/outdoor carpeting inside each house, as well as a scratching pad on the roof. Approximate size: 16" w. × 48" l. × 25½" h. Best of all, you can order a similar version of this house as a four-unit home, a duplex, or as a beautiful single unit for just one cat. Inquire about customization.

Accommodations for Four, $309.99 + $21.95 S&H
Accommodations for Three (shown), $229.99 + $18.95 S&H

Accommodations for Two, $159.99 + $16.95 S&H
Accommodations for One, $99.95 + $13.95 S&H (N.J. res. add 6% sales tax)

Kittytowne, USA
308 Duff Ave.
Wenonah, NJ 08090
(609) 468-3183

Baby-Kitty Nest

If my Himalayan Bella got pregnant, I would immediately do two things. First, I'd call the vet and ask for my money back—she's supposed to be spayed. Second, like all anxious fathers, I'd do whatever it took to make everything go as smoothly as possible. Whelping Nests are wonderful: small circular nests for newborn animals that help control the body heat of these little babies. Cold is the single greatest danger to the newborn. This nest keeps baby kitties warm by electricity and radiant heat to within 1° of the desired body heat for their health and comfort. They can snuggle up next to one another and be warm as toast. If Mama Cat happened to wander off or get distracted, I'd rest easily as the proud father, knowing that the little ones are safe.

T. E. Heated Whelping Nest, $199.95 + $7.50 S&H (Ind. res. add 5% sales tax)

T. E. Scott, Inc.
9927 U.S. Highway 36
Avon, IN 46168
(800) 989-4178

Kitty's Dinosaur

Give Kitty her own furniture for scratching. Baby Dino measures 30″ l. × 24″ h. An ideal viewing, napping, and scratching place, it's made from thick, durable carpeting and has a base for stability and a level area on Dino's back for sacking out. Particulary nifty if you have young children in the house.

Baby Dino, $99.99 + UPS S&H (Penn. res. add 6% sales tax)

Discount Master Animal Care Catalog
1 Mazlewood Dr.
Hazleton, PA 18201
(800) 346-0749

Hold-the-Beans Bed

Cool taco bed is big, comfortable fun for your cat. Folded over like a taco, it's made of tortillalike cotton fabric on the outside, plush fake fur on the inside, and trimmed with cotton "lettuce" and "cheese." Machine-washable; 20″ dia.

Cat Taco Bed, $30 + $4 S&H (Calif. res. add $2.18 sales tax)

Small Town Ideas, Inc.
P.O. Box 1905
Lower Lake, CA 95457
(707) 994-0552

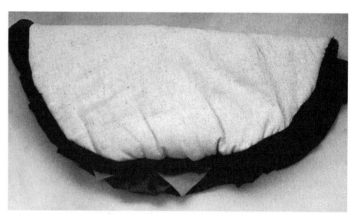

Feline Restroom Throne

During long New England winters, Frank and Judy Gatta of Woburn, Massachusetts, created one of the most unusual—and practical—litter boxes I've ever seen. Here's how it works: It looks like a little house, and when you lift the roof you'll find a refillable compartment you can load with up to 25 lbs. of clean cat litter. Pull out the childproof "safety lock" handle—just below the windows—and new litter falls into the litter box, just below it (make sure the cat's not in there when you do this!). The old litter drops through a false bottom in the litter pan into a plastic bag when you pull another lever, hidden in a compartment behind the steps. Completely manual, simple, reduces litter-box odors, uses no electricity, and it looks great! Handmade with painted white and red windows; the birch wood frame is treated with marine varnish to resist staining and liquids. Plush, carpeted stairway leads Kitty to the "rest stop." You'll never handle kitty litter again! Patented. Custom designs available.

According to Judy, there were two jobs Frank hated around the house: taking out the trash and taking out the kitty litter. Frank is a happier man today, and you will be, too!

Feline Restroom, $389.95 and up, + UPS S&H (Mass. res. add 5% sales tax)

Superior Pet Products
5 Donna Rd.
Woburn, MA 01801
(617) 938-9258

TRUE CAT FACT

Moving Your Cat Indoors

Need a good reason to turn your outdoor cat into an indoor cat? Indoor cats easily live twice as long as outdoor cats.

So let's say you've made the decision. How do you go about it? Start by neutering/spaying your pet, if you haven't already done so. It's difficult to adapt an unaltered pet to indoor life. Next, confine the cat to one room, with a litter box and food. To ease the adjustment, mix some real soil in with the litter. Keep the cat in this room for three or four days. Each time you visit, play with the cat, and put him in the litter box. After this adjustment period—and if he's using the litter box—allow the cat to roam the house. Put him back into the room at night and when you're not home.

Your cat has been used to exploring the world. Make him an "armchair traveler" by letting him watch special action videos for cats, or creating a good spot by a window where he can observe the world. Provide plenty of toys for mental and physical exercise. There's no excuse for boredom!

Dinner with a View

Given a choice, many cats would love to eat on a feeding platform, off the floor. This clever Cat Cafe mounts on an indoor window sill, keeping cat food out of reach of the family dog and children. Kitty feels safe and secure up there, and the transparent wall that surrounds the front and side of the feeder allows you to watch him enjoy his meal.

Cat Cafe Feeding Platform, $39.95 + $5 S&H (Calif. res. add sales tax)

Adams Precision Design, Inc.
P.O. Box 591036
San Francisco, CA 94159
(800) 600-3643

Scratching the Dog

This is something cats have dreamed of for centuries! Cats Bow Wow is a wall-mounted 24″ scratching post in the shape of a black-and-white-spotted dog. Also known as "Getting Even," it's hand-painted and carpeted. Brackets for mounting included. It's about time cats had their day.

Cats Bow Wow Scratching Post, $34.95 (N.Y. res. add 8.25% sales tax)

Cat Cottage
133 Lafayette Ave.
Holbrook, NY 11741
(516) 981-6685

Catcalls, British-Style

This is a real conversation piece. This charming, funny, cozy cat bed is imported from England. It's one of the few cat beds in the world suitable for keeping in the living room, even when you have guests. Made of high-density foam, painted viscose, and acrylic fur fabrics. Bright red! Machine-washable. Measures 15″ × 15″ × 27″.

Telephone Bed, $49 + $6 S&H (Mass. res. add 5% sales tax)

The Catnip Trading Company
P.O. Box 451
Lexington, MA 02173
(800) 822-8647

I'll Take My Nap Here!

My cats love to try new resting spots. Put down a mat or a pad, and they're right there to sit on it. This bright red Cat Mat with cat logo makes an inviting spot. Washable, comfy, and warm.

Cat Mat, $12 + $5.45 S&H (Tenn. res. add 8.25% sales tax)

The Zerick Company
837 Country La.
Walland, TN 37886
(800) 977-1650

Natural Kitty Furniture ®

This is almost like being in the woods. Each piece is unique because the wood is natural, made of maple, box elder, mulberry, oak, cherry, or ash to create an unusual environment. This version stands 3′ tall, and it's a great rest stop, especially since there's catnip hidden within the plush carpet.

Natural Furniture Cat Tree, $75

Information:
American Cat Emporium
103 Oakdale Rd.
Camp Douglas, WI 54618
(800) 752-6228

All I Need to Know I Learned from My Cat ®

Cats have the luxury of time. They may seem indolent, but all that time makes them extremely well-equipped to contemplate life. This small paperback of cat musings contains useful life-lessons for humans. Life is frantic enough. Relax, read, amuse yourself with this light book of cat philosophy. It's not rocket science, but then again, when was the last time you paused to enjoy the moment? Cats do—all the time. It's a good thing to remember.

By Suzy Becker, 1990, 88 pp., $5.95

Workman Publishing
708 Broadway
New York, NY 10003
(800) 722-7202

TRUE CAT FACT

Crazy Cat Games

Cat looking bored? Is she going nuts at night running around the house? Well, cats are nocturnal, and they need to burn off energy. One potential solution is to feed her just before your bedtime. But that might make a fat cat. Try making a real effort to play with your cat—even 10 or 15 minutes a day keeps her healthy and interested in you. There are marvelous "interactive" toys in this book that are proven cat favorites. And here are some simple games:

- **Light Hunt:** Turn out all the lights in the room, grab a flashlight, and watch Kitty pounce away.

- **Food Search:** Hide some little nibblies (kibble, dry cat food) around a room—under the sofa, behind a bureau, under a cushion—be creative. Have Kitty watch you as you do it. Feed her a piece first, then watch her look for the buried treasure.

- **New Room:** Cat brains need to be engaged! Gently place your cat in the top of your closet, or some other place you don't let her go. Let her explore something new. (Make sure you're available when she's done checking the place out.)

When a Pole Is More than a Tree

The Cat-A-Pole is more than just another cat tree. It requires no tools for assembly, and the combined shelves and tension rod make for added stability. There are two other varieties: Sleeper and the Cube. Catnip-scented, handcrafted, all wood with quality earth-tone carpeting. A 6′ cat climb to the ceiling.

Cat-A-Pole, $79

Information:
American Cat Emporium
103 Oakdale Rd.
Camp Douglas, WI 54618
(608) 427-6875

Walking Up the Fence

What a great way to get up a fence! The Kitty Walk (shown in 10′ length) attaches securely to plaster, wood, brick, concrete, or chain link, and comes complete with two 12″ l. × 10″ w. sitting perches. Reduces chance of injury to your kitty, eliminates scratch marks on your fence. Weatherproofed with a water-based white stain finish and can be installed indoors or outdoors to complement your home.

The Kitty Walk, $149.95 + $12.95 S&H
(Calif. res. add 7.75% sales tax)

Avcon Products
10162 Orangewood Ave.
Garden Grove, CA 92640
(714) 530-4828

A Gathering of Cats

Deep in her 14 acres surrounded by the virgin forest of the Catskills, Era Zistel observed nature and animals, particularly cats. As the seasons passed in her quiet world, she compiled the stories of many cats that entered her life. The result is a remarkable paperback collection of 14 stories that celebrate the complexity of cat personalities. These cats might seem ordinary at first, but first impressions can be deceiving. The author had many quiet hours to sit, observe, and take notes; her writing exudes the reassuring calm and peace of nature and country life. My favorite story is "The Wild Cat."

By Era Zistel, 1993, 126 pp., $11.95 + $2 S&H

J. N. Townsend Publishing
12 Greenleaf Dr.
Exeter, NH 03833
(603) 778-9883

Living-with-Cats Furniture

Interesting idea: furniture for you, *and* the cats. After all, they live here, too! This cat-friendly end table, part of a new line of furniture, is 23½″ h., and the surface is 18″ × 24″ × 1½″ oak butcher block. The oak legs are tightly wrapped with 200 ft. of imported Brazilian sisal. In other words, it's both a very attractive table and a functional scratching post for Kitty!

Living with Cats End Table, $139 + S&H (Mass. res. add 5% sales tax)

The Catnip Trading Company
P.O. Box 451
Lexington, MA 02173
(800) 822-8647

Cherry Cat Beds

These beds are authentic miniature reproductions of famous rice planters' beds from the post–Civil War rice plantations found throughout the South. Posts are carved from solid cherry wood and bedframe has a fine cherry veneer. Headboard and footboard come preassembled, side rails are easily attached with screws provided. A lovely canopy cover is also available (not shown). Price of the bed includes mattress with washable cover. Cream-colored bedding is all cotton and washable. Absolutely beautiful.

Rice Planter Kitty Bed, $130 + S&H
Bedding, $65 + S&H

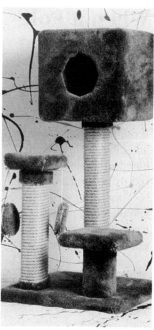

Canopy & Cover, $50 + S&H (N.C. res. add 6% sales tax)

Jessie's Treasures
Rt. 3, Tower Rd.
Thomasville, NC 27360
(910) 475-3422

Lifetime Furniture

The Mini Playground with optional sisal rope not only looks good, it's guaranteed for life. Solid-wood construction with quality carpeting. The sisal makes a superior scratching post. Combines Kitty's sleeping quarters with a play-and-exercise area. Measures 38″ h. × 19″ w. square base. Many other models from which to choose.

Mini Playground, $149.95 + freight

Catalog: $1
Abeta Products
5021 Tara Tea Dr.
Tega Cay, SC 29715
(803) 548-1019

California Cat Futon

Futons are foldable beds with cotton sleeping pads. This one's for cats. Specially downsized for the feline physique, it's the same design and quality as a "people" futon.

The sturdy frame is made of solid pine, with a cushion of soft, warm acrylic lambswool on one side and designer fabric on the other. Folds down into a flat bed. Available in small (20″ × 24″) or large (24″ × 30″) cushion sizes. It could only come from California!

Cat Futon, $69.95 (small); $89.95 (large); includes S&H (Calif. res. add 8.25% sales tax)

Allie Cats
c/o Pacific Fulfillment
P.O. Box 2474
Martinez, CA 94553
(800) 444-5917

Cottage in the Woods ®

A real tree holds up the carpeted platform and two sisal rope toys next to this carpeted cat house. Kitty can snooze inside the wood house, on the roof, on the platform, or just scratch it all up at will. House is 24″ tall, tree is 30″ tall. Nice kitty country resort.

Cat Cottage, $79

Information:
American Cat Emporium
103 Oakdale Rd.
Camp Douglas, WI 54618
(608) 427-6875

California MouseHouse

This is great! Cats love the specially designed acrylic lambswool interior. Sturdy kitty and heart beads double as a play toy. Measures 26″ l. × 15″ h. × 13″ w. For a small cat, an ironic kitty-in-a-mouse-house for napping and observing the world.

MouseHouse, $36
(Calif. res. add 8.25% sales tax)

Allie Cats
c/o Pacific Fulfillment
P.O. Box 2474
Martinez, CA 94553
(800) 444-5917

Walkway to the Stars

Perfect for reaching that favorite viewing window, the Kitty Walk Deluxe (3′ window height shown) includes a dangling play ball with a natural sisal scratching area. The 15″ l. × 12″ w. perch supports a 25-lb. cat. Includes carpeting in assorted colors and assembly and installation instructions, as well as a training guide

to walking felines through the standard steps. Superior quality, available for 3′, 4′, and 5′ window heights.

Kitty Walk Deluxe, $79.95 +
$12.95 S&H
(Calif. res. add 7.75% sales tax)

Avcon Products
10162 Orangewood Ave.
Garden Grove, CA 92640
(714) 530-4828

Teepee Kitty! ®

This cute lined teepee is just right for a cozy nap or hanging out. Thick white base pad provides plenty of comfort, and the colorful "Santa Fe"

Southwest look matches any decor.

Kitty Teepee, $30

Information:
Dogloo, Inc.
1241 Old Temescal
Corona, CA 91719
(909) 279-9500
E-mail: dogloo1@aol.com

Diary of a Cat ®

If cats could write—and we all know they certainly think—they just might put down musings similar to the "true confessions and life-long observations of a well-adjusted house cat" found in this hardcover. Here's a cat who has it made, knows his neighborhood, and has something to say about everything—including kids, holidays, other cats, and why he stares at that spot on the wall for so, so long.

By Leigh W. Rutledge, 1995, 70 pp., $12.95

Dutton
375 Hudson St.
New York, NY 10014
(212) 366-2000

In the Cave

Time for a nap? Secure cave uses thick foam wall construction and several decorative fabrics, including this lively kitty-fabric pattern. Floor is of black faux fur. Cave measures 16″ h. × 17″ w. × 16″ dia.

Hideaway Lodge

Need a break? This cedar lodge provides the perfect getaway when Kitty feels the need for privacy. Interior is completely lined with denim and padded with thick 100% natural unbleached cotton for maximum comfort. Ample bottom cushion is removable for laundering. May also be adapted for outdoors. Other customization choices available.

Lodge (shown), $150
Lodge with covered porch, $200
Lodge with covered porch & outdoor cedar shake roof, $250
Price includes free home delivery within the U.S., except Alaska and Hawaii.
(Tex. res. add 6.75% sales tax)

House of Cats International
25011 Bell Mountain Dr.
San Antonio, TX 78255
(800) 889-7402

Pet Cave, $39.00

Information:
Caddis Manufacturing, Inc.
3120 N. Highway 99W
McMinnville, OR 97128
(503) 472-3111

Fluffy Mat

Handmade in Montana, this durable, warm cat mat is machine-washable and -dryable. A fluffy, affordable instant bed to put in the sun or on your sofa.

The Cat Mat, $15 + S&H

Pet Pals, Inc.
107 Sun Ave.
Livingston, MT 59047
(800) 999-5366

Sleepy Circle ®

Cats love a cozy, soft bed, and the "egg crate" molded foam bottom (with no CFCs) makes this one especially comfortable. The 7″ sides help reduce drafts while allowing Kitty to keep an eye on things. Cover is machine-washable with elastic around the bottom for easy removal. Inside fabric is white sherpa, outside is a nice kitty-print design. 15″ dia.

Cat 'n' Round, $20.95

Information:
Caddis Manufacturing, Inc.
3120 N. Highway 99W
McMinnville, OR 97128
(503) 472-3111

The Top Cat's Home

For the kitty who demands distinction, consider the Victorian (shown), Federal, or Colonial Executive Kitty Homes. These are beautiful, made of sturdy plywood and completely covered in bold red, white, and blue catnip-scented carpet. Features several easy-access entries as well as removable roof with openings for Kitty to peek out from. Two-story layout measures 30″ w. × 20″ dia. × 24″ h. All homes are available in assorted designer colors, and come complete with a house deed and a home warranty. That's Groucho peeking out of the Victorian model!

Executive Kitty Home,
$379.95 + $12.95 S&H
(Calif. res. add 7.75% sales tax)

Avcon Products
10162 Orangewood Ave.
Garden Grove, CA 92640
(714) 530-4828

Tropical Furniture

Bright tropical colors and palm-tree designs liven up this great furniture. Each story is accompanied by a carpeted shelf and also allows access to the next story. Heavy, quality carpeting portrays palm trees with tan trunks and gorgeous green palm fronds. Two-Story Condo measures 21½″ h. × 18″ dia. Three-Story is 21″ h. × 18″ dia. A reminder to both of you that somewhere the warm sun is shining on palm trees.

Two-Story Condo, $72.99 + UPS
Three-Story Condo, $99.99 + UPS
(Penn. res. add 6% sales tax)

The Little Red Wagon

Perhaps you had and loved a little red wagon as a child. Now here's one for your kitty. Fully carpeted, with fun handle to push it around. Put Kitty in and give her a ride. Nice to sleep in, too!

The Little Red Wagon,
$81.99 + UPS (Penn. res. add 6% sales tax)

Discount Master Animal Care Catalog
P.O. Box 3333
Mountaintop, PA 18707
(800) 346-0749

Floral Kitty Couch

This is cute. Couch has an upholstered look, with a variety of fabrics to choose from. Or you can supply your own fabric for a custom couch to match your decor. Made with quality foam, cotton fabric with zippers for easy removal, and a sturdy plastic frame support. Replacement cushions and extra covers also available.

Kitty Couch, $129 + $24 S&H
(Calif. res. add 7.75% sales tax)

Critter Couch Company
13315 Simon La.
Los Altos, CA 94022
(800) PET-BEDS

Natural Lighting for Pets

Ott lights have been on the scene for many years. The Valentine company, started 50 years ago, sells a complete selection of these remarkable full-spectrum lights. They were created by Dr. John Ott, who discovered, as a photographer, that he could not grow indoor plants with artificial lighting. Ott went on to invent the first total-spectrum radiation-shielded light sources. Light—full-spectrum natural light—plays a subtle but very important role in how we function as living creatures. These natural lights can make a difference in the life of you and your cat. They're available as reading lamps, overhead fixtures, and for desks. To learn more, and to check out Valentine's many other cat products, just give them a call.

Ott Lights, prices vary

Valentine, Inc.
4259 S. Western Blvd.
Chicago, IL 60609
(800) GET -STUF

Treasure Your Thoughts ®

A blank hardcover with ruled pages for your greatest thoughts, and a cat or kitten picture on each page. Perfect as a diary, idea book, recipe keeper, you name it. All those little notes you've been jotting on scraps of paper would fit in here nicely.

Cats Anything Book, $7.99

Outlet Books, Inc.
40 Engelhard Ave.
Avenel, NJ 07001
(800) 733-3000

Wild Litter Boxes

Moortser sells eccentric decorated litter boxes that verge on the creatively bizarre. From the Valentine (red roses and hearts, trimmed with red and white ribbons, silk roses topped with ceramic cupids) to the Troll (trimmed with beads and seashells, sprayed to provide the feel of sand), these designs are one of a kind. There's a design for every interest: shell collecting, crapshooting, sports, cartoons, hot mama, Christmas, gold glitz, Cleopatra, flower garden . . . it's endless. Their catalog is a scream!

Decorated Litter Boxes, each $65 + $7.95 S&H (Fla. res. add 6% sales tax)

Moortser, Inc.
2620 N. Miami Ave.
Miami, FL 33127
(800) 557-4228

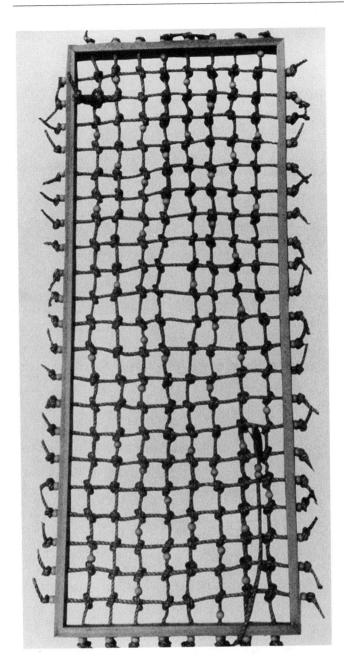

Modular Kitty Furniture

The Kitty Klimber arrives at your door in seven individual pieces that slide snugly together with no tools. It's fun furniture for napping, viewing, and scratching. Solid-wood construction; choice of color combinations to match your decor.

Kitty Klimber, $149.95 + UPS shipping
(Calif. res. add sales tax)

Animal Attic
P.O. Box 1305
W. Sacramento, CA 95691
(800) 65-ATTIC

Warm, Cozy Rest Stop ®

We all need a snug, safe spot to call our own for cat-naps. This fits just right. Durable simulated fleece interior insulates from cold, damp floors. It's warm in winter, cool in summer. Soft polyfoam core with a removable machine-washable cover. Catnap Central.

Kozy Kup, $33.99

Information:
Flexi-Mat Corporation
2244 S. Western Ave.
Chicago, IL 60608
(312) 376-5500

Climbing the Walls

There is genius at work here. Your made-to-order Climbing Net is created with your choice of sisal or manila rope. It's woven and tied in 2″ squares, then stretched over a frame of natural cedar. Order this incredible net by the square foot to fit the dimensions of your wall. Cats love to climb, and protruding feather toys and movable wooden beads are inter-spersed within the net for their batting enjoyment. May also be used as a ladder or for spanning spaces (from entertainment centers in other locations). Brilliant.

Climbing Net, $30 sq. ft. Price includes free home delivery within the U.S., except Alaska and Hawaii.
(Tex. res. add 6.75% sales tax)

House of Cats International
25011 Bell Mountain Dr.
San Antonio, TX 78255
(800) 889-7402

"I'll Rest Here, Thank You" ®

How about a nice, thick fluffy pad (or several) for Kitty to rest on every now and then during her usual tour of the house? Soft, cozy fleece provides plush comfort and orthopedic pressure reduction. Stain-resistant, reversible, nonallergenic. Toasty warm in winter, cool in summer, plus it folds easily for travel. You bring your pillow, she brings her Flexi-Fleece. Machine-washable and -dryable.

Flexi-Fleece, (15″ × 20″) $13.99; (20″ × 30″) $20.99; (30″ × 40″) $36.99

Information:
Flexi-Mat Corporation
2244 S. Western Ave.
Chicago, IL 60608
(312) 376-5500

Room to Move

This is a great idea. What if you're traveling, or you need to be someplace with your cat for hours? Do you keep her bunched up in a carrier? The Home Stretch is a patented, portable, collapsible cat shelter/enclosure that makes sense when you're on the move. Made of water-resistant nylon, it has staking tabs for outside use and a tab to attach a cat leash. The "house" comes with either a 3′ or 4′ screened, zippered "run," and the whole unit fits into its own carrying case. Four sizes, from mini to large. Particularly handy if you need to shelter your cat in the event—God forbid—of an earthquake or other natural calamity. Housing a cat is a big problem to people if they suddenly have to leave home. If you grab the Home Stretch, the litter box, and food, your cat is protected.

Home Stretch, $127 (small); $192 (large) + $6.25 S&H (Calif. res. add 7% sales tax)

Stopgap Enterprises
1240 S. Grade Rd.
 Alpine, CA 91901
          (619) 445-8856

Scratching from the Start

Cats will scratch, do what one may. They have to: It's healthy. If you have an adult cat, give serious thought to the Claw Dandy (16″ dia. × 3″ thick), luxuriously padded and shaped to resemble an attractive quilted pillow. Kittens have their own Kitten Trainer (12″ dia.). Many breeders think that a kitten can be trained, early on, to scratch a preferred surface.

The kitten learns to scratch only that, or a similar surface, instead of wreaking havoc on your sofa and drapes. Both are high-quality scratching pads, and they look good. As you might expect, many cats wind up using the pad as a bed, too!

Original Claw Dandy, $19.95 + $5.50 S&H
Kitten Trainer, $9.95 + $4 S&H
(Ill. res. add 6.75% sales tax)

Dandy Products
P.O. Box 12
Lombard, IL 60148
(708) 627-7155

Felines: Great Poets on Notorious Cats ®

No other animal has inspired so much devotion or literary attention as the cat. Accompanying beautiful linocut (similar to woodblock) illustrations are the musings of 20 famous poets, including Marianne Moore, Emily Dickinson, Ogden Nash, Alice Adams, J. R. R. Tolkien, Pablo Neruda, and William Carlos Williams. Attractive hardcover with thoughtful—occasionally irreverent—reflections on our buddy, the cat.

Compiled by Fly Productions, linocuts by Martha Paulos, 1992, 64 pp., $14.95

Chronicle Books
275 Fifth St.
San Francisco, CA 94103
(415) 777-7240

Cabitat

This could be something out of a *Star Trek* show. An ultramodern, beautiful house made of washable polyethylene, it's available in nine colors to match your house interior. Cats need their own personal space. Removable, washable carpet included. Measures 24″ l. × 14.5″ w. × 12″ h.

Cabitat, $47 + $6 S&H

Innovative Design, Inc.
P.O. Box 172001
Memphis, TN 38187
(901) 452-6222

Scratch It to Bits! ®

All cats need to scratch, and this door-hanging 100% natural sisal scratcher gives them a rough, tough texture they love to dig their claws into. Sisal's also great for conditioning claw muscles and removing old claw coverings. It sure beats getting your sofa torn up! Cats love it; for them it's like going to the gym.

Clawtuff Natural Sisal ScratchR, $19.60

Information:
Clawtuff Corporation
13602-12th St.
Chino, CA 91710
(800) 252-9883

Landlords & Cats

Before you move into a new place, always check your lease for a clause that prohibits pets. If there is such a clause but you really want the new place, be prepared to convince the landlord that you're a responsible cat owner. Here's how. Set up a meeting with the landlord and take Kitty along in a pet carrier or on a leash. Introduce the cat to your landlord as you would a person. Hand the landlord a brief written resume about your cat: name, age, personality, special traits that endear her to you. Include your vet's name and phone number. Include references from past landlords who will vouch for the fact that your cat didn't spray or tear up the place. Offer, if necessary, a modest, refundable security deposit for your cat as an act of goodwill. This personal approach will often work.

Patio Cabana

Cats are masters of leisure. The Kitty Cabana offers the upscale advantage of all-cedar construction with a strong Plexiglas sunroof to allow light onto the enclosed stainless-steel litter box. Kitty can lounge on a suede or hand-washable denim or canvas cushion, stuffed with 100% natural unbleached cotton. What could be better? Dynamic design elements include natural oak branches and a kinetic, sculptural quality in all-natural wood or the finish of your choice. Customized features available. Measures 27″ h. × 36″ w. × 8″ dia. Superb.

Kitty Cabana, $500
Price includes free home delivery within the U.S., except Alaska and Hawaii.
(Tex. res. add 6.75% sales tax)

House of Cats International
25011 Bell Mountain Dr.
San Antonio, TX 78255
(800) 889-7402

The Literary Cat: Quips, Quotes, and Observations ®

Tiny, illustrated paperback of quips, quotes, and musings by writers and artists. In the words of Mark Twain: "If man could be crossed with the cat, it would improve man but deteriorate the cat." Amusing . . .

Compiled by Running Press, 1990, 38 pp., $4.95

Running Press
125 S. 22nd St.
Philadelphia, PA 19103
(215) 568-2919

Royal Seat Cover ®

Where's your cat's favorite spot? Most have a favorite chair or other resting area. The problem with that is the cat fur all over your furniture. (Well, we both know it's not really *your chair,* anyway.) This luxurious plush throw might just solve that fur and soiling problem. With a paw-print design in three colors (blue, green, or beige), the throw measures 30″ × 36″, is machine-washable, and won't shrink or fade. The Sofa Throw is larger, measuring 30″ × 60″. Great for use at home or in the car.

Paw-Print Plush Chair Throw, $24.99
Sofa Throw, $35.99

Information:
Flexi-Mat Corporation
2244 S. Western Ave.
Chicago, IL 60608
(312) 376-5500

Chapter Three

Classy Cat Clothing and Jewelry

Classic City Cat

From the Classic Collection of
L. Coffey Ltd. come these stunning
Perfect Purrls for Cats. Your kitty
will look oh-so-beautiful wearing
these classy pearls on a loose-fitting
collar that includes five bright, dangling fish. What could be more
upscale and uptown? You must get
Linda Coffey's catalog of other
incredible kitty gifts.

Perfect Purrls for Cats,
$15 + $3.50 S&H

L. Coffey Ltd.
4244 Linden Hills Blvd.
Minneapolis, MN 55410
(800) 448-4PET

Meeting Other Cat Lovers

Show off your love of cats with this
attractive white sweatshirt. You'll get
more compliments than you'd believe.
Quality white shirt with letters in red,
black, brown, orange, and white.
Interesting way to advertise your love
of cats and meet other cat lovers.
Additional color choices, too.

Pet Lover Sweatshirt,
$24.99 + $3.95 S&H
(N.J. res. add 6% sales tax)

W.R.S. Marketing
207 Stahls Way
N. Plainfield, NJ 07060
(800) 815-2606

Cloisonné Artistry

The enameled jewels of Merry Lee Rae are dramatically different from anything you've ever seen, the personal expression of this warm and enthusiastic artist. This neckpiece is made of 18k gold and cloisonné enamel, 5″ wide, from an edition of nine. To be worn with an 18k gold chain, provided. The white cloisonné face of the Creampuff pendant can be worn as either a pin or as a necklace with the sterling silver chain included. Measuring 1⅜″ × 1½″, made of sterling silver and enamel, it's affordable custom cloisonné. From an edition of 36. Unique and beautiful statements of your love of the cat.

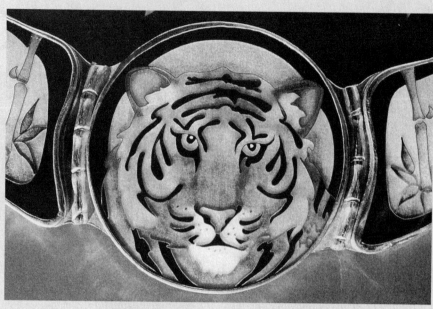

Tiger Neckpiece/Collar, $8,600 + $5 S&H + $25.80 insurance (Calif. res. add 8.25% sales tax [$709.50])
Creampuff Cloisonné, $360 + $5 S&H + $1.20 insurance (Calif. res. add 8.25% sales tax [$29.70])

Merry Lee Rae
Rae Studios
P.O. Box 536
Aptos, CA 95001
(408) 761-2844

Nine-Lives Shirt

Fun artwork of nine cats is embroidered in muted colors on this dressy white cotton shirt. Ask about the silver Cat Button Covers. This could be your lucky shirt. Fits sizes 6–14. Machine washable.

Nine-Lives Blouse,
$60 + $7.95 S&H
Cat Button Covers,
$18 + $4.95 S&H
(Tex. res. add 7.25% sales tax)

Accessory Pet
5836 Pathfinder Trail
Plano, TX 75093
(800) 558-7387

The Unexplainable

The phenomenon of cats finding their owners in a place they've never been before is scientifically known as Psi-trailing. Many well-documented stories tell of cats that have walked hundreds, even thousands of miles to find their owners. One cat walked all the way from Florida to California. Another walked from New York to Denver. One cat took two years to find her owner, who had moved to another state.

These are irrefutable, carefully researched facts. How do we explain them? One theory is that cats possess extraordinary psychic abilities, far beyond human capacity or understanding. Some scientists believe that cats can tune in to other dimensions of reality which we, as humans, have lost the ability to sense (aside from our occasional brushes with ESP and déjà vu).

Garden Kitty Nap

Artist Siri Schillios portrays a beautiful orange kitty "napped out" in bright flowers and green leaves. Fabulous colors and brilliance on a T-shirt you'll love to wear. Subtle, classy.

Helping in the Garden,
$19.95 + $3 S&H
M, L, XL, & XXL
(Add $1 for XXL)

Catfish Designs
P.O. Box 40326
Portland, OR 97240
(800) 441-8522

Who's Who of Cats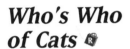

Here they are: hundreds of very short stories about individual cats, some with pictures. As the book cover succinctly states, "extraordinary lives of ordinary cats." The paperback alphabetically focuses on the lives of cats throughout America in brief, fascinating narratives as told to the author by their *companions*. A snapshot look into the lives of hundreds of cats.

Edited by John Breen, 1994, 504 pp., $7.95

Workman Publishing
708 Broadway
New York, NY 10003
(212) 254-5900

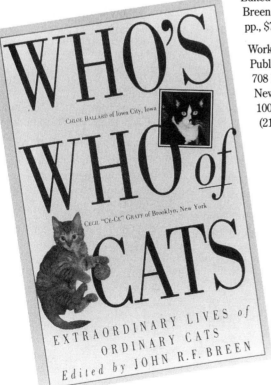

Cats To Wear

Beautiful full-color cat paintings on quality T-shirts and sweatshirts, all sizes, incredible range of styles and designs, including kitschy cartoons—clawing up the sofa, litter-box humor, other goofy, fun cat behavior. More than 100 to choose from. Sizes up to 6XL.

Good Vibrations
Shirts from $15.99,
Sweatshirts from $25.99

RR #2, Box 317
Englishtown Rd.
Old Bridge, NJ 08857
(908) 251-5959

Wear Your Love for Cats!

The art on these beautiful T-shirts is based on original paintings by artists from the American Northwest. Made to last and last. Silk-screening on 100% heavy-weight cotton makes the colors *pop!*

The Calico Cat T-shirts, $16 + $3.50 S&H 1st shirt (additional shirts $1 S&H) M, L, XL

Calico Cat
640 W. 1st Ave.
Eugene, OR 97402
(503) 686-6631

Calvin (not Klein) Face

Who could resist a face like this! Now you can wear it on a great 100% cotton T-shirt created by Siri Schillios. Her fanciful felines have delighted cat lovers worldwide, and her art is featured in the popular *Art Cats* calendar published by Pomegranate Calendars and Books. Beautiful, subtle pastels.

Calvin T-Shirt, $19.95 + $3 S&H M, L, XL, & XXL (Add $1 for XXL)

Catfish Designs
P.O. Box 40326
Portland, OR 97240
(800) 441-8522

The Personality of the Cat ®

If I had to choose just one cat book to take on vacation, it would be this one. What is it about cats that inspires such creativity? From T. S. Eliot to Colette, Don Marquis and Pablo Picasso, Edouard Manet and Jean-Jacques Rousseau, Émile Zola and Rudyard Kipling, Paul Gallico and Saki (H. H. Munro) and Lewis Carroll . . . such incredible talent and so many good stories about cats, with illustrations of their unique presence.

THE PERSONALITY OF THE CAT

A cat lover's collection of stories, poetry and pictures by T.S. Eliot, Rudyard Kipling, Colette, Lewis Carroll, and others
EDITED BY BRANDT AYMAR

The best collection of cat short stories I've ever read—and I've read a few! Fabulous story by Paul Gallico on Jennie teaching Peter how to behave like a cat.

Edited by Brandt Aymar, 1958, 342 pp., $9.99

Random House Value Publishing
Wings Books
40 Engelhard Ave.
Avenel, NJ 07001
(800) 733-3000

TRUE CAT FACT

The Door to Love

The Spanish word for a cat door is *gatera*. The *gatera* was cut into the door of old Spanish homes to provide the cat with easy passage in and out of the house. It also provided many a young man with the door to his lady's heart. Young Spanish suitors sometimes conducted courtships by talking through the cat door. When the girl's balcony was too high for courting conversations, the boy and girl would lie on the floor on either side of the door and flirt through the hole, even reaching their arms and hands through it. Anything for love.

Catspells ®

This collection of more than 50 magic spells was gathered by the author from journals belonging to her great-grandmother, a Victorian-era wise woman. You'll learn the ancient tradition of naming a kitten to influence her individual personality and to encourage certain traits. You'll learn to cast spells for healing and good luck by weaving a few loose hairs from your cat's coat into a special token and how to interpret portents of love and dreams by reading the flick of a tail or being the object of an intense feline gaze. Magic cat rituals from another century in this hardcover.

By Claire Nahmad, 1993, 88 pp., $12.95

Running Press
125 S. 22nd St.
Philadelphia, PA 19103
(215) 568-2919

Speak to Me, O Great Hat

Put this hat on your head and it blinks as you walk. Another version blinks and meows. What an attention getter! This company also makes quality cat T-shirts, tote bags, aprons, sweatshirts, and nightshirts. If you want cat clothing items from their Pet Lover line in bulk for your child's class or your softball team, you can buy in quantity and they'll give you nice wholesale prices. Hat happy.

Blinking Cat Hat, $13.99 + $3 S&H
(N.J. res. add 6% sales tax)

W.R.S. Marketing
207 Stahls Way
N. Plainfield, NJ 07060
(800) 815-2606

Thoroughly Catatonic

Artist Thomas Mann, down in steamy New Orleans, has come up with utterly unique cat pins. Nobody else has quite his style. The two Catatonix Pins (top two) come in your choice of bronze or nickel, with dimensions of 1½″ × 1¾″. The Catatonix Collage Pin is made of nickel, bronze, brass, and laminated Lucite, and it is indeed wearable art. Mann explains:

"My love of making jewelry actually means more than producing pretty things for people to wear; it can be a means of expression that might affect people in a much more serious and purposeful way—in effect, real communication of ideas. Techno-Romantic is the end result. The pieces combine industrial materials with romantic imagery, and can provide, for those who are receptive, the links to the intuitive that everyone has—but may not be paying attention to!"

Catatonix Pin, $60 + $8 S&H
Catatonix Collage, $95 + $8 S&H
(Louis. res. add 9% sales tax)

Thomas Mann Design, Inc.
1810 Magazine St.
New Orleans, LA 70130
(504) 581-2111

Phoebe & Moon Shadow Cats

Another great design from artist Siri Schillios: This kitty basks in brilliant pastel colors with incredibly lifelike designs. Exceptional art on a 100% cotton T-shirt. Her Moon Shadow Cat includes an illustration of a kitty and a cat-moon face named Pie in the Sky. Great colors, extra-pretty.

Phoebe or **Pie in the Sky,** $19.95 + $3 S&H M, L, XL, & XXL (Add $1 for XXL)

Catfish Designs
P.O. Box 40326
Portland, OR 97240
(800) 441-8522

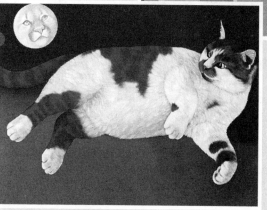

Look Deep into My Eyes

Bright yellow cat eyes on this T-shirt are a sure attention getter. Black face and paw, red dot on nose. Extra-long length, good-quality cotton, made to last.

Pet Lover T-Shirt, $14.99 + $3 S&H (N.J. res. add 6% sales tax)

W.R.S. Marketing
207 Stahls Way
N. Plainfield, NJ 07060
(800) 815-2606

Sterling Enamel Pins

What do you get when you mix talent, a love of cats, sterling silver, and enamel? Enanimals! Michele Raney's Cheshire Cat pin—with a perpetual grin—measures 1¼″ × ¾″. You're actually looking through the enamel to a carved image from Alice in Wonderland. Available in indigo/green, black/wine, rose/copper, or sage green/green. The Sleeping Kitty—of sterling and enamel—has a brilliant silver background and a choice of black, tan, indigo, sage green, wine, or brown kitties. The artist studied hand engraving and enameling at Sir John Cass Polytechnic in London. She works in the traditional style of Basse-Taille.

Cheshire Cat Pin, $54 + $3 S&H (Calif. res. add $4.46 sales tax)
Sleeping Kitty, $46 + $3 S&H (Calif. res. add $3.80 sales tax)

Enanimals by Michele Raney
P.O. Box 1917
Freedom, CA 95019
(408) 722-1975

Legacy of the Cat ®

This picture book features the work of photographer Tetsu Yamazaki, whose technique includes playing with cats and then snapping the shutter to freeze their spontaneous action. A brief history of cats precedes a thorough look at genetics, as revealed by studies of cat fur and eye coloration. This will be of particular interest to folks who show their cats. The author is an all-breed judge of cats, and a genetics instructor for the International Cat Association. Includes profiles of 37 breeds, strikingly photographed, with a brief history and defining characteristics of each breed. The superb photographs make this a must-have hardcover for your cat library.

By Gloria Stephens, 1990, 144 pp., $16.96

Chronicle Books
275 Fifth St.
San Francisco, CA 94103
(800) 722-6657

Solid-Gold Cats

Solid-gold cat coins make stunning jewelry. Hallock Jewelry offers solid-gold or pure-silver cat coins depicting many different breeds, including coins made into bracelets, earrings, money clips, cuff links, and tie tacks. Shown here is the Japanese Bobtail, engraved on ⅕ of an ounce of pure gold. These coins are produced off the coast of England, on the Isle of Man, home of the Manx cat, and each year a new variety of cat is featured. Previous years of rare cat coins also available. Just add the gold chain of your choice.

⅕ **Oz. Pure Gold Japanese Bobtail Cat Jewelry,** $329
(Calif. res. add $25.50 sales tax) Prices can vary based upon the market value of precious metals.

Hallock Jewelry
2060 W. Lincoln
Anaheim, CA 92801
(800) 854-3232

The Cat That Rides the Hand

The creative imagination of silversmith James Yesberger never stops. Next to his rabbit companion, a sterling silver kitty rides atop your finger as you move through the day. When ordering, specify ring size and inquire about this artist's other highly imaginative and beautiful rings that feature cats.

PegaPuss Ring, $90
(Conn. res. add 6% sales tax)

One Is Silver
James Yesberger
214 Child Rd.
Woodstock, CT 06281
(203) 974-3081

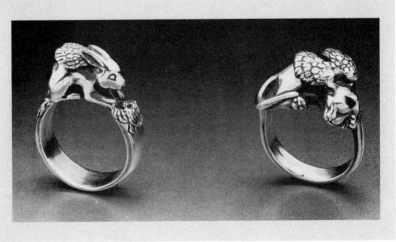

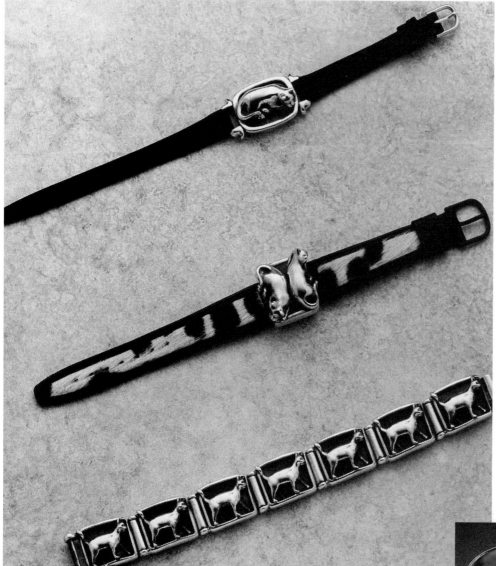

The Art on Your Wrist

With exquisite attention to detail, master gold- and silversmith James Yesberger has created extraordinary art for your wrist. The look is stunning and dressy. Choose from the sterling silver Cat Strap with black leather band (top), the sterling silver Two Cats Strap with "tiger-spotted" brushed fur recessed into a black leather band (center), or the sterling silver Cat Links with seven regal—almost Egyptian-looking–cats parading around your wrist (bottom). Superior quality.

Cat Strap, $160
Two Cats Strap, $180
Cat Links, $1,000
(Conn. res. add 6% sales tax)

One Is Silver
James Yesberger
214 Child Rd.
Woodstock, CT 06281
(203) 974-3081

Cloisonné Black Leopard

Enamelist Merry Lee Rae specializes in jewelry and small sculpture cloisonné. Ribbons of fine silver or gold separate and define the colors and shadows of transparent glass enamels. The metal framework of the piece is made by bending these ribbons to match the outlines of preliminary artwork. Once each tiny piece is in place and gently fired to hold its position, the process of wetpacking the enamels into the design can begin. A thin layer of color is packed into each division and then fired in a kiln at 1475° F. The amazing color and depth that Merry Lee achieves comes from blending and adding more and more layers of the fine glass. At least five, and as many as twenty, layers and firings go into each piece.

The Black Leopard pendant shown is 18k gold and cloisonné enamel, measuring 2¼″ × 2½″, worn with a 14k chain, included. Colors are black with a ruby-red background, yellow tint, and burnished gold. Extraordinary cat art from an edition of 17.

Black Leopard Cloisonné Pendant, $3,200 + $5 S&H

+ $9.60 insurance (Calif. res. add 8.25% sales tax [$264])

Merry Lee Rae
Rae Studios
P.O. Box 536
Aptos, CA 95001
(408) 761-2844

Panzer Mona Lisa

Panzer is the Mona Lisa of cats, with her inscrutable, delicate face and background of pansies by artist Siri Schillios. A lovely, cheery pastel kitty, sure to bring smiles as you stroll in your 100% cotton T-shirt.

Panzer, $19.95 + $3 S&H
M, L, XL, XXL (Add $1 for XXL)

Catfish Designs
P.O. Box 40326
Portland, OR 97240
(800) 441-8522

The Noble Cat ®

The classic coffee-table cat book, with more than 700 color photographs of cats, both domestic and wild. Author Howard Loxton—drawing upon the expert knowledge of zoologists, ethnologists, veterinarians, breeders, show judges, and pet owners—has brought together in this hardcover a complete picture of the whole cat family, so that cat lovers and wildlife enthusiasts alike can gain a deeper understanding of the domestic cat and its wild kin.

By Howard Loxton, 1994, 335 pp. $29.99

Random House Value Publishing
Crescent Books
40 Engelhard Ave.
Avenel, NJ 07001
(800) 733-3000

Highbred, Lowbrow?

Some of the nicest, smartest, healthiest cats in the world are called moggies or moggys. Sometimes they're called mongrels. Whatever you call them, all the common existing names for cats that aren't purebred or pedigreed have a nasty edge to them. They're put-downs.

Something needs to be done about this. We need a new name for the millions of good old garden-variety buddy cats who don't have upscale parents, who could care less about Cat Fancy cat shows, who are just perfect the way they are. We need a nice, dignified name with class, instead of this guttural, unpleasant *mongrel* talk.

So next time you discuss a cat with no clearly documentable parentage, how about calling him a world cat or a California hybrid (or Texas or Massachusetts, etc.) or a hybrid champion? You know. Something nice for those of us who love cats for their personality, not their lineage.

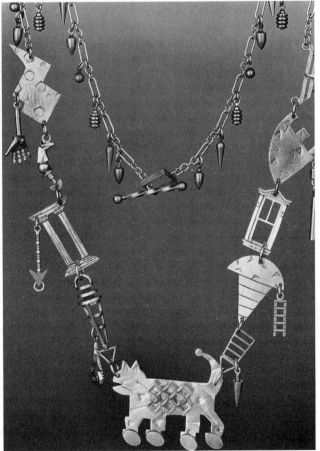

Your Beautiful Fetish

Thomas Mann lives and works in New Orleans, where he oversees a jewelry studio, sculpture studio, and two design galleries. A 20-year veteran of the American Craft circuit, he exhibits his jewelry and sculpture in more than 180 galleries nationwide. His latest offering is the Cat Fetish Necklace, a unique creation 26″ in length, made of silver, brass, bronze, and copper. The center cat is silver. A wild, lovely piece of power and magic.

Cat Fetish Necklace, $295 + $8 S&H (Louis. res. add 9% sales tax)

Thomas Mann Design, Inc.
1810 Magazine St.
New Orleans, LA 70130
(504) 581-2111

The Artistic Cat ®

Praise and poems by many artists and writers fill this miniature hardcover of cat paintings. It's small enough to fit in the palm of your hand—small words, great inspirations.

Compiled by Running Press, 1991, 100 pp., $4.95

Running Press
125 S. 22nd St.
Philadelphia, PA 19103
(215) 568-2919

Wearing the Magic

Worn loosely around your neck with a braided sterling silver chain (included), this beautiful Cat Bell Pendant chimes quietly as you move. Superior detailing and quality; a magical pendant to be with you always.

Cat Bell Pendant, $300
(Conn. res. add 6% sales tax)

One Is Silver
James Yesberger
214 Child Rd.
Woodstock, CT 06281
(203) 974-3081

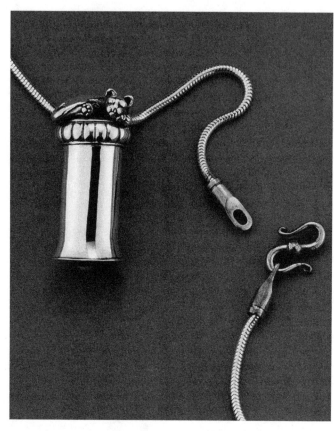

Precious-Metal Cats

Maria Irene Aufiero comes from a family of jewelers and silversmiths dating back to the 18th century in Lamella, Holland. Her designs are sculpted in clay or wax, then cast in silver and gold. One of her favorite themes is nature abundant with animals, including cats, and you can see her work at juried art shows and through private commissions. Her Cat Ring is available in silver or 14k gold, with glowing tourma-

line eyes. The textured sterling silver Cat Pin or Cat Buckle mea-

sures 2″ × 2″, and has deep, dark onyx eyes. Quite extraordinary. True collectors' pieces for the feline aficionado.

Cat Ring, $80 sterling silver;
$550 14k gold
Cat Pin/Buckle, $150
(N.Y. res. add 8.25% sales tax)

Leopardo d'Oro
444 E. 86th St.
New York, NY 10028
(212) 249-9198

Bastet, the Egyptian Cat Goddess

Were cats important to the Egyptians, or what? In ancient Egypt, Bastet, the daughter of the Sun God, Ra, represented the power of the sun and was known as the Cat Goddess of Joy. Many bronze cat figures were dedicated in her now-ruined temple in the northeast African Delta. Bastet has now moved far, far away to San Jose, California, where she offers Cat Goddess Pendants, Cat Goddess Mugs, T-shirts, tote bags, Cat Crystal Earrings, even a black shirtdress, all with the Cat Goddess design. Note the 4″ bronze Cat Goddess statue on a black basalt base, also available in a smaller 3½″ black cat on black basalt base. All remarkable and mystical.

Cat Goddess Jewelry, inquire for prices
Cat Goddess Statue (bronze), $20 + $4 S&H
(Calif. res. add 7.75% sales tax)

Cat Goddess
2530 Berryessa Rd., #935
San Jose, CA 95132

PMS Pin

A bit on edge lately? Dubbed the PMS Pin (but not by me!), you can presumably wear this and signal a warning to any of the irritating nuts that happen to cross your path. The pewter cat, approx. 2½″ h., looks totally annoyed. Ready to scratch and bite. Should scare off most problem people.

PMS Pin, $19 + $5 S&H

The Cat House
110 Crowchild Train, NW
Calgary, Alberta T2N 4R9
Canada
(800) MEOW-CAT

Glitzy Cats

After 23 years teaching high school, Sharon Brown decided she'd had enough. She took early retirement, designed some kitty pins for herself, and then her friends all wanted them. The rest, as they say, is history. Her stuff is really amazing: incredible, expressive cat-face pins for you to wear, wood boxes with tiger faces and feathers, gorgeously painted 8″ × 10″ photo frames that remind me of another century. The pins are absolutely unbelievable.

Cat Pins, $20 each + $3 S&H
Wooden Cat Boxes, $35 + $3 S&H

Cat Photo Frame,
$35 + $4 S&H
(Conn. res. add 6% sales tax)

Glitzy Lady
86 Crown St.
Trumbull, CT 06611
(203) 268-5195

Ticking After All These Years

Now this is a clock to watch. All sorts of stuff going on each and every second . . . the kitty rolls his eyes, his tail flicks back and forth. He first became popular many years ago, and now he's back by popular demand. Black acrylic, 15″ from head to tail, fits on any wall, uses two C batteries (not included).

The Original Kit-Cat Clock, $39.95 + S&H (Minn. res. add 6.5% sales tax)

Wireless Catalog
Rivertown Trading
Company
P.O. Box 64422
Saint Paul, MN 55164
(800) 663-9994

Sparkle's Tidbits of Advice for Cats (and Their Owners)

Sparkle is a feline prodigy who gives humorous and meaningful tidbits of advice to cats and their owners. Written from her own kitty perspective, she talks about naming kittens, exercising properly, staying healthy, glamour grooming, handling stressful situations (such as thunderstorms and visiting the vet), and more. Includes cat poetry and a Cat Assessment Test.

By Charlotte Dalton, 1995, 68 pp., $9 (includes S&H; Tex. res. add 50¢ sales tax)

Sparkle Enterprises
6022 Morning Dew Dr.
Austin, TX 78749
(512) 892-6969

Mother-of-Pearl Cats

Mother-of-pearl has a special iridescent glow that shimmers as the light plays upon it. Pin any of these remarkable hand-carved fashion accessories to your favorite outfit and prepare yourself for more compliments than you could ever imagine. Size is 1½″ h. to 1½–2″ l. No two are alike. Also ask about their mother-of-pearl cat buttons.

Mother-of-Pearl Collectible Cat Pins, $9 to $19 + $2 S&H (Calif. res. add $1.57 sales tax)

Cara Maia
5532 Woodruff Ave., #164
Lakewood, CA 90713
(800) 656-7509
E-mail: KHOB@ix.netcom.com

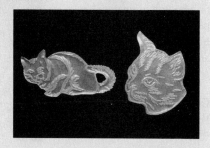

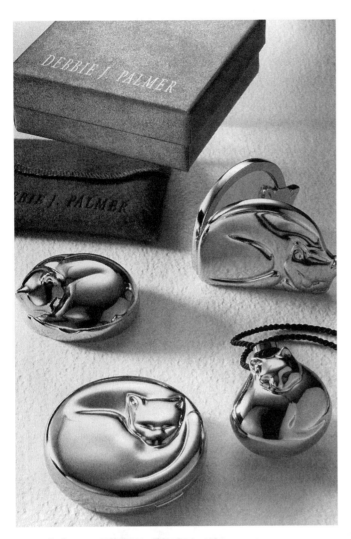

Gold in Your Purse

Gorgeous cats rest comfortably in these 18k gold-dipped Contented Cats, from the Debbie J. Palmer Collection. Clockwise from upper left, the plastic-lined Cat Pill Case measures 2″ × 1¾″ and could make a pleasing resting place for your earrings and rings. The folding Cat Mirror (perfect for your purse) measures 2½″ × 1¾″ and includes two high-quality mirrors: one actual-size and one magnifying. Cat Flacon, measuring 1½″ × 1¾″, is designed to hold approximately ¼ oz. of your favorite fragrance. Carry it in the distinctive pouchette, or wear as a necklace (includes a dipping wand attached to its closure). Cat Compact, measuring 2¼″ round, holds standard 50 mm refills of your favorite pressed powder, available from most leading cosmetic companies. They're as nice to have as they look.

Cat Pill Case, Cat Mirror, Cat Flacon, Cat Compact, $29.50 each + S&H: (less than $50, add $4.95; $50.01–$100, add $6.95; $101.01–$200, add $9.95)
(N.Y. res. add 8.25% sales tax)

Debbie J. Palmer Design, Inc.
19 W. 36th St.
New York, NY 10018
(212) 714-1710

Tips for Allergic Owners

No matter how much you love them, others in your family might be allergic to cats. Here are some ways to lessen allergic reactions:

- Keep Kitty out of the bedroom. Sleeping and breathing dander all night is sure to aggravate allergies.

- Have someone who is not allergic brush the cat every few days, and bathe Kitty every week or so to help reduce dander.

- Vacuum every few days. Use a good-quality vacuum that has a water or filter system to keep dander from blowing back into the house.

- Check your furnace and air-conditioner filters. Keep them clean, and use the finest possible mesh recommended by the manufacturer to keep dander from circulating in the house.

- Consider a room air cleaner that can help eliminate dander particles from individual rooms. Keep these rooms off-limits to the cat.

- Minimize upholstered furniture that traps dander and dust particles. Wash curtains and bedding on a regular basis to eliminate dust buildup. Consider replacing your wool blankets with combed cotton.

- Thick wool carpeting can be a major reservoir of dander and dust. If you have a choice, consider replacing it with a low-pile carpet or with wood or linoleum flooring.

African Cats

The gorgeous necklace, earrings, and stickpin, from Sandy Hamman, use age-old African techniques of pattern making. Each is individually handcrafted with brass and cork, beads and rhinestones; no two are alike. Stunning work.

African Cat Necklace, $74.71
Earrings, $25.95
Stick Pin, $25.95

Art Design, Ltd.
15 Janet Way, # 5
Tiburon, CA 94920
(415) 388-1328

The Rose and Night Cat

Claire Willett of San Antonio makes some fine-quality cat jewelry. Her Rose Cat Earring is suspended from an 8 mm Swarovski rose-quartz crystal, above which is a 4 mm bead of faceted Czechoslovakian glass, pale peach in color. The cat is gold-plated, and the earhooks are sterling silver. The Rose Cat Necklace includes genuine Swarovski rose-quartz crystal and sterling-silver beads with a sterling-silver clasp. The Rose Cat Bracelet features four silver-plated cats. The Night Cat Earring is suspended from an 8 mm bead of black Chinese cloisonné and a 6 mm bead of hematite, with a gold-plated cat and gold-filled ear hook. The Night Cat Necklace and matching bracelet is made of genuine freshwater pearls, hematite, Chinese cloisonné, and Czechoslovakian glass, with four gold-plated cats and a gold-filled clasp. Length is approx. 22″. Huge selection of color-coordinated bridal party jewelry, custom creations, and a gift subscription service called The Necklace Club.

Rose Cat Earrings, $15 + $1 S&H
Rose Cat Necklace, $48 + $2 S&H
Rose Cat Bracelet, $32 + $1 S&H
Night Cat Earrings, $15 + $1 S&H
Night Cat Necklace, $48 + $2 S&H
Night Cat Bracelet, $32 + $1 S&H

Claire R. Willett Jewelry
999 E. Basse Rd., Suite 180
San Antonio, TX 78209
(800) 315-1615

Losing Time, Lost Time, Time Flies, Save Time

I stumbled onto Susan Castle's mixed-media brooch watches at a California gift show. All of her wonderful clock-motif designs have something to do with time, and each brooch is a handmade original. Running Out of Time consists of five cats surrounding a mouse. Styles and colors may vary, but the rest of the brooch is identical to this one. Intriguing jewelry inspired by the ways in which we spend our time. Superior craftsmanship.

Running Out of Time,
$22 + $1.50 S&H
(Calif. res. add 7.5% sales tax)

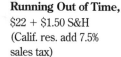

Time and Materials
Collage Jewelry by Susan Castle
334-D Payran St.
Petaluma, CA 94952
(707) 769-1729

TRUE CAT FACT

Why Should I Spay My Cat?

Aside from the nasty fact that millions of lovely cats are euthanized each year, there are real practical health benefits to spaying or neutering your cat. Your cat will have a glossier coat and a lessened chance of contracting a variety of diseases, including cancers of the reproductive tract. Spaying and neutering helps keep Kitty "people-friendly," more playful, less likely to roam.

Holographic Cats

Photos of holograms never do them justice, because they are three-dimensional images that appear to move as you view them from different angles. The Royal Holographic Art Gallery uses Russian pulse-camera technology on glass plates to assure superior-quality cat holograms. You can choose beautiful cat images, a stunningly designed cat wristwatch, or commission a custom-made watch using a holographic image of your cat. The watches make incredible gifts.

Persian Cat Hologram
(9″ × 12″), $185
Cat Holographic Wristwatch,
$44.95 + Canadian 7% GST
(B.C. residents add 7% PST)

Royal Holographic Art Gallery
1 Market Square
560 Johnson St.
Victoria, B.C.
Canada V8W 3C6
(604) 384-0123
http://www.islandnet.com/
~royal/
index.htm

Persian Gold

Cat coins are hot. This ⅕ oz. solid-gold Persian coin could be just the start of your collection. Other breeds include the Manx, American, Norwegian, Siamese, Maine coon, and Japanese Bobtail. Various weights, from ⅟₂₅ oz. up to 1 oz. coins, and most are available as wearable pendant jewelry or as bracelets. The heavier the coin, the more you save on the actual gold content. The 1 oz. version is slightly less than twice the cost of the ⅕ oz. version, though it contains five times more gold by weight. Many are also available in pure sterling silver, which is very affordable. Get the color catalog and start collecting!

Solid Gold ⅕ oz. Persian Cat Coin, $359
Sterling Silver 1 oz. Persian Cat Coin (not shown), $49

Carlson Cat Coins
15 College St.
Arlington, IL 60004
(847) 255-0015
E-mail: carlson@email.
starnetinc.com

Classic "Cats Coming and Going" II

This is the classic T-shirt first created in 1986. Hep Cat's most popular shirt; you'll find many versions in their color catalog. Great clothing, and they'll put in a free cat calendar with your order.

T-Shirt, $17.95
Sweatshirt, $27.95
Nightshirt, $20.95
Longsleeve T-Shirt, $22.95
(S, M, L) Add $3.95 S&H per order (Tenn. res. add 8.25% sales tax)

Hep Cat
P.O. Box 40223
Nashville, TN 37204
(615) 298-2980

The Cats from New York City

Jeffrey Edelman of SoHo Design makes NYC T-shirts and baseball hats, including this two-sided Soul Cat design on a heavyweight, preshrunk, 100% cotton shirt. Vivid reds, yellows, teals, blues. Very New Yawk. Very alive. His entire catalog is available on the World Wide Web.

Soul Cat T-Shirt, $15.99 + $3.25 S&H (N.Y. res. add 8.25% sales tax)

Kitty Time

Send a quality photo of your kitty to this company, and they'll make a nice men's or women's watch with your kitty's face on the dial. It takes about 21 days for completion and you get to wear the watch for years.

Kitty-Face Watch, $34.95 + S&H (N.Y. res. add 8.25% sales tax)

Hour Image
2316 Delaware Ave.
Suite 248
Buffalo, NY 14216
(800) 671-5646

SoHo Design
10 Main St.
Dobbs Ferry, NY 10522
(914) 478-7953
http://www.
infomall.org/
sohodesign

© *Gravity Graphics*

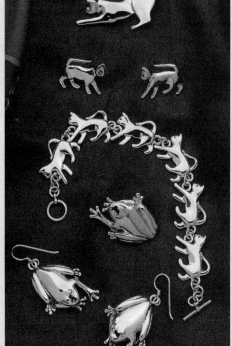

Playful Cats

Artist/composer Roger Nichols lives along the banks of the Deschutes River in Bend, Oregon. He left the fast life in L.A. after writing many well-known classic songs, including "We've Only Just Begun" and "Rainy Days and Mondays." These days he puts his creative energy into creating beautiful jewelry, including the Playful Cat Pin (top), available in sterling silver or 14k gold; Cat Earrings (post or French wire); a fabulous Cat Bracelet (measures 7″ long, sterling silver or 14k gold); and those cute frogs you see below the cats. His color catalog of jewelry is extensive, and he does wonderful custom work, such as placing small diamonds, rubies, sapphires, or emeralds in any of his pieces, usually as eyes for animals.

Playful Cat Pin, $49.50 (sterling silver); $375 (14k gold)
Cat Earrings, $49 (sterling silver); $395 (14k gold)
Cat Bracelet, $145 (sterling silver); $995 (14k gold)

Roger Nichols Studios
2445 NE Division St.
Bend, OR 97702
(800) 235-0471

Can I Show My Beautiful Pet Cat?

Your cat does not have to be a purebred to be in a cat show. There are gorgeous cats with mixed parentage who are champions in cat shows. Your cat can take a ribbon in any of these categories: Household Pets, which includes all spayed/neutered cats—purebred and mixed-breed—with no papers; Purebred Kittens, Intact (not spayed/neutered); Purebred Cats; and Spayed or Neutered Purebred Cats. There's a nice democracy to all of this: Basically, any cat with claws (most declawed cats are not allowed in cat shows) and good looks can be recognized as the champion you know she is!

Poetry for Cats ®

Henry Beard—cofounder of *National Lampoon* magazine and author of *French for Cats* and *Advanced French for Exceptional Cats*—is at his amusing best in these musings. Perfect illustrations of the voice of one cat's thoughts.

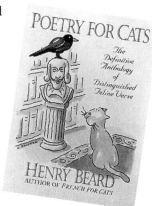

By Henry Beard, 1994, 96 pp., $12.95

Villard Books
201 E. 50th St.
New York, NY 10022
(212) 572-2211

Caring for Your Sick Cat ®

I hope you never need this paperback, but it will definitely help you in an emergency, or if your pet is ill or recovering from an injury. Complete descriptions of cat diseases and how to recognize symptoms. Useful advice on giving medications, caring for wounds and broken bones, seeing your cat through pregnancy, and much more. Sound advice from a compassionate, expert author.

By Carol Himsel Daly, D.V.M., 1994, 182 pp., $8.95

Barron's Educational Series
250 Wireless Blvd.
Hauppauge, NY 11788
(516) 434-3311

Sterling Cat Pins

It's an understatement to say that Kit Carson is a master gold- and silversmith. His Cat Pin (top) measures $1\frac{1}{4}'' \times 1''$ in sterling silver. The Cheshire Cat Post Earrings measure $\frac{3}{4}'' \times \frac{1}{2}''$ in sterling silver, with a sterling silver post and back. The Cheshire Cat Pin (below) measures $1\frac{1}{8}'' \times 1\frac{1}{2}''$, in sterling silver. Everything Carson makes and sells is the best.

Sterling-Silver Cat Pin, $28
Sterling-Silver Cheshire Cat Post Earrings, $34
Sterling-Silver Cheshire Cat Pin, $44

Kit Carson Design
P.O. Box 22298
Santa Fe, NM 87502
(800) GIT-DOWN (448-3696)

Costumes for Your Cat ®

Fun costumes for the willing kitty. Hold a party, dress up the cat, get into it! Easy do-it-yourself outfits: New Year's Kitten (all you need is a cloth diaper and two safety pins), Thanksgiving Cat, Easter Bunny. The Modern Dance Cat costume includes 20 1″ pieces of glow-in-the-dark tape and a boom box (use your imagination). Includes excellent directions for dressing your cat as a One-Cat Band. Period costumes (including Cave Cat) contribute to general nuttiness and fun in this hardcover.

By Lynn Chang, 1995, 42 pp., $6.95

Chronicle Books
275 Fifth St.
San Francisco, CA 94103
(800) 722-6657

Beaded and Sequined Cat Appliqués

These easy-to-use cat appliqués from Camerin Lucas look great, and they work well on a variety of fabrics. Imported, handmade, no sewing required. Simply glue them onto the fabric of your choice with the 100% nontoxic adhesive included. Not suited for soft leather, fine fabric, fabric with a cut pile, or angora sweaters. Brilliant designs and colors add life to clothing.

Persian Kitty (top left),
Siamese Kitty (top right),
$5.95 each
Medium-Size Sitting Kitty (lower right), $10.95
Two Large Striped Kitties (center and lower left), $13.95 each
Add $2.50 S&H
(Calif. res. add 7.25% sales tax)

Cielle Appliqués
P.O. Box 414
Tiburon, CA 94920
(415) 435-1392

Short Sleeve, Long Hair

Artist Linda Messenger renders this detailed black-and-white pen-and-ink drawing of a longhaired cat onto white 100% cotton short-sleeved T-shirts. Many other designs are available, along with note cards, mugs, and matted art prints. Visit her Internet site for more information.

Longhaired Kitty T-Shirt, (S, M, L, XL, XXL), $19.95 + $2 S&H (Wash. res. add 7.9% sales tax)

L. Messenger Studio
5815 138th Pl., N.E.
Marysville, WA 98271
(360) 659-4737
http://www.everett.net/users/sculptor/

Cat-Print Dress for Toddlers

Little girls will love to play in these adorable dresses printed with whimsical cats. Available in toddler sizes 1T, 2T, 3T, and 4T. Fabrics will vary, but all feature cats. Of 100% cotton, made in the U.S., machine-washable and -dryable. Brochure available upon request from dressmaker Diane Current.

Toddlers' Cat-Print Dress, $32 + $4 S&H (Calif. res. add 7.25% sales tax)

Current Image
1040 Lea Dr.
San Rafael, CA 94903
(415) 492-8864

Kliban for All!

The whimsical tabby we all know and love is back, ready to launch a bowling ball. Sweatshirt is an $^{80}/_{20}$ cotton blend, with adult sizes of S (34–36), M (38–40), L (42–44), and XL (46–48). Kliban's cats are lovable, and your bowling buddies will look great wearing this at the lanes! Unconditional 100% money-back guarantee from the folks at that terrific Wireless Catalog.

Kliban Alley-Cat Sweatshirt, $42 + S&H
Regular delivery, $5.95; rush, $10.95; overnight, $15.70

Wireless Catalog
Rivertown Trading Company
P.O. Box 64422
Saint Paul, MN 55164
(800) 663-9994
http://www.giftcatalog.com

Wise Words T-Shirts

Field Crafts has a nice line of white 100% cotton T-shirts with clever sayings. All the usual sizes. Unusually good artwork, from sublime to sarcastic.

Cat Chex or **House Cats,** $14.99 + $3.25 S&H (Mich. res. add 6% sales tax)

Field Crafts, Inc.
1058 Michigan Ave.
Benzonia, MI 49616
(800) 332-3131

Chapter Four

Collectible Cat Art

Pet Portraits

There's more than one way to paint a cat. Eugenia Talbott of Mayhew, Mississippi, is a fine artist who can capture the expression of your pet in many mediums, working from photographs you provide. Painted Pets (oil on wood, from $100 to $300) may be used as decorative accessories. Or perhaps your pet would be best portrayed on a fire screen ($550–$750). Pencil sketches ($75 & up), watercolors ($150 & up), oil on canvas ($250 & up), and pastels ($150) are all available for your framing. Room-divider screens ($1,500 & up) offer the opportunity to portray your pet in many different poses and moods. Talbott is well known for her wildlife illustrations and museum exhibits. She's also the spokesperson for the Cedar Hill Animal Sanctuary, a home to lost, forgotten, abused, and abandoned pets. Wonderful custom art.

Pet Portraits, prices vary

Eugenia Talbott
P.O. Box 39
Mayhew, MS 39753
(601) 328-5534

The Whimsical World of Judie Bomberger

Judie's colorful cat sculptures can be seen at art shows, but they would look even better in your house or yard. Her metal art is superior, with a unique, whimsical personality. Each piece you see is available painted in bright colors or with the natural deep red-brown patina of rusted metal. Her Sitting Cat in blue and pink measures 19″ h. × 14″ w. and comes with a base for display. The Lying Cat measures 14″ h. × 17″ w. and includes a display base. Bird on Cat (Friends) is a black-striped white cat with a brightly colored bird friend, measuring 15″ h. × 20″ w. Cat Fish, painted in vibrant purple, red, yellow, blue, and turquoise, measures 22″ h. × 12″ w. Whichever you choose, you'll be pleased. Custom work available.

Sitting Cat, $65 + $12 S&H
(Calif. res. add $7.71 sales tax)
Lying Cat, $65 + $12 S&H
(Calif. res. add $7.71 sales tax)
Bird on Cat, $60 + $12 S&H
(Calif. res. add $4.35 sales tax)
Cat Fish, $65 + $12 S&H
(Calif. res. add $7.71 sales tax)

Judie Bomberger
1181 Midway Ct.
Novato, CA 94947
(415) 883-3072

Why Cats Paint: A Theory of Feline Aesthetics ®

It's plausible that your cat is a latent Picasso. Just look at this paperback's cover. It's so well done that it's tough to separate fact from fiction: The more you read it, the more credible it seems. But in fact, it's an elaborate goof, a put-on, with convoluted theories about cat personalities, and interpretations of feline painting styles. Cats paint, monkeys paint, turtles paint, humans paint. Everything can paint. Ants could paint. Amusing, convincing!

By Heather Busch and Burton Silver, 1994, 96 pp., $14.95

Ten Speed Press
P.O. Box 7123
Berkeley, CA 94707
(800) 841-BOOK

Tyber Katz

Tyber Katz are museum-quality cat dolls, produced in small quantities, signed and numbered by Oregon artists Peter and Patricia Tyber. Life-size, exquisitely hand-carved from linden wood, and painted, they are the *crème de la crème* of cat dolls. The wooden form is attached to a soft muslin body, with finishing touches such as real horsehair whiskers. Many unusual cats in all sorts of imaginative poses and situations. Fishin' Cat is just one design. Displayed on a hardwood base (bubinga wood shown above). Also available are custom sculptures and commissioned portraits from photographs of your cat. Winner of the 1990 Niche Award for Excellence in American Crafts. I could go on and on with raves, but let's just say that Tyber Katz are fabulous, and leave it to you to call for a catalog. Perfect for the feline fancier and folk-art collector.

Tyber Fishin' Cat, $1,800
Sculpture Cat, $5,000

Color catalog: $3
Tyber Katz
P.O. Box 1367
Sutherlin, OR 97479
(503) 459-0806

Leaping-Cat Wind Machine

Spectacular cat art for your yard or home. The Leaping Cat whirls and spins in the wind, frozen in motion, eternally chasing an imaginary mouse as a propeller spins on the end of its paw. Lovingly handcrafted in wood. Choose from an orange tabby, black-and-white-striped (shown), or have a Leaping Cat custom painted to match a picture of your kitty. Back in the old days, these used to be called whirligigs. Personally, I think they're almost too good to leave outside. You can display this art in your living room with the display base (shown).

Leaping-Cat Wind Machine, $230 ($250 for special orders) + $7 S&H

Amazing Wind Machines, Inc.
410 Great Rd.
P.O. Box 619
Littleton, MA 01460
(508) 952-2478

Your 3-D Kitty!

Take pictures of your cat and send in your best color photo or negative. Sculpt' Art will make either an 8″ × 10″ three-dimensional "pop-out" portrait of your kitty (shown with tabby kitty) or a silhouette of Kitty with no background. Vivid colors, nice for your desk at the office or on your bureau with photos of the kids. Takes 7 to 10 days, and they send back your original photo or negative in perfect condition. Also ask about Life-Size Photo Pet Pals. You can order a 6′ long

photo of your kitty on GatorBoard or Plexiglas. These people can do almost anything with your cat photos. The ultimate gift.

Three-Dimensional Kitty, (5″ × 7″) $34.95; (8″ × 10″) $42.95; + $4 S&H
Silhouette Kitty, (5″ × 7″) $31.95; (8″ × 10″) $39.95; + $4 S&H
Optional personalization, $3
(Fla. res. add 6.5% sales tax)

Sculpt' Art
299 SW 8th St.
2nd Floor
Miami, FL 33130
(305) 860-1345

Wildcat Tables

These unusual tables are carved in Bali by one family of craftspeople. Made from a fast-growing, nonendangered wood called bentawas, they are individually unique and vary in detail depending upon the carver. Perfect as side tables, or place a piece of glass on top of two and use as a coffee table. Stunning brown/orange stain with black markings.

Available in two sizes: The leopard is 30″ l. × 6″ w. × 16″ h.; the smaller tiger is 24″ l. × 6″ w. × 14″ h. Exceptional native art for your home.

Leopard, $90 + $5.50 S&H
Tiger, $65 + $5.50 S&H
(Calif. res. add 7.75% sales tax)

Just-Cats
P.O. Box 60028
Santa Barbara, CA 93160
(800) 805-CATS

Ways of Drawing Cats ®

Anyone with an interest in drawing or painting cats will enjoy this hardcover. It's full of practical information and hints and tips on drawing, and it's also a guide to observing and interpreting cat behavior. Every page has cat illustrations in many different styles, including images from the great masters. Fascinating discussion about artistic approaches, techniques, and learning to "see" what you draw.

Compiled by Running Press, 1994, 64 pp., $12.95

Running Press
125 S. 22nd St.
Philadelphia, PA 19103
(800) 345-5359

High-Wire Cats

These are fun! Amusing wire sculptures of cats in bright colors, doing almost everything imaginable. From left, tennis cat Devo (8″) stands on a mini tennis court; Leni (5″) contemplates the meaning of life on her litter box; Elmo (7″) has been caught by a big red fish and his trusty cat pole; Tyrone (5″) is having a beer while lounging in a small blue Jacuzzi; Moe (8″) is try-ing to make par as he putts a tiny white ball on a tiny green; Arlo (5″) wears his best red scarf as he takes his shiny silver plane out for a spin. Smart desktop gifts for cat lovers and sports fans. Also available: holders for paper towels, napkins, and toilet tissue; Christmas cat; and other wild and crazy designs.

Devo, $15; **Leni,** $12; **Elmo,** $23; **Tyrone,** $15; **Moe,** $15; **Arlo,** $23; + $5.95 S&H

Guy's Cats
P.O. Box 1339
Avalon, CA 90704
(800) 392-9037

How to Live with a Jewish *Cat*

This zany paperback includes modern-day fairy tales to tell Jewish kittens, your cat's horoscope, true-blue Jewish breeds, all the Yiddish your cat wants you to know, a guide to overseas travel, psychotherapy for the meshugge cat, Ten Commandments a cat will ignore, plus much more irrepressibly nutty stuff.

How to Live with
A *Jewish* Cat
By Sig and Pat Heavilin
Illustrated by Tracy Ellington

Your Cat's Horoscope

Modern Fairy Tales For Jewish Kittens

The Joy of Cooking For Your Jewish Cat

The True Blue Jewish Breeds

All the Yiddish Your Cat Wants You to Know

Your Cat's Guide To Overseas Travel

Psychotherapy for The Meshugge Cat

Ten Commandments A Cat Will Ignore

And much more . . . !

#1 BEST SELLER AT SOL'S NEWSSTAND

"Zaniest cat book ever!" (If you're not Jewish, you'll wish you were.)

A Cerebral Hollow Press Book

Cerebral Hollow Press
890-75 Robinhood Dr.
Reno, NV 89509
(800) 928-5280

By "Sig" and Pat Heavilin, 1994, 108 pp., $10.95

Clock & Ink by Cossman

Howard Cossman took a deep breath. Sat down. And then put several hundred hours of drawing into creating this one-of-a-kind Cat Art Clock. He's a professional illustrator with a few special products that feature only cats, in pen and ink. This 11″ × 11″ wall clock is made of aluminum and powered by battery-operated quartz movement. Cossman's intricate artwork is reproduced in a gleaming finish of ebony-and-ivory enamel. Cat print postcards and high-quality 18″ × 24″ prints are also available. Artistry that celebrates cats.

Cat Art Clock, $39.95 + $5 S&H
Pen-and-Ink Cat Postcards (set of 8), $10 + $2 S&H
Postcard Art Prints (18″ × 24″), $10 each + $2 S&H (Calif. res. add 8.5% sales tax)

Sophisticats
P.O. Box 4564
North Hollywood, CA 91607
(818) 879-0339

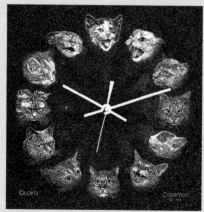

Cats
Leslie Baker

The Art of Leslie Baker

Leslie Baker is the award-winning author/illustrator of children's books such as *The Third-Story Cat* and *The Antique Store Cat.* Her light, ephemeral watercolors include *Cat Chasing Butterfly, Cat with Boxes, Cat Smelling Flowers,* and *Cat Sleeping.* Her paintings have been chosen for inclusion in the prestigious Society of Illustrators Original Art Exhibition in New York City. Five cards of four subjects—the same curious cat in different settings—with twenty envelopes. Isn't it time you sent a nice letter to somebody?

Leslie Baker Cats Boxed Notes, $12.95 + $3.95 S&H (N.Y. res. add 8.25% sales tax)

Galison Books
36 W. 44th St.
New York, NY 10036
(212) 354-8840

Painted Faces

It's nice to have an artist depict you and your cat in a custom charcoal, oil, or pastel portrait. Lylanne Musselman does a nice job with the photo you provide her. She also does Poetry Portraits, which combine your pet's portrait with a special poem. Many choices of size and medium. Makes an unusual gift for a friend.

"All I need is several photos, or one clear photograph. I do all my work freehand, so if I can't see the eyes clearly, I feel I can't do my subject justice. If there are any special markings, be sure they are visible as well."

Portraits and Poetry, $65 to $90 and up

Lylanne's Purr-Sonalities
400 S. Jefferson St.
Hartford, IN 47348
(317) 348-4359

A Box of Dreams

Lifting the lid on this exquisite sterling-silver cat bed reveals a tiny box to hold your most precious possessions. Napping quietly, a 14k gold cat sleeps on a bed of stars. Wonderful things come in small packages: This extraordinary creation measures only 1¾" long.

Cat on Bed Box, $700
(Conn. res. add 6% sales tax)

One Is Silver
James Yesberger
214 Child Rd.
Woodstock, CT 06281
(203) 974-3081

TRUE CAT FACT

Cat's-Claw

Growing to more than 100 feet tall in the highlands of the Peruvian Amazon in South America, cat's-claw (known in Spanish as *una de gato*) has been used for hundreds of years as a tribal medicine for arthritis, gastritis, and other illnesses. It's now being tested in America and many European countries for its health benefits. When it's harvested, the root is spared to avoid killing the plant. It's called cat's-claw because the thorns on the vine—found wrapped around rain-forest trees—resemble the claws of a cat.

Pet Portrait Rocks by Mona

Imagine your cat's lifelike portrait on a rock! No kidding; they're called Pet Portrait Rocks. Painted on smooth Arizona river rock, finished with a clear, nonyellowing sealer for years of durability. Includes a handmade satin-like pillow that fits the base of the rock. *So* cool. Mona Truhlar is a great artist. She also does Attack Cats Doorstops, fun little items with fuzzy faces next to your doormat. Send her a few good photos of your cat, protected between cardboard in an envelope, and that's about it. Include an exterior picture of your house, and she'll paint it on your Attack Cats Doorstop.

Pet Portrait Rocks, $54
(includes S&H and insurance)
Attack Cat Doorstops, $34.95
(add $3 for each extra cat face; first two cat faces are included in price)

Mona Truhlar
1911 W. Broadway, #13
Mesa, AZ 85202
(602) 985-6651

Kitty in a Shoe

Vicki Opseth has made this charming illustration available as a black-and-white T-shirt for you to wear proudly. Good quality, fine detail.

Kitten in the Boot T-shirt, $12.95 (S, ML, XL); $14.95 (XXL) + $2.50 S&H (N.Y. res. add $1.10 sales tax)

Tropicats
98-151 Pali-Momi St., #195
Aica, Hawaii 96701
(888) 876-7228

Vicki Opseth 96

A Cat ®

Thoughtful observations and line drawings by award-winning author Leonard Michaels capture the many moods and feelings of cats. Much more than trite, cute fluff: Michaels understands the mind of the cat, and you will see much truth in his reflections.

By Leonard Michaels, 1995, 96 pp., $14.95

Riverhead Books
200 Madison Ave.
New York, NY 10016
(212) 951-8400.

Awaiting Your Correspondence . . .

That wonderful moment—opening awaited correspondence—is especially fulfilling if you're using this elegant Parade of Cats letter knife, exquisitely hand-crafted by master gold- and silversmith James Yesberger. The mundane letter knife reaches new heights: a tool that opens correspondence and actually *means* something. Not recommended for utility bills, insurance bills, and the like. Save it for love letters. Bronze or sterling.

Parade of Cats Letter Knife, $500 (Conn. res. add 6% sales tax)

One Is Silver
James Yesberger
214 Child Rd.
Woodstock, CT 06281
(203) 974-3081

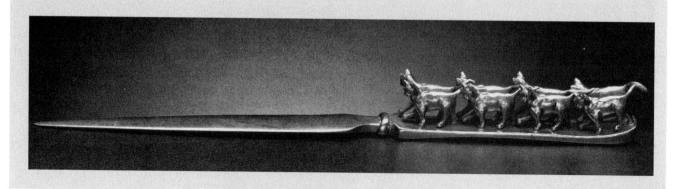

The Art of Claire Murray

Artist Claire Murray has gained worldwide recognition for her hooked rug designs. Each rug is hand-hooked with the highest-quality 100% wool, and then backed with latex to anchor the stitches and prevent sliding. Or, if you'd like some quiet time, consider making a rug yourself. Many of Claire's designs are available as kits: needlepoint rug, latch hooking, needlepoint pillow, and counted cross stitch.

Country Cat Rug
(26″ × 32″, oval, #R240), $149

Country Cat Needlepoint Kit
(14″ × 14″, #K419), $79

White Cat Needlepoint Kit
(14″ × 14″, #K414), $89

Cat Fancy Runner
(27″ × 67″, #R257BK), $249

Claire Murray
Route 5
Ascutney, VT 05030

Finished Rug Orders:
(800) 252-4733
Kit Orders:
(800) 345-KITS

TRUE CAT FACT

Earthquake Cats

According to studies funded by the U.S. Geological Society, it appears that cats can predict an earthquake several hours before it takes places. Some female cats know to carry their kittens outside before an earthquake; and in China, cats have been used successfully for years to forecast their occurence. In 1975, cat seismologists in Haicheng, near the Great Wall, indicated an oncoming earthquake. City officials ordered an immediate evacuation of the city, and within 24 hours a massive earthquake caused tremendous damage. Here are some more stories.

A three-year-old cat named Sister awakened her Chinese family at 4 o'clock one morning in the town of Baojang. Needless to say, the family was annoyed. But they took note of her frantic scratching at the window, and trusting her instincts, headed out the door. A few minutes later, an earthquake collapsed the family's mud dwelling.

Just before an earthquake in Messina, Italy, a merchant noticed that his cats were in a very agitated state, running around and scratching the door to get out. When he opened the door, his cats took off. He followed them all the way out of town. When an earthquake occurred a short time later, the merchant's house was one of many that were totally destroyed.

It is not known how cats sense that an earthquake is on the way, but there are several theories. One is that cats are more sensitive to earth vibrations than even the most sophisticated instruments. Another is that earthquakes generate a subtle change in the electrical environment of the earth, which cats can sense.

HONOR HEAD
THE
ARTFUL
KITTEN
A tribute, with 60 portraits

The Artful Kitten: A Tribute, with 60 Portraits ®

This book was first published in England, a country that has a long-standing love affair with the cat. Devoted solely to kittens, this collection combines poetry with paintings that visualize the poems. Family Portraits, Learning and Exploring, Looking for Mischief, Making Friends, Days Out, and Celebrations (including Christmas) are among the many moments in a kitten's life. Very pretty hardcover you could proudly display in your living room.

By Honor Head, 1993, 128 pp., $19.88 (+ $2.50 postage and handling)

Running Press
125 S. 22nd St.
Philadelphia, PA 19103
(800) 345-5359

Kitty Stationery & Friendship Cards

Pat McLaughlin has a great selection of cat note and birthday cards, pet sympathy cards (her best-sellers), stationery, Christmas cat greetings, friendship cards, too much to list. Wildly eclectic catalog. Something for everyone.

Catalog: $1.00
Art Studio Workshops
17611 Potomac St.
Forest Lake, MN 55025
(612)464-5623

A Kitty Cameo

Perhaps you've been thinking about a beautiful cameo of your kitty's breed. That's what you get with these 3-D domes with a fine, textured glass bead finish. Choose from Siamese, Persian, calico, tabby, Himalayan, Abyssinian breeds. Cameos come in an attractive wooden frame.

Kitty Cameo, $17.95 + $3 S&H (Md. res. add 5% sales tax)

Deer Park Craftworks
6513 Deer Park Rd.
Reisterstown, MD 21136
(410) 526-4357

Cat Window Art

Knowing you love cats is one thing—now you can show it. Cat art takes many forms, including these window decals that look like real etchings. They look great in your car, on a living-room window, wherever you want them seen. No glue, no mess, easy to remove and reapply somewhere else. Your choice of long-haired cat (Persian), Siamese, or American shorthair. Fun for the kids, too!

Cookie's Window Art, $5 (all orders shipped UPS COD)

C. Cookie Driscoll, Inc.
530 Flohrs Church Rd.
Biglerville, PA 17307
(717) 334-4117

The 100 Cats of Paws Valley!

Nina Stamus of Boulder, Colorado, spent a long time painting this 16″ × 20″ poster of more than 100 cats. She's also the creator of beautiful cat Christmas cards you could send this year for the holidays.

"Inspired by the detailed, panoramic works of the artist Brueghel, I strove to blend a wide array of sleeping, playing, growling felines—young and old—from the forefront largest cats, to the tiniest ghost cat in the background."

Paws Valley Poster, $17.95 + $4 S&H (Colo. res. add 7% sales tax)

Catalog: $1
Stamus Art
6 Burton Ct.
Rehoboth Beach, DE 19971
(302) 226-2268

Cats: Book of Days ®

Fat cats, black cats, mat cats, and lap cats pad their way through the pages of this delightful book of days. Famous and favorite pussycat poems fill the months in a celebration of cats from the cutest of kittens to cantankerous old bundles of paws and claws. These literary tales and snippets of superstition and feline myth are sure to delight every cat lover. Feminine, pretty hardcover makes a nice gift.

By Rhoda Nottridge, 1995, 140 pp., $12.99

Random House Value Publishing
Crescent Books
40 Engelhard Ave.
Avenel, NJ 07001
(800) 733-3000

TRUE CAT FACT

We're *not* crazy.
We just love our cats.

Need proof? Here we go: Fifty-three percent of cat owners celebrate their cats' birthdays at least some of the time. Fifty percent of cat owners buy their pets Christmas gifts. Forty-four percent allow their cats to sleep with them in their beds. Twenty-two percent feel closer to their pets than to their spouses (oops). All true.

Mountain Metal Art

Up in the Blue Ridge Mountains of North Carolina, Kathleen Doyle and Tom Reardon are making some of the nicest cat art objects you'll ever see. I found their work at an art show. The Alley Cat, on the left, is a gorgeous creation featuring a sterling-silver house with a window shade of gold fill. The fence and lamppost are of bronze. The Cat on a Fence with Tree (shown) is made of pattern-rolled sterling silver and gold fill, with a cast bronze cat and a gold-filled window shade. The tree is a brilliant niobium metal pattern, rolled in purple and green hues, with a dark trunk. Both art works are stunning and measure approx. $2'' \times 1\frac{1}{2}''$. Fine art you can wear as a pin or pendant.

Alley Cat, $72 + $6 UPS
Cat on a Fence with Tree,
$84 + $6 UPS
Pendant Attachment, $7
(N.C. res. add 6% sales tax)

Catalog: $2
Portfolio Metalwork
130 Norwood Ave.
Asheville, NC 28804
(800) 729-1664

The Cat in the Hat ®

What child has not read Dr. Seuss's classic tale of two bored children who stare out the window on a cold, wet day, with nothing to do? In bursts the cat, and the fun begins! Originally published in 1957, this wonderful story, here in paperback, will never go out of print.

By Dr. Seuss, 1985, 62 pp., $7.99

Random House
400 Hahn Rd.
Westminster, MD 21157
(800) 733-3000

TRUE CAT FACT

Your Used Car Is Their Ride Home!

Many nonprofit humane societies will resell a donated used car. You'll receive a nice tax deduction, and you'll be helping the societies reunite lost animals with worried owners, give sick and injured animals a second chance at life, and find new, loving homes for unwanted animals. Everybody wins! Call your local humane society and lend a hand to life.

Aglow in the Night

Night-lights have become beautiful. Fine artist Curtis Benzle—whose work is found in museums and the White House—makes extraordinary cat night-lights for your home. Each is made from the highest-quality translucent porcelain, and was created using a technique called lithophane, which dates back to the 1800s. The night-lights provide a subtle and beautiful glow that's esthetically appealing as well as functional.

"The lithophane technique was prized in Victorian times as a unique method of creating an image through the variation in light and shadow seen in translucent porcelain. An original model is carved in beeswax. The finished carving is then transferred via plaster mold to the porcelain object. The image reflects the original scene, but only when illuminated by a backlight. Without the appropriate light, the darkened porcelain appears to be only a series of random relief markings. When lit, the image comes magically back to life."

Cat night-light, $23.50 (Ohio res. add 5.75% sales tax)

Benzle Applied Arts
6100 Hayden Run Rd.
Hilliard, OH 43026
(614) 876-5340

The Light That Shines on the Garden Cats

Tom Haas is an award-winning artist with a penchant for animals, especially cats. His work is seen in galleries, and has been widely reviewed in magazines. The "Gardener's Cats" color print measures 24″ h. × 18″ w. and is a high-quality reproduction of his original oil painting. His use of light and exceptional mastery of colors—orange tabby kittens, bright red flowers, cobalt blue vase, glowing orange wall—make this an exceptional print, well worth framing.

The Gardener's Cats, $25 (includes S&H & sales tax)

Tom Haas Studio
1750 W. Lodge Dr.
Phoenix, AZ 85041
(602) 243-3146

A Sleepy Kitty for Your Bedroom

The charming art of Vicki Opseth would look especially nice in your (or your child's) bedroom. A sleeping kitty drawn in pencil adorns an 18″ × 20″ print. Sweet dreams!

Sleeping Kitty Print, $14.95 + $2.50 S&H (N.Y. res. add $1.27 sales tax)

Tropicats, Inc.
98-151 Pali-Momi St., #195
Aica, Hawaii 96701
(888) 876-7228

Cat Artists & Their Work ®

You may have read about the latent artistry of cats in *Why Cats Paint* (page 93). This book of 48 postcards shows cats "painting" in gardens, on apartment walls, refrigerators, and windows, and artistically shredding sofas, chairs, and window blinds. Rip one out and mail it to another cat fanatic. Some people think cats mark their territory, others think they're creative geniuses. You decide.

By Heather Busch and Burton Silver, 1994, 48 pp., $7.95

Ten Speed Press
P.O. Box 7123
Berkeley CA 94707
(800) 841-2665

Dimensional Cats

Anne Engert has a knack with cats. Pick one or more of the 60 cat shapes from her catalog. Specify the coat and eye colors of your kitty, and send her a few good photographs. She'll translate your photo into a work of art, sawing wood into the shape you've chosen, bonding it, and giving it the painted likeness of your kitty's fur. Ching Chang (reclining cat, brown with yellow eyes or black with green eyes, measures 6″ h. × 17″ l.) and Sapphire (Ocicat with brilliant markings, measures 11″ h. × 10″ w.) are just two of her cat shapes. None of her cats are mass-produced; each is an individual work of art. Pricing based upon customization. It usually takes 4 to 6 weeks to receive your order. Artistic work that you will treasure for years!

Ching Chang, starts at $34
Sapphire, starts at $34
Custom Painting, $20
Add $5 S&H (each additional cat $3) (Calif. res. add 7.35% sales tax)

Catalog: $1
Anne's Calico Cat Originals
1688 Mark Ct.
Oakdale, CA 95361
(209) 847-9046

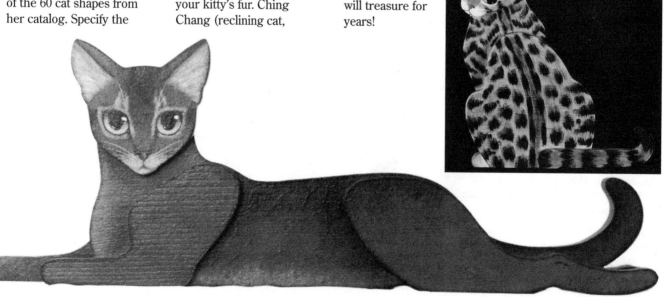

Whatever Happened to Amelia?

Looking every inch a world-famous aviator, Amelia Aircat prepares for her trip round the world. The image area of this quality art print is approx. 12″ × 16″ and ready for framing. A signed edition is also available. Created by artist Kragh Lillethorup and marketed by his sister Galen; together they've created Sibling Press. Perfect gift for your cat-loving aviator friends!

"Amelia Aircat was the most famous feline aviation pioneer. She and her navigator, Fred Nooncat, disappeared in 1937 while trying to fly their Lockheed Electra around the world. There has been much controversy about her fate. Did she crash? Many pilots believe that Aircat not only survived, but that she can still be found quietly watching over airplanes in the dark corners of hangars all over the world."

Amelia Aircat,
$14.95 + $4 S&H

Signed & numbered print, $24.95 + $4 S&H
(Nebr. res. add 6.5% sales tax)

Sibling Press
1012 Douglas St.
Omaha, NE 68102
(402) 341-4011

Catkin ®

An imaginative, moving tale of a tiny cat and a child. When friendly little gnomes mistakenly adopt the child, a resourceful golden cat named Catkin is called to the rescue, summoning all his cleverness to solve three cunning riddles and return the child to her heartbroken parents. Magical story, fabulous illustrations by P. J. Lynch, hardcover.

By Antonia Barber, 1994, 42 pp., $16.95

Candlewick Press
2067 Massachusetts Ave.
Cambridge, MA 02140
(617) 661-3330

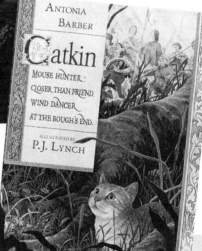

Southwest Cats

There's a special magic to the Southwest desert and adobe towns such as Santa Fe and Taos. The light of the sky is different, the adobe is smooth and blends into the landscape. And cats live there, too, under the wide-open sky. Here's a wonderful collection of eight charming note-cards with photographic art by Lynn Cox. Images of cats, chile ristras, and adobes. Each captures the feel of the Southwest. Box of eight blank cards with envelopes, two each of four designs. You'll be pleased!

There's also a beautiful poster of the Chile Cat (on the stump, in the sun with chiles) available separately.

Cats of the Southwest, notecards $10 + $3.95 S&H
Chile Cat Poster, $20 + $4.95 S&H
(Calif. res. add 7.75% sales tax)

Landmark Fine Art
P.O. Box 1713
Goleta, CA 93116
(800) 562-3986

Cat Butler & Bench

I remember the first time I saw Bonnie Miburg-Mumford's incredible cat butlers and benches at a San Francisco American Crafts Council show. People thronged around these amazing art creations, awed. Needless to say, they'd be incredible in your home. The Cat or Lion Butler—weighing 30 lbs. and standing an impressive 5'5" tall—has bendable arms and comes fully dressed as a male or female in "people" clothing. Or you can select your own duds. You can order a model with roller skates for easy movement, believe it or not, or choose the seated model. The hands work like clips, so they can hold things—trays, tambourines, signs, you name it. Commissioned works available. The Cat Bench is airbrushed canvas with a wooden form. Nobody you know has one of these! Limited editions available.

Cat Butler, male or female, $800
Lion Butler, male or female, $825
Cat Bench, $850
Add $50 S&H for any of the above (Calif. res. add 8.25% sales tax)

Bonika
41 Ridge Ave.
Mill Valley, CA
94941
(415) 383-3225

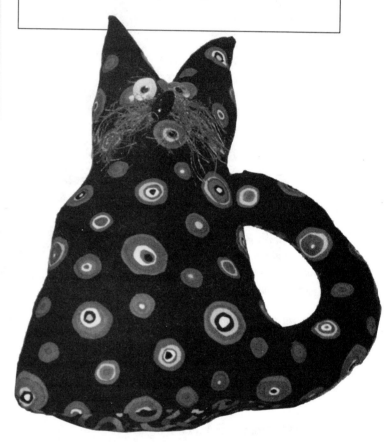

Great Big Stuffed Cats

Artist Carol Van Horn's great big (20" tall) stuffed cats look as if they've had a few snacks too many. Super quality, handcrafted, absolutely unique pillow-art, with amusing button eyes, yarn and ribbon whiskers, colorful prints, and distinctive tails. Many designs available, including ribbon, color block, graphic, dressier, window pane, and triangle. Carol also makes custom journals and specially designed Queen Anne chairs as soft sculptures to hang on the wall.

Carol Van Horn's Cat Pillows, $60 + $5.75 S&H (Iowa res. add 5% sales tax)

Big Stuff
34 Fox Creek Dr.
Waukee, IA 50263
(515) 987-1405

Kittens: An Illustrated Treasury ®

Kitten paintings accompanied by poetry are the theme of this pretty book dedicated to those fleeting moments when a cat is not yet a cat, but a kitten about to become a cat. Victorian paintings, modern art, nicely illustrated. Also a nice, gentle book for children.

By Courage Books, 1994, 48 pp., $6.98 + $2.50 S&H

Running Press
125 S. 22nd St.
Philadelphia, PA 19103
(800) 345-5359

Ceramic Companions for Your Home

Considering their quality, Lisa Harris's ceramic cats should cost much, much more than they do. A big selection, including kittens, mother and kitten, nursing cat with kittens, Cat Plant Stand, and Longhair Cat, all with remarkable attention to detail. More than 30 cats in all, with your choice of colors and markings. A quiet friend for your home, or a prized addition to your cat collectibles.

Longhair Ceramic Cat (11½" h.), $35.95 + $6 S&H

Large Cat Plant Stand (14" h., 16" l.), $45.95 + $7 S&H

CAT FAMILY—Order individually or as a group:

Standing Kitten, $24.95 + $1.25 S&H; **Sitting Kitten,** $24.95 + $1.25 S&H; **Large Sitting Cat,** $35.95 + $7 S&H; **Lying Medium Cat,** $35.95 + $7 S&H (Ind. res. add 5% sales tax)

Brochure: $1 (include #10 S.A.S.E.)

Lisa's Pieces—Ceramics
110 S. 29th St.
Lafayette, IN 47904
(317) 447-7876

Father's Cattery

We would like cat lovers all over the world to know that we are a monastic order of monks—Notre Dame de la Confiance. Our primary act of mercy is in the breeding and raising of Persian and exotic shorthair cats which, we have found, are the most easily trained breeds. We teach them from kittenhood to respond to simple commands. They become agitated when someone is knocking at the door or when the phone rings. As contemplative monks, we have the time to invest in the love, affection, and patience it takes to accomplish this, and the rewards are great.

"Where do our cats go? The majority are given, not sold, to senior citizens who have been neglected or abandoned by their children, relatives, and friends.

"The love and assistance that these cats have given to so many seniors is its own reward."

Fr. B. Roberts
Notre Dame de la Confiance
P.O. Box 278 N.D.G. Station
Montreal Q.C.
Canada H4A 3P6
(514) 277-1717 (telephone)
(514) 272-9955 (fax)
E-mail: bobrob@cam.org
http://www.cam.org/~bobrob/index:html

The Painted Cat ®

Thirty elegant portraits by the world's great artists make the postcards in this attractive book rather difficult to part with. Removing one postcard at a time, the book will slowly shrink in size. But you might simply choose to keep these cats —from a somber black cat and a princely Persian to an inquisitive kitten and a mis-chievous calico. It's not an easy call.

1994, 60 pp., $7.95 + $2.50 S&H

Running Press
125 S. 22nd St.
Philadelphia, PA 19103
(800) 345-5359

TRUE CAT FACT

The Swimming Cat

The Turkish Van is a breed of cat that loves to swim! Originating near Lake Van in eastern Turkey, Vans have no woolly undercoat like most longhaired cats, so they dry out relatively quickly after a swim. Sometimes they swim to hunt fish and frogs. The Van is a pretty brown-and-white cat with a white patch on its forehead, which Turkish legend calls the thumbprint of Allah.

Pet Angels Always

C. J. Collins's animal portraits capture the feel of a medieval icon through his technique of hand-painting a traditional wood panel and the inclusion of a golden halo or ivory wings. Presentation includes a golden Baroque-style frame, not as elaborate as the one pictured above. Collins works as most pet artists do: Send him a good photo of your cat and the cat's bio information, choose the size portrait you want (and the medium— oils, pencil sketches, etc.), and he'll work with you to produce a quality portrait.

"Because of three special animals in my life in recent years, I decided I would do their portraits. For color and composition guidelines, I studied the ancient methods of traditional icon paintings and Persian miniatures. I chose these styles because they both are designed to 'tell stories' about honored individuals and events in this life and the next. The complete portraits turned out to be beautiful, unique lifetime remembrances of my 'Moses,' 'Tux,' and 'Lucky.' Friends and strangers alike who saw the personalized portraits then began commissioning me to paint their pets, and that is how Pet Angels got started."

Pet Angels Portraits (4″ × 6″), $175; (5″ × 7″), $225; + $9 S&H (N.Y. res. add 8.25% sales tax)

C. J. Collins' Pet Angels
73 Leonard St.
New York, NY 10013
(212) 431-8639

Lighting Your Life

The astonishing artistry of James Yesberger reveals itself in these incredible solid-bronze cat lamps, each measuring 24″ tall. A purchase of this nature requires discussion with the artist.

Bronze Cat Lamps, $6,000 each (Conn. res. add 6% sales tax)

One Is Silver
214 Child Rd.
Woodstock, CT 06281
(203) 974-3081

Silent Companions

You can keep these remarkably lifelike stones by your front door, ready, waiting, and watching. Many designs are available, including a custom-painted stone, personalized to look like your cat. Beautiful, expressive detail makes each cat look very real. Might be nice in your office, a child's room, or even a child's kindergarten classroom.

Hand-Painted Cat Stone
Small (9″ × 6″), $90 (Custom: $95) + $8.95 S&H
Large (14″ × 8″), $130 (Custom: $135) + $9.95 S&H (Tex. res. add 7.25% sales tax)

Accessory Pet
5836 Pathfinder Trail
Plano, TX 75093
(800) 558-7387

Balinese Companion

Looking for an exotic cat that requires absolutely no care? These big cats are carved by a family of craftspeople in a village in the mountains of Bali. Bentawas, a fast-growing, nonendangered wood, is used for this piece, which has a lovely burnt umber/ orange patina with black markings. Each piece is one of a kind, depending on the shape of the wood and the carver. Approximately 3′ tall. These collector's items let you affordably display native art in your living room or office.

Cheetah, $115 + $7.50 S&H (Calif. res. add 7.75% sales tax)

Just-Cats
P.O. Box 60028
Santa Barbara, CA 93160
(800) 805-CATS

Heavenly Hevener Portraits

Dr. Fillmer Hevener of Farmville, Virginia, might paint you or your cat, if you ask. Nice work. Here's a picture of "Goldie" done as a pastel, painted from a photograph. Give him a call to talk it over (graphite, pastel, oils?) and get a price list.

Cat Portraits, various prices, starting at $255

Fillmer Hevener Studio, Inc.
Rt. 2, Box 1425
Farmville, VA 23901
(804) 392-6255

Clock-A-Doodles

You won't find Doreen Nagle's humorous cat clocks in most stores. Here's your chance to own a truly eccentric timepiece. She uses her two cats as models for her illustrations. The full-color reproductions are then printed on paper; bonded to recycled fiberboard; and cut, trimmed, sanded, and sealed by hand. They're lightweight and keep good time with a standard AA battery and quartz movement. Each is loaded with personality, and you have a choice of five.

Clock-A-Doodles, $25 each + $3.50 S&H
Catnip Thyme, measures 10″ × 6½″, hangs or stands; **'Twas the Night Before,** measures 8″ × 6½″, hangs or stands; **Cat on a Hot Red Chair,** (shown above), measures 5¾″ × 7″, hangs or stands; **Keep a Window Open,** measures 8½″ × 6½″, hangs or stands; **How Do I Love Thee,** measures 5″ × 6″, stands only

Doreen Nagle
312 Auburn St., Suite A
San Rafael, CA 94901
(415) 454-2521

Keeping Track of Friends ®

Changing address books is always a task. Transferring all those numbers and addresses, updating everything. If, however, your old book is just a tattered mass of scribbles, consider replacing it with this attractive, high-quality address book. Features a good, solid binding that should last you for years, with alphabetical tabs for phone numbers and addresses. Oh, yes—don't forget the beautiful full-color cat paintings by renowned artist Susan Powers.

Cats Address Book, $17.95
Add $3.95 S&H (N.Y. res. add sales tax) when ordering direct.

Galison Books
36 W. 44th St.
New York, NY 10036
(212) 354-8840

The American Shorthair Cat

Look in any city or state and there they are: short-hair cats. How'd they get here? Who are their common ancestors? How do you show purebred short-hair cats? This is a wonderful self-published hardcover by Dr. Ingeborg Urcia, who just loves cats and who has something worthwhile to say. Topics include the history, appearance, and personality of the American shorthair, and the CFA standards. The practical stuff—from acquiring your first purebred kitten to training, health care, housing, and breeding your cat —provides plenty of tips on successfully raising this very popular cat, with more than 75 black-and-white and color photos. Ask about her other book, *The Russian Blue Cat.*

By Dr. Ingeborg Urcia, 1992, 172 pp., $14.95 + $2 postage (Wash. res. add $1.20 sales tax)

Ellis Holl Press
P.O. Box 36
Cheney, WA 99004
(509) 239-4450

Darcee's Cat Portraits

Send Darcee three clear close-up photos of Kitty (preferably taken outdoors, without a flash) and a 50% deposit by check or money order. She'll call you to discuss the individual characteristics of your cat, and you'll choose a background color. Your photos are returned with your finished portrait. You may choose from chalk pastel, watercolor, or oil on canvas. She'll mail you free information, or call her.

Cat Portraits—Pets Painted with Love
Chalk pastel or watercolor (9″ × 12″), $65; (22″ × 30″), $175
Oil on canvas (9″ × 12″), $85; (24″ × 36″), $275

Darcee Duerholz
4335 O'Conner Way
Sacramento, CA 95838
(916) 922-3166

SMOKE PERSIAN *Asia Minor.* Placid, gentle nature, easily adjusts to new places. Ideal show cats. Full rounded body, long, flowing coat, profuse ruff. "Smokes" are magnificent looking. Colors: (smoked) black, blue, cameo (red), tortoiseshell, blue-cream. Eyes: brilliant copper.

Framing the World of Cats

The Wonderful World of Cats is a Cat Fanciers Association–approved informative poster in which 47 breeds of cats have been beautifully and lovingly rendered in brilliant color. Brief descriptions give the country of origin, interesting legends, personality traits, and body and coat type as well as coat and eye color. Measures 24″ × 36″ for standard framing; mailed in a sturdy tube.

A colorful, framable wall poster for anyone who loves cats.

The Wonderful World of Cats Poster, $9.95 + $2.50 S&H (N.Y. res. add 8.25% sales tax)

Patie Ventre
The Wonderful World of Cats
P.O. Box 350122
Brooklyn, NY 11235
(718) 332-8336
E-mail: Venad@aol.com

TRUE CAT FACT

Cat Greetings

We all enjoy a friendly greeting from the cat. It starts with a nuzzling of the head, and then a rubbing of the tail area against your leg. What she's doing is placing a subtle scent on you from special glands near her temples and mouth, and at the base of her tail. When you come home from time away, she's making sure you smell like her once again. It's reassuring and comforting to her.

Fine Porcelain Collector's Plates

Porterfield's sells fine art in limited editions. The Cattails plate by Jamie Perry is 8¼″ in dia., made of the finest quality porcelain with a 2 mm 24k gold band, a gold hand-numbered backstamp on the reverse, and the author's signature mark. The plate comes with a hand-numbered certificate of authenticity, a story written by the artist about 24 cats in the underbrush,

and a free stand for display purposes. Moonglow is the second issue in Ms. Perry's "Inspurrations" plate series. Ask for more information about other plates in the series.

Cattails Collector's Plate, $29.90 + $2.93 S&H
Moonglow, $29.20 + $2.93 S&H

Porterfield's
12 Chestnut Pasture
Concord, NH 03301
(603) 228-1864

Cats in Life

Deirdre Drohan Forbes makes her fabulous prints of cats available in three matted sizes. Booklovers II is two cute kitties, close buddies, conked out on a book. Moon Dance features a cat named John Moon, who has the soul of Nijinsky and the heart of Fred Astaire. All photographs signed on both the mat and the back of the print. Great shot of a Labrador watching a cat eat his food, entitled *He's at It Again.* Hilarious.

Booklovers II or **Moon Dance,** (5″ × 7″, 8″ × 10″ mat), $20; (8″ × 10″, 11″ × 14″ mat), $30; (11″ × 14″, 16″ × 20″ mat), $40; + S&H
(N.Y. res. add 8.25% sales tax)

Deirdre Drohan Forbes
Catlife Photography
4 Ridgedell Ave.
Hastings-on-Hudson, NY 10706
(914) 478-3825

Alice in Wonderland Cheshire

Owning this clock is owning a work of art. I remember meeting this guy at a gift show—he looks like the actor/ playwright Sam Shepard—and staring at the wildly improbable, incredible clock he has created. He's a genius. I hassled him (nicely) by phone and fax, all the way down to New River, Arizona, until he sent me this picture with a price. The Alice Clock, with Cheshire cat perched on top, right, measures 8″ h. × 5½″ w. × 4″ d. It has a bronze body with a dark green finish. Eight sterling silver images from *Alice in Wonderland* surround the clock's dial, which reads, "It's Always Tea Time." It's battery-operated with quartz movement. *Very* limited edition of 20.

Alice Clock, $2,400

Kit Carson Design
P.O. Box 22298
Santa Fe, NM 87502

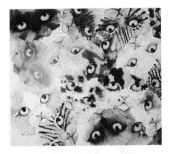

I Get the Feeling Someone's Watching

Actually, many cats are watching. This unusual painting, titled *The Eyes Have It,* is a limited-edition fine-art print published from an original watercolor painting by the artist Pat Ciccolella. Each print is signed, and all are consecutively numbered. The image size is 12″ × 16″ and the colors are beautiful, picking up the blues, yellows, and golds of cats' eyes. Check out Pat's print and an online catalog of cat products. The future has arrived.

The Eyes Have It, $50 + $5 S&H (Nev. res. add $3.50 sales tax)

Cat's Meow
2234 Paradise Rd.
Las Vegas, NV 89104
(702) 734-7337
http://bearing.com/cat'smeow/

TRUE CAT FACT

Where's the Cat Gone to Now?

If the cat isn't around for meals, he's either hiding or lost. Where can a cat hide in most houses? You'd be surprised at the number of places a wily kitty will go.

- Inside drawers. Cats can get behind a bureau and climb up into the backs of drawers.
- Inside suitcases
- Filing cabinets
- The chimney
- Closets (check even if closed)
- The refrigerator (it happens)
- The clothes dryer (common) and clothes washer
- Behind and under all appliances (the motor may emit warmth when running)
- Box springs and mattresses (cats can nestle into a tear in the lining and be almost undetectable)
- Behind books in a bookshelf
- Inside the walls or floors through heating ducts and openings for plumbing
- Kitchen cabinets (some cats can open cabinet doors)

The other day I closed the door on the clothes dryer to finish drying some towels, walked away, and heard a *thump, thump* sound as if sneakers were bumping around. Then the door flew open and Bella, my Himalayan, came flying out at a million miles an hour, heading straight under the bed. Thank God the door flew open, but who would've thought she'd be in the dryer? She had three or four good spins, like astronaut training. Only her pride was hurt—but it could have been a disaster.

Mary's Amazing Dolls

Mary Pierce is a doll maker—equal parts designer, sculptor, crafter, painter, pattern maker, and seamstress. Her pieces are remarkable and whimsical, crafted of cellulose clay and fabric. There's the Royal Lion (12″ l. × 11″ w. × 14″ h.) on his wooden throne; the Tigerr (25″ l. × 5″ w. × 7″ h.); Musical Cats (each is 13″ l. × 4″ w. × 14″ h.) with a rat thrown in for good measure; and King Rat (6″ l. × 9″ w. × 14″ h.). All are first-rate, collectible pieces with tremendous personality. Mixed-media, signed originals.

Royal Lion, $210 + $15 S&H
Tigerr, $180 + $15 S&H
Musical Cats, (each) $135 + $10 S&H
King Rat, $210 + $15 S&H
(Colo. res. add 7.5% sales tax)

Ottist
Mary Pierce
1824 S. Washington St.
Denver, CO 80210
(303) 733-9234

That's Cats: A Guide to Understanding Your Cat's Behavior ®

Understanding my cat's behavior? You've got to be kidding. Well, Grace McHattie actually knows what she's talking about. Most North Americans haven't seen this broadcaster and top feline psychologist on TV since she lives in England, but there are more than a few words of wisdom in this paperback that go a long way toward explaining the difficulties you may be having with Mr. or Mrs. Fuzzy. Cats do think. They have a "comfort level" we can all understand, and most cat behavior or misbehavior has a reason behind it.

Grace has a few choice words for you in her inimitable British style, and she knows from whence she speaks. You might have to hunt a bit to find this in your bookstore, but do ask.

By Grace McHattie, 1993, 192 pp., $19.95, published by David & Charles, Devon, England

Distributed by: Sterling Publishing Co.
387 Park Ave. S., 5th Floor
New York, NY 10016
(800) 367-9692

Catfish & Lionfish

Ruth Cardin's whimsical soft sculptures are individually handcrafted, made of silky jewel-toned fabrics. The Lionfish has a real feather mane. Both are available in gold, teal, and fuchsia, sizes S and L. Great for you or the kids, but not for children under the age of three.

Catfish, $5 (small, 5″); $12.95 (large, 15″)
Lionfish, $7 (small, 5″); $14.95 (large, 15″)
Add $2.50 S&H (up to 3 fish)
(Calif. res. add 7.25% sales tax)

Cardin's Crazy Critters
26 Mendocino La.
Novato, CA 94947
(415) 898-6875

Cat in Art

The vivid paintings of Ruth Manttari capture the spiritual Aztec—and Indian—feel of South America, where the jaguar and other wild cats assume magical dimensions. The power of her work makes these oils an exceptional find for the cat fancier.

Ruth Manttari Oil Paintings, color catalog (prices vary), $5

PurrPLE Kat Pet Designs
P.O. Box 262151
San Diego, CA 92196
(619) 689-6412

A Cat in Waiting

This full-color print, called *Waiting,* is a signed edition by artist Mike Barr. Image size is 8″ × 10″. One of many affordable cat prints in this nice color catalog.

Waiting (color print), $26 + $5 S&H (Mass. res. add 5% sales tax)

Hoof Prints
P.O. Box 1917
Lenox, MA 01240
(413) 637-4334
(800) 741-5054
E-mail: Hprints@aol.com

Thirty Cat Models

Karen Sin, who works in Marin County, California, and shows at numerous galleries, lives with thirty-something felines of all ages and colors, all former strays or someone else's rejects. At your request, she'll create a custom commissioned sculpture of your kitty, in her unique impressionistic style. Each of her cats is handbuilt of various clays, fired in an electric kiln to earthenware or mid-range stoneware temperatures. Many beautiful styles and glazes from which to choose.

Ceramic Cats, $50 to $500, depending on size (Calif. res. add 7.25% sales tax)

Karen Sin
P.O. Box 685
Forest Knolls, CA 94933
(415) 488-9825

TRUE CAT FACT

Finding a Lost Cat

Sometimes, even if you look in every possible place for your cat, he's just plain lost. Don't panic, but here's a partial list of things to try when your cat is truly missing.

- Check out places where you have been recently: the garage, attic, shed, perhaps a neighbor's garage or building. Trace your steps. When was the cat first missing? Where were you at the time? Make up flyers with your kitty's picture and description. Distribute and post them in your area. You should always have a good current picture of your kitty on hand in case you need it.

- Take the flyer to local vets, the laundromat, and anywhere else in the neighborhood where people gather.

- Check local animal shelters every few days.

- Put an ad in the newspaper offering a reward.

- Your cat knows your smell. Take off your shoes and walk around barefoot in your neighborhood, to the door of your home, back and forth. This seems crazy, but your cat might stumble across your smell and follow it home.

- If it's okay with them, post your flyer at nearby elementary schools. Young kids have an uncanny ability to remember pets they've seen.

- Walk the neighborhood calling your cat's name. Go slow. Your cat may be too scared to come out. Walk, stop, call, listen for a meow.

- Leave a piece of used clothing outside your door, something worn by the cat's favorite person, and not recently washed. This will identify your house by smell as "home" to your kitty.

- Used kitty litter is a marking device for your cat's scent. Spread it around the perimeter of your yard to let Kitty know this is home.

But most important, even if Kitty is sleeping happily next to you as you read this book, get him a tag or other ID. *Make it a priority this week.* Most cats wind up at shelters and are never claimed because they have no ID.

Cat Love Letters ®

Passionate, burning, all-consuming love. Had any lately? Lucky cats do. Revel in these wild letters between cats and their felines of desire. Hilarious kitty series of steamy "tails on fire" missives between star-crossed lovers. It's not literature. It's passion. Wonderfully illustrated hardcover.

By Leigh W. Rutledge, 1994, 112 pp., $14.95

Dutton
375 Hudson St.
New York, NY 10014
(212) 366-2215

Cats in Art

Periwinkle's Pet Gallery offers a huge collection of awesome cat art, imprinted on everything from baseball shirts to jackets to sundresses, tote bags, and high-quality sweatshirts. Choose the cat you like from their impressive catalog. Outstanding artwork!

Maine Coon (Fo Fum), Catalog (prices vary)

Periwinkle's Pet Gallery
9801 Copeland Dr.
Manassas, VA 22110
(703) 369-0244

TRUE CAT FACT

Cat Behavior and What It Means to You

How does the average well-fed adult domestic cat spend its day?

Sleeping: 16 hours

Grooming: 5 to 6 hours

Sitting around: 1 hour +

Patrolling territory: 15 minutes

Playing, fighting, and hunting: 15 minutes

Eating and drinking: 10 minutes

Eliminating: 5 minutes

Big Sky Cats

Creative Art Treasures is a family-owned and -operated business in Turner, Montana. They make personalized sculptures of your cat in either hand-painted resin or bronze. They also make a highly convincing line of breed kitties, crafted in exact detail. Their Comedy Cats line includes the fabulous rock 'n' roller you see here; as well as 10 neighborhood cats engrossed in a high-stakes poker game. All are produced in limited editions.

Personal Cat Sculpture, $125 (resin); $250 (bronze)

Cat Breed Sculpture, $79.95 (specify breed)

Comedy Cats, $39.95 + up
Add $4.95 S&H

The C.A.T. Company
Creative Art Treasures
HC 67, Box 5
Turner, MT 59542
(406) 379-2323

Pencil Cats

These colorful hand-sculpted and -painted cats stand 8″ tall and offer a quaint early-American touch that will complement any cat lover's home. The Gracious Lady wears a long mauve dress with matching hair bow and holds a pot overflowing with colorful flowers. The Dapper Gentleman is outfitted with a vest, bow tie, and umbrella. Set of children also available. Made in the U.S. of sculpted crushed pecan shells.

Pencil Cat, $26 + $ S&H
Pencil Cat Set, $48 + $7 S&H
(Mass. res. add 5% sales tax)

Kensington Cat Company
162 Main St., Suite E
Wenham, MA 01984
(800) 772-6615
E-mail: kenscat@aol.com

The Eyes Have It

The wildlife originals and custom portraits by Kayomi Harai are worthy of your serious consideration. Detailed, gallery-quality work from an artist born in Osaka, Japan. Portraiture based upon size of finished artwork. Her work appears in galleries and on collector plates for the Danbury Mint. Request her catalog, or check the Internet.

Cat Portraits, $95 (8″ × 10″); $160 (11″ × 14″); + S&H. Other sizes available (Calif. res. add sales tax)

Kayomi Harai
ArtyCAT Studio
1667 Wyndham Dr.
San Jose, CA 95124
(408) 266-1634
http://members.aol.com/artycat/home.htm

Big Cat Sculpture

Artist Linda Messenger specializes in wildlife. Her cougar sculpture is cast of fine-ground sand and resin, then hand-painted in exacting detail. Collectible art

mounted on a wood base, measures 11″ l. × 5⅕″ h. × 5½″ w.

Cougar, $59 + $6 S&H
(Wash. res. add 7.9% sales tax)

L. Messenger Studio
P.O. Box 13214
Mill Creek, WA 98082
(206) 337-0432
E-mail: sculptor@everett.com

Chapter Five

The Healthy, Well-Groomed Kitty

No More Scratches

Here's an interesting alternative to declawing and trimming your kitties' claws. Soft Paws are vinyl nail caps that keep cats' nails blunt and harmless four to five times longer than routine nail trimming. They slip over the claws and are especially useful for people with medical conditions that scratches will aggravate. Perfect for kitties who just won't stop shredding your furniture, and much more humane than declawing. Voted one of the 10 Best New Cat Products of 1993 by *Cat Fancy* magazine.

Soft Paws, $15 to $20

Drs. Foster & Smith Catalog
Smart Practice
3400 E. McDowell
Phoenix, AZ 85008
(800) 826-7206

French Kitty Bath

Sometimes giving your cat a bath just isn't enough (or she won't stand for it at all). This spray-on cologne is nontoxic, smells good, and lasts for up to 24 hours. Use it as a "French bath" between groomings to freshen things up. Just right for sweetie pie when she's snuggling up to you.

Four Paws Cologne for Cats, $7.39

Information:
Four Paws
Products, Ltd.
50 Wireless
Blvd.
Hauppauge,
NY 11788
(516) 434-1100

Twisted Whiskers: Solving Your Cat's Behavioral Problems

What the heck is she doing? And why? That's a common refrain in many cat households. Let's face it: Cats do things we don't understand —unless we take the time to know their minds. This is a great hardcover on behavior modification and communicating with your cat. Emphasis on a natural approach that includes things like the Bach Flower remedy and play therapy. Eating Behavior, Litter-Box Problems, Scratching Behavior, Aggression, Stress and Nervousness, Introducing a Companion Pet, and even Helping a Depressed Cat are included, as well as fun things you can do to keep your cat happy—no boredom

allowed! Author Pam Johnson is a well-known feline behavior consultant.

By Pam Johnson, 1994, 166 pp., $12.95

The Crossing Press
P.O. Box 1048
Freedom, CA 95019
(408) 722-0711

A Soothing Bath . . . for Both of You

Sometimes even the nicest cats hate to take baths. It starts with scratching and hissing and water flying all over the place. Maybe even some biting! A nightmare for both of you. But you still need to do it; although cats naturally keep themselves clean, sometimes they really need some soap-and-water, especially if fleas are a problem. This strong mesh bag—with a lifetime warranty—is shaped like the sleeve of a sweatshirt. Just slip it over Kitty's body,

and it holds her snugly. Bathe, remove the Cat Bag, dry the cat, and everybody's happier! Useful for flea dipping, manicuring, transporting, and medicating any cat in a bad mood.

CalmCat Cat Bag (S/M, L/XL), $19.95 + $3 S&H (Ga. res. add 6% sales tax)

Vital Visions
P.O. Box 566005
Atlanta, GA 30056

Purr-fect Shiatsu: Tender Touches for the 90's Cat

Shiatsu is an ancient Asian healing practice that involves applying pressure with your fingers on various points of the body. Skeptics are everywhere these days, but if you've ever had this done—getting your pressure points worked by skilled hands—you'll swear you just had a two-week vacation. Many of the natural-healing arts are crossing over to pets, from shiatsu to chiropractic. This amusing, practical paperback teaches you shiatsu massage for your cat. Humorous illustra-

tions. Your cat will appreciate all the attention.

By Jeffrey Ranbom, 1993, 96 pp., $9.95

Weatherhill, Inc.
420 Madison Ave.
15th Floor
New York, NY 10017
(800) 437-7840

Flea Fact II: Health Problems Caused by Fleas

Fleas are more than just an annoyance. They can cause a wide range of health problems. In kittens, fleas can cause anemia. Adult cats are often allergic to flea bites, and develop a nasty skin irritation called flea-bite dermatitis. A single bite can set off a highly allergic reaction with intense itching that can result in a secondary bacterial infection. Many people are also highly allergic to flea bites. Fleas that are swallowed by cats can transmit tapeworms. All are very good reasons for keeping a collar on your cat and paying immediate attention if you see Kitty scratching suspiciously.

Hair Today, Gone Tomorrow

Our long-haired Himalayans shed so much that sometimes I think I should take up weaving. Here's a nifty device to run over the sofa, carpet, and bedding to pick up those pesky hairs. My son uses it on his baseball cap.

Pet Hair Remover, $24.99 + $5.29 S&H (N.Y. res. add sales tax)

Pedigrees
1989 Transit Way
Brockport, NY 14420
(800) 548-4786

Video with Booklet

How To

Bathe, Brush & Comb

Your Cat

Sylvia & Suzette

Imagine your dear grandmother making you her very own instructional video on bathing your cat. Sylvia Ross and Suzette, a lovely white cat with unlimited patience, are the main actors in this humorous homemade video. You'll find wonderful instructions on bathing as well as tips for keeping Kitty clean and healthy. Sylvia looks into the camera and flubs her lines now and then, but it doesn't really matter. And Suzette puts up with all sorts of things as Sylvia rubs and scrubs, combs and brushes. There's a hilarious scene with Sylvia brushing Suzette's teeth. Given that bathing a cat can be a wild experience, Sylvia provides good advice with a very gentle approach. Includes a handy booklet that summarizes the video's main points.

How to Bathe, Brush & Comb Your Cat, 60 minutes, VHS, $19.95 + $4.95 S&H + sales tax

Mercury Gift
P.O. Box 5004
S. San Francisco, CA 94083
(415) 583-0572

Potty Training for Cats

This looks like a toilet seat. It *is* a toilet seat—for cats. You really can train your cat to use the toilet, if you're patient. How's it work? Here's the short version. Fill the cup in this special seat with cat litter. Slowly, slowly, over time, raise the House Pet Potty to the level of your toilet. Put what you see on your toilet, with the lid up. Gradually begin to use less litter. Start to open the opening in the potty. Do everything in slow motion. Eventually—and you must, must, must be patient—your cat will use the toilet instead of a litter box. Sensible product with detailed instructions. Think of what this could mean to your life.

"Should your pet discontinue using the Pet Potty at any time, go back to the stage where it was being used and allow more time at that stage. Sometimes older pets require more time to train. Be patient and reward your cat when successful. Remember—you didn't learn so quickly either!"

House Pet Potty Trainer, $14.95

Valon Products International
26 Locust La.
Huntington, NY 11743
(516) 427-4695

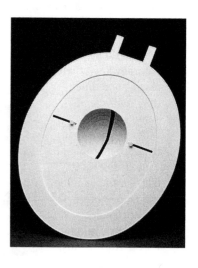

Dr. Jim's Animal Clinic for Cats ®

Dr. Jim is a talented vet with a big heart who hosts a weekly national cable television show called *Pet Care Magazine.* He's answered more than 35,000 questions from pet owners on his syndicated talk-radio show, *Dr. Jim's Animal Clinic.* His style is friendly and easy to understand. He's got great advice on declawing; dental health; spaying and neutering; grooming; behavior and training; fleas, ticks, and parasites; nutrition and diet; skin diseases; senior cats; and general medicine. For example, it might be news to you, but cat allergies are rampant among their owners. Dr. Jim estimates that 25 to 30 percent of people are sensitive to

their pets. Excellent paperback from a man who loves all life.

By Jim Humphries, D.V.M., 1994, 238 pp., $15

St. Francis Productions
4444 Westgrove Dr.
Suite 300
Dallas, TX 75248
(800) 232-PETS

Bad Bug Bites

Certain varieties of ticks can infect people and pets with Lyme disease. These medically tested pliers slide under a tick's body without squeezing it, enclosing its mouth parts without cutting them. It holds the tick safely as you lift it away —you never have to touch the tick. Plus, a 20X magnifying lens lets you check to make sure all the tick is gone. Works on pets and people alike.

Tick Nipper, $5.95 + $2 S&H (N.Y. res. add 6.75% sales tax)

Josyln Designs, Inc.
650 Union Valley Rd.
Mohapac, NY 10541
(914) 628-0364

Reflection Protection ®

Safety for your cat—at night, on the streets—is so important. This clever little safety reflector provides needed visibility for your cat. It comes with a hook that you just snap on to your pet's collar. Safety first!

Pet Safe Tag, $1.99

Information:
Molor Products Company
1350-A Shore Rd.
Naperville, IL 60563
(708) 416-6840

On-the-Go Litter Box

Traveling with Kitty? This disposable litter box comes filled with recycled, biodegradable newspaper litter pellets. My cats took to it with no qualms. Makes ecological and practical sense. Just pop it open, use, and discard. No cleaning. Great for vacationing, motor homes and hotels, weekend trips, and cat-sitting. Who wants to haul along all that other stuff?

Travlin' Cat disposable litter box, $8 to $9 each

Amturf, Inc.
850 Old U.S. 23 Highway
Brighton, MI 48116
(800) 632-5640

Quick-Groom Kitty

My cats love to be brushed with this nifty tool. It's gentle, and it attracts their loose hair like a magnet. Brush, gather up the hair on the brush, and discard. Great as a shampooer or scrubber when bath time rolls around. Simple and easy to use. Works great!

ZoomGroom, $5.99 to $6.99

Information:
The Kong Company
11111 W. 8th Ave.
Lakewood, CO 80215
(303) 233-9262

Taking Care of Your Cat: A Young Pet Owner's Guide

A lovely, simple way to show young children how to take care of their kittens and cats. Answers all the basic questions, such as "How do I choose a kitten," "How do I train it and keep it happy," "What should I do when my cat looks ill," and much more. The healthy basics, from supplies to TLC. Perfect beginning paperback for a child's first cat.

By Helen Piers, 1992, 32 pp., $4.95

Barron's Educational Series
250 Wireless Blvd.
Hauppauge, NY 11788
(516) 434-3311

A Young Pet Owner's Guide

Homeopathy for Cats

Homeopathy isn't new—millions of people around the world have used it. Now it's available for cats. This video and the accompanying remedy kit are intended to help you treat a wide range of common symptoms. If there's a serious problem there's no substitute for a good vet, but some vets also embrace this new approach to treating cats. Narrated by Christina Chambreau, D.V.M., the video describes five common homeopathic remedies, effective for such ailments as feline acne and

other skin infections; itching; joint pains; arthritis; nervousness; and digestive disorders such as gastritis, flatulence, and hiccups. Keep an open mind.

Homeopathic First Aid for Pets (video only), 21 minutes, VHS, $19.95 + $4 S&H
Remedy Kit, $24.95 + $4 S&H
Video and Remedy Kit, $39.95 + $4 S&H

Video Remedies, Inc.
P.O. Box 290866
Davie, FL 33329
(800) 733-4874

Finding Cat Odors in the Carpet

You know the feeling. You smell cat urine, somewhere. Unless you caught the cat in the act or feel like crawling on your hands and knees feeling for the wet spot or sniffing every inch of your carpet, you're probably not going to find it. And if you can't find it and clean it up, the cat will probably continue to use that spot. The smell (and your aggravation) will get worse. In some instances, people give up and get rid of the cat, which

generally amounts to a death sentence. It might seem dopey, but actually this is a very, very important issue to many cat owners.

Pets 'N People sells a special carpet cleaner to be used with a black light. Amazingly, cat urine shows up under black light when it won't show up under regular light. Plug in the light (which you can buy through them or at a pet store, or also *rent* from vets or pet shops), shine it over the

area you suspect, and you will see the stain. Treat the stain, and work on housebreaking the cat. Resolve the problem, and keep the cat.

Nature's Miracle Stain & Odor Remover, $6.99 (pt.); $9.95 (qt.)
Black Lite, $39.95

Information:
Pets 'N People
930 Indian Peak Rd.
Suite 215
Rolling Hills Estates, CA 90274
(310) 544-7125

Flea Fact III: Treating Your Cat the Natural Way

Many excellent natural products exist for ridding your cat of fleas. (Treating your cat is just one step of the process. You've still got to de-flea the house and yard.) Here's how to start.

Herbal Shampoos with conditioning and cleansing agents plus flea-killing and -repelling properties are very effective. Ingredients include orange oil, which kills both larvae and adult fleas; essential oils of citronella, cedar, eucalyptus, and bay, which have been shown to be effective insect repellents; and botanical pyrethrum, a product made from the crushed flowers of the chrysanthemum. Dried, pulverized leaves of certain plants make excellent herbal flea powders. Herbs found to be effective in deterring or repelling insects are: wormwood, rosemary, bay, lemongrass, and rue.

Herbal Collars contain safe, natural oils such as citronella, eucalyptus, cedar, and bay, and can be effective in keeping fleas off your cat. Natural collars offer an alternative to the more toxic chemical collars commonly available, and reduce the possibility of allergic or toxic reactions.

Brewer's Yeast and Garlic: Many pet owners report positive results in controlling fleas when their pets are fed products containing brewer's yeast and garlic. This hasn't been scientifically proven, but if it works, it works! Brewer's yeast and garlic can be found in specialized cat foods, cat treats, and supplements.

Power Up Your Cat! A healthy cat is a stronger cat, and more likely to fight off allergic reactions and irritations caused by fleas and parasites. It may cost a few pennies more per meal, but you really ought to be feeding your cat superpremium natural pet foods that have been formulated to provide 100% complete and balanced nutrition. Your cat doesn't need foods with added chemical preservatives such as Ethoxyquin, BHA, or BHT, artificial flavors, or appetite stimulants.

Help! The Quick Guide to First Aid for Your Cat

This is a valuable reference for everyone involved with cats, from cat owner to cattery proprietor and professional breeder. A huge range of medical techniques are covered, including CPR; stopping bleeding; head-to-toe exams; and first aid for burns, bites, and poisoning. Thorough discussion on restraint and transport and first-aid supplies while traveling and for the home. There's even an interesting mental exercise, which involves you figuring out the solution to hypothetical emergency situations.

By Michelle Bamberger, D.V.M., 1995, 150 pp., $9.95

Macmillan Publishing USA
Howell Book House
201 W. 103d St.
Indianapolis, IN 46290
(800) 858-7674

Cloning Your Cat

The future is now. It's possible to send a sample of your cat's blood to this company, where they will store it in liquid nitrogen. Assuming the technology arrives—and it just might, according to the newspapers—it may be possible someday to produce a genetically identical twin—a clone of your cat.

Geneti-Pet, Inc.
Set-up Fee, $75; Annual Fee, $100

Geneti-Pet, Inc.
P.O. Box 1897
Port Townsend, WA
98368
(800) PET-GENE

Kitty Sunburn? ®

It makes sense for you to use sunblock to protect your skin outdoors. But how about your cat? SunSpot offers protection for pets in a spray. With an SPF of 15, it provides shelter from cancer-causing UVA/UVB rays. Ingredients include natural oils that emolliate skin and coats, help prevent dermatitis, and keep bugs away, too! Ideal for cats with light-colored skin and coats, short-groomed or clipped-back cats, and show cats.

SunSpot, $11.99 (8 fl. oz.) (Mass. res. add 5% sales tax)

Information or to order:
Biochemics, Inc.
7 Faneuil Hall Marketplace
Boston, MA 02109
(617) 242-9282

Magic Cat-Pill Crusher

You'll wish you had this next time you give Kitty a pill. Here's an example: If your cat has fleas, it probably has tapeworms. The vet will give Kitty a shot for tapeworms, and *you* will also need to give Kitty a pill. It isn't always easy, and here's the solution. Drop the pill in this magic crusher. Close the lid. Turn the handle. The pill is now powder—easier to get in the cat's mouth, easier to swallow with food. Bright idea!

E-Z Swallow Pill Crusher, $10

American Medical Industries
330½ E. Third St.
Dell Rapids, SD 57022
(605) 428-5501

The Fresh-Air Machine

If you keep the litter box in a small bathroom, or if you have allergies or asthma, you might want to think about getting an air purifier. They come in lots of different models.

This one helps remove odors, chemical gases, pollen, dust, cat dander, smoke from tobacco, stoves, and fireplaces, plus mold spores, mildew, and bacteria. How does it work? Using no filters (they need to be replaced, just another chore you don't necessarily want to do), it pulls in the room air and creates negative ions and ozone (created naturally by electricity during thunderstorms). It purifies your air and knocks out a lot of junk particles that might be aggravating your allergies. Just what you need—less aggravation.

The XL-15 Air Purifier, $595 + $10 S&H (wood case); $650 + $10 S&H (clear acrylic case)

A&R Air Purification
1404 Hickory Heights Dr.
Waverly, IA 50677
(319) 352-4191

Natural Ways to Care for Kitty ®

Here's a reliable source for natural products for household pets, including cats. Consider the Pet Vita tablets (in a dried liver base for good taste) and Pet Calcium Tabs with balanced doses of calcium, phosphorus, and vitamin D-3 for bone strength in growing kitties. The benefits of brewer's yeast are well-known, including a very high digestible protein (more than 30%), plus it's fortified with B-complex vitamins and 5% garlic with a liver flavor cats love. Cat-Plex powder helps move hair balls and combat litter-box odors, with natural ingredients from the yucca plant and DL-methionine, an essential amino acid. When it's time for a shampoo, try Citrus Natural, which contains 10% aloe vera and lanolin (10 times the level found in most pet shampoos), as well as 10% d-Limonene, an extract from the peels of citrus fruit that works as a potent deodorizing agent. Herbal Guard shampoo contains mild cleansers derived from coconut oil, and active herbal extracts, including oils of melaleuca, lavender, rosemary, and sage, and 10% aloe vera to help soothe skin and condition Kitty's coat.

Pet Vita tabs, $5.99 (60)
Pet Calcium tabs, $5.49 (60)
Brewer's Yeast & Garlic tabs, $4.49 (250)
Cat-Plex, $9.99 (8 oz.)
Citrus Natural shampoo, $8.59 (16 oz.)
Herbal Guard shampoo, $8.39 (16 oz.)

Information:
Revere Manufacturing
9151-B Rehco Rd.
San Diego, CA 92121
(619) 453-8372

Flea Fact IV: Treating Your Home and Yard for Fleas

Treating your cat is the first step, but you must eliminate all stages of the flea life cycle in your home and yard.

Inside: Thoroughly treat high-traffic areas and locations where your pet spends time. Bedding should be washed and dried in high heat. Mop, vacuum, and treat the basement, garage, and laundry room. Discard the vacuum bag since hundreds of eggs may have been picked up during cleaning.

Natural pyrethrum powders are very effective and can be used safely indoors. Apply powder on floors, along baseboards, under pet sleeping areas. Pyrethrum is to be used indoors; it breaks down quickly and harmlessly when exposed to sunlight.

Outside: Treat your yard with diatomaceous earth, especially favorite spots where Kitty likes to catnap in the shade. This natural, nontoxic product is made from one-celled plants called diatoms that settle onto lake bottoms. Mined and dried, the inert, finely ground fossil material kills fleas both indoors and outdoors by absorbing or removing the insects' outer coverings.

Chasin' That Cat Away

Easy-to-use spray that's effective in keeping the cat away from furniture, carpet, trees, the garden, you name it. Works indoors and out. Sometimes you have to apply the spray repeatedly until Kitty's gotten the message. Think of it as a training aid; be consistent, and after a while you won't need it anymore.

Four Paws Cat and Kitten Repellent, $5.89

Information:
Four Paws
Products, Ltd.
50 Wireless Blvd.
Hauppauge, NY
11788
(516) 434-1100

Newspapers for Cats

Bio-Flush Cat Litter is made from 100% recycled newspapers. Your cat won't be able to read a thing, but this new pellet litter is four times as absorbent as clay litter; it's biodegradable, flushable/burnable, 99% dust-free, and especially recommended for declawed cats. Each ton of paper that's recycled will save 17 trees, divert three cubic yards of material from landfills, and save 7,000 gallons of water! Recycling helps reduce the flood of trash into our landfills. My cats have tried lots of different litters, and they like this one. Big advantage for you is they can't track it all over the place.

Bio-Flush Cat Litter, $5 to $7 (10 lbs.)

Amturf, Inc.
850 Old U.S. 23 Highway
Brighton, MI 48116
(800) 632-5641

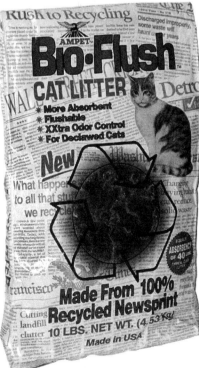

Home Vet Supply Shop

Nothing fancy about this photocopied, thick catalog, stapled together and tossed in the mail. But the content is amazing, mostly items you can use at home that you'd ordinarily buy from a veterinarian's office. This catalog is for the cat "do-it-yourselfer"—hundreds of products from antibiotics to disinfectants, vaccines, wormers, shampoo and insecticides, ointments and topical lotions—and it's perfect for folks living in remote areas who can't get to a vet easily. Helpful, very knowledgeable staff, all of whom have worked in vet hospitals in varying degrees. You won't feel like a dweeb asking them dumb questions. They will give you a 10% discount on your first order, and even send you a three-ring binder in which to keep the catalog and their monthly newsletter.

Catalog:
Amturf, Inc.
850 Old U.S. 23 Hwy.
Brighton, MI 48116
(800) 632-5641

Hold That Tiger

Some cats love to travel in cars. Like most things, it's a matter of practice: If you take your cat for enough rides, it'll become a common part of his life. Now, *you* wouldn't drive without wearing a seat belt, right? So why put your pet in danger? Here's a seat-belt system for cats on the move. It allows the cat to lie down or sit up, but prevents him from roaming around the car. The Cat Seat Belt fits most modern American and foreign-made cars, and simply snaps into existing seat-belt buckles.

Cat Seat Belt, $19.99 + $3.50 S&H (Nebr. res. add 7% sales tax)

Omaha Vaccine Pet Catalog 3030 L St. Omaha, NE 68107 (800) 367-4444

A Feline Affair: A Guide to Raising and Breeding Purebred Cats ®

Cat breeding is an art and a science. In this hardcover you'll find everything you need to know about breeding: birthing and newborn kittens; feline economics; marketing purebred cats; kids and kittens; grooming and bathing; diet and nutrition; and cat shows. Authoritative. Includes sales agreements, litter records, gestation chart.

By Elaine Wenner Gilbertson, 1993, 176 pp., $19.95

Alpine Publications P.O. Box 7027 Loveland, CO 80537 (800) 777-7257

Animal Talk

Have you ever wondered what your cat or dog or tortoise is thinking? Do animals think? Much of this progressive-minded, compassionate paperback is devoted to what the author calls "tried and true telepathic communication techniques."

The purpose is to transform people's relationships with other species on all levels—physical, mental, emotional and spiritual. Extraordinary stuff. Requires a big open mind. But is it really that strange? Most people talk to their pets, and it seems that a nonverbal, telepathic communication is possible between many living things. The only way you will ever know is to try it. This book qualifies as the official road map to your pet's mind.

By Penelope Smith, 1995, 96 pp. $6.95

Pegasus Press P.O. Box 1060 Pt. Reyes Station, CA 94956

Cat Safety Collar

All cats that go outdoors should wear tags—too many cats are sitting in animal shelters simply because their owners can't be found. This safety collar stretches to avoid choking the cat in case it gets snagged on something. Good idea, nice-looking, lots of color choices: black & white; purple & pink; red, yellow & green; teal, purple & black.

Stretch Cat Collar, $9 + $4.95 S&H (Tex. res. add 7.25% sales tax)

Accessory Pet
5836 Pathfinder Trail
Plano, TX 75093
(800) 558-7387

Natural Kitty Goodies ®

More natural cat products:

- Diatom powder kills insects by removing their outer waxy covering. Insects cannot become immune to this long-lasting, odorless, nonstaining, nontoxic powder. Great for flea problems.
- Herbal Flea Powder is a natural herbal powder made from the flowers of the African chrysanthemum, the best flea killer ever.
- Coat Enhancer blends fresh herbs and essential oils with lanolin, aloe, and other natural ingredients into a natural water-based formula that relieves dry, itchy skin and enhances coat condition. Earth-friendly pump spray.
- Shampoo & Dip Concentrate contains five essential oils and vegetable glycerin in a mild coconut shampoo base—smells great!
- These Yeast and Garlic Bits help drive fleas away, and they're blended with essential amino acids, vitamins,

minerals, and healthful herbs. You know what Grandma said about garlic? Well, it's true.

Diatom Powder, $6.95 (5 oz.) + $3.50 S&H
Cat Herbal Flea Powder, $4.95 (2.6 oz.) + $3.50 S&H
Cat Coat Enhancer, $24.95 (64 oz.) + $3.50 S&H

Cat Shampoo & Dip Concentrate, $7.95 (8 oz.) + $3.50 S&H
Yeast & Garlic Bits, $9.95 (2 lbs.) + $3.50 S&H (Fla. res. add 6% sales tax)

Information or to order:
Natural Animal
7000 U.S. 1, North
St. Augustine, FL 32095
(800) 274-7387

Removing a Tick

Ticks are more than just a nuisance. These nasty bloodsuckers transmit Lyme disease, which is estimated to affect nearly 50,000 people each year in the U.S. It doesn't stop there. Ticks transmit tick-borne encephalitis, Rocky Mountain spotted fever, tularemia, Colorado tick fever, babesiosis, tick paralysis, and relapsing fever. Whew! This handy pocket pack contains a patented, pressure-specific stainless-steel instrument for precision tick removal, an alcohol wipe, a magnifying glass, and an instruction booklet.

TickPick, $9.85 + $3.75 S&H (Pa. res. add 6% sales tax)

Scandinavian Natural Health & Beauty Products, Inc.
13 N. Seventh St.
Perkasie, PA 18944
(215) 453-2505

TRUE CAT FACT

Everything You Ever Wanted to Know About Cat Litter

Cat litter comes in all sorts of materials—Fuller's earth, corncobs, wheat husks, recycled newspaper pellets, cedar shavings, alfalfa chaff, orange peels, oat flakes—almost anything that's absorbent and will reduce cat-box odor.

The most common type is Fuller's earth. It's made of little pieces of clay and can be bought almost anywhere, cheap. It attracts and absorbs virtually any liquid it comes in contact with. (FYI, a close cousin of Fuller's earth, kaolin, is the primary ingredient in the antidiarrheal Kaopectate.) Clay is also used to coat the slick paper of magazines. It's all over the place.

The largest known deposit of Fuller's earth is along the eastern border of Florida and Georgia. Other major deposits are in Mississippi, Louisiana, California, and Oregon. It's mined in huge open-pit operations, using steam shovels the size of small houses. They scoop the clay into giant dump trucks that transport their loads to automated factories where the clay is crushed, passed over a screen that sorts by size, briefly washed, and then sterilized in tumbling ovens. Once the clay has cooled, some manufacturers add a secret blend of chemical additives to control litter-box odor.

Now you know!

Get Wet!

Bath time again? Talking about it and doing it are two different things. Unless your cat is a fan of water, bath time can turn into a contest of wills—and scratches, and bites. Here's a practical spa that's used by thousands of vets, groomers, animal shelters, and pet owners. The spa restrains the cat for easy washing and rinsing. It comes with an instructional videocassette, a quick-release collar and D-ring, a rinse hose and showerhead, two removable floor plates, a sliding resistant top, and an easy-to-use drain. In short, everything you need to give your cat a bath except the all-natural sham-poo (which you can find, for example, on page 127).

Pet Bath Treatment Spa, $69.95 + $6 S&H (Calif. res. add $5.78 sales tax)

The Image Plant
8722 Airlane Ave.
Los Angeles, CA 90045
(800) 636-8080

If You Let Me Look in Your Ears, I'll Buy You a New Coat! 🐾

That doesn't sound very romantic. Except—we're talking about the cat! Consider that fur coat she's wearing. A bit frayed around the edges? Shedding, itching, dandruff? Maybe the way to work on it is from the inside out. Consider adding Dream Coat to your cat's food. A combination of natural oils will improve your cat's fur and skin, and Garlic and Evening Primrose Oil are organic immune-system boosters.

Now, about those ears. Cats, like people, can get waxy ears. Sooner or later it can reduce hearing ability. Gently cleaning your cat's ears can be important. Use Natural Herbal Ear Wash, herbal extracts blended in a witch-hazel base, to get rid of waxy buildup and associated problems such as odor and infection.

Dream Coat, $9.98 (8 oz.) + $4.50 S&H
Natural Herbal Ear Wash, $9.98 (4 oz.) + $4.50 S&H (Fla. res. add 7% sales tax)

Halo, Purely for Pets
3438 E. Lake Road, #14
Palm Harbor, FL 34685
(800) 426-4256

Cat Owner's Home Veterinary Handbook ®

Packed with information, this book is an interesting collaboration between a D.V.M. and an M.D. Though written for home use, it's so thorough and complete it could serve as a reference for practicing veterinarians. Massive, detailed hard-cover of basic care also includes diagnostic infor-mation, sick-cat pho-tographs (not for the faint of heart), and rec-ommended treatments. Definitely not a "cute kitty" book.

By Delbert Carlson, D.V.M., and James Giffin, M.D., 1983, 392 pp., $22.50

Macmillan Publishing USA
201 W. 103d St.
Indianapolis, IN 46290
(800) 858-7674

Cat Owner's HOME VETERINARY Handbook
by DELBERT G. CARLSON, D.V.M. and JAMES M. GIFFIN, M.D.

Throw Out the Litter Box

This is one of the very best videotapes I've seen on how to wean your cat off the lit-ter box and onto the toilet. It's not that tough if you're patient and really want it to happen. How long will it take? Well, Jill, on the video, trained her cat Stormy in 10 weeks. Basically, you take an extra toilet seat, tape an aluminum pan under the seat, tape that contraption to an empty litter box, use old phone books to raise the lit-ter box over time to the height of a toilet, put it over a functioning toilet seat, gradually cut a bigger and bigger hole in the aluminum pan, and eventually you have your cat using the toi-let instead of the litter box.

This is a great tape for the cat owner suffering from litter-box burnout. Well pro-duced, with step-by-step instructions and a time-lapse sequence showing Stormy actually using the training toilet and ultimately the real toilet. You'll need some basic, cheap supplies, and plenty of patience. Remember, every cat goes at its own pace.

Toilet Training the Feline, 30 minutes, VHS, $19.95 (includes S&H)

PetAvision, Inc.
P.O. Box 102
Morgantown, WV 26507
(800) 822-2988

"Toilet Training the Feline"

A step-by-step guide to conditioning your kitten or cat to use the flush toilet.

Veterinarian Approved

Let's Hit the Road, Kitty Cat

So, you've been thinking of taking a trip with Kitty. Here are some helpful hints to make it work for both of you.

- Check with the vet to make sure your cat is healthy. Explain your travel plans, and if the vet suggests tranquilizers, give them a trial run with your cat before you leave.

- Take along a copy of your cat's heath certificates. Airlines, international customs, and kennels will expect to see them. Depending on where you're going, ask your vet about special vaccines, areas with epidemics, and quarantines.

- Call the airline before traveling with your cat. You'll need to make advance reservations, and there are rules about crate sizes and documents. Most airlines will allow cats in a carrier in the passenger compartment. Insist on this to prevent trauma to your cat in the luggage compartment from flight delays, pressurization problems, and extreme heat and cold.

- To prevent upset, don't feed your cat before travel-ing. Two hours is best if traveling by car, six hours when flying. A trip is not the time to try out a new cat food.

- Heat is dangerous to all pets. While traveling, take along adequate water and ice cubes for drinking. Never leave a cat alone in a hot car, even with the windows cracked in the shade. If necessary, leave the air conditioner on. In an emergency, cool your cat down with water. If cats get too hot, they will start to pant.

- Most cats don't like new lodgings. If you're staying in a hotel, put out the Do Not Disturb sign so the maid doesn't barge in. First unpack the litter box (or consider bringing along a disposable box) and cat bed and toys, then let the cat out and con-fine it to one room that can be closed off.

A Shocking Experience

If keeping your cat off the kitchen counter is really important, the parakeet can't take too much more terrorizing, there's a toxic plant that Kitty really loves to eat, he's determined to walk on a narrow, dangerous windowsill, or she's destroying the Christmas tree . . . these just might be cases for using the Scat Mat. It delivers a low-level electrical shock, similar to static electricity. The effect is immediate. Most cats associate the mild shock with the location or object, and avoid it thereafter. The mat comes in various sizes, including thin and narrow for windowsills, and circular to go around the Christmas tree. You plug it into a wall socket, set one of three adjustments, and that's it. Hopefully, you can put it away after a couple of days. Is this humane? The shock level is very low and it might be a lifesaver.

Scat Mat, many sizes and prices Extensive product & safety information.

Contech Electronics, Inc.
P.O. Box 115
Saanichton, British Columbia
Canada V0S 1M0
(800) 767-8658

Shining Cat

It's a rough world out there, so make sure your precious kitty can be seen by cars at night. This extra-wide collar is visible up to 1,000 feet away! The elastic band holds a special reflecting material that stretches for safety. Included is a brass key ring (not shown) to attach tags and bells. Available in white Reflexite on black or red, ⅝″ webbings.

HIVIS Reflective Collar, $8 + UPS shipping (Calif. res. add 7.75% sales tax)

Metropolitan Pet
354 Oaktree Dr.
Mountain View, CA 94040
(800) 966-1819

Watching Where You Step!!!

Like most great ideas, this one is simple and effective. Here's a litter box with extra-high walls that prevent Mr. Fuzzy from blasting cat litter (and other unmentionables) all over the floor. Made of waterproof, washable white acrylic, measures 20″ × 12″ × 19″. Good idea for cats who "love to fire over the rim or kick sand in your floor's face."

High Wall Wizard, $37.50 + $7.50 S&H (Calif. res. add 7.5% sales tax)

Architectural Plastics
1299 N. McDowell Blvd.
Petaluma, CA 94954
(707) 765-9898

What's That Spot on My Ankle?

Oh, dear. There's no feeling quite like looking down at your ankle and seeing a small, dark spot that wasn't there a second ago. You guessed it. Fleas. I once boarded our flea-free cats and they came home crawling with the little monsters. Took an all-out war to get rid of them. Dr. Goodpet's Flea Relief and Dr. Goodpet's Scratch Free provide an interesting solution to fleas and the suffering caused by itching and scratching.

Flea Relief, $8.95 (1 oz.) + S&H
Scratch Free, $8.95 (1 oz.) + S&H

Dr. Goodpet
P.O. Box 4489
Inglewood, CA 90309
(800) 222-9932

Muzzling the Cat?

I've seen some pretty strange cat stuff, but this is intense. Looks like something made for the Marquis de Sade. I keep asking myself, why would you want a cat you need to muzzle? What kind of pet is that? But, if you've got a cat you love and he's determined to chew you up every time you take him to the vet, or give him a bath, well then, I suppose this makes sense.

Quick Cat Muzzle, $9 + $2 S&H (specify S, M, or L) (Minn. res. add 6.5% sales tax)

Four Flags Over Aspen, Inc.
34402 15th St.
Janesville, MN 56048
(800) 222-9263

Guide to a Well-Behaved Cat ®

Well-behaved cat? That might be an oxymoron to you, like giant shrimp. This book focuses on correcting weird cat behavior. It encourages you to understand your cat—its personality, the way it thinks—and explains basic and advanced training. It's the only cat book I've ever read that shows you how to teach your cat tricks—yes, *tricks*—lots of tricks, many pages of tricks. Easy steps for getting your cat to come when called, to obey rules of the house, to walk on a lead, sit up, roll over, jump through a hoop, shake hands. Amazing. Who said cats can't learn? Your children might actually have the patience to teach the cat even if you don't, and will find it fun to try. How'd you like your cat to walk over and shake hands with the

guests at your next party? You must have this paperback!

By Phil Maggitti, 1993, 138 pp., $10.95

Barron's Educational Series
250 Wireless Blvd.
Hauppauge, NY 11788
(516) 434-3311

New Looks in Litter Boxes

Litter boxes from artist Susan Clay are a witty, stylish, and practical alternative to the typical exposed litter box. The Palm Desert is a sleek, sturdy, thoroughly modern design. The Country Look with brass hinges is available with a cactus-green, cobalt, or natural-pine finish. The Traditional (shown) includes light- or dark-wood stain and ornate molding flourishes with brass hinges and handles. All are very attractive and functional—just lift up the front lid and slide in your standard plastic litter container. Finished with a clear polyurethane varnish in matte or semigloss. Don't forget the cloth canopy, optional on all models, which offers your cat privacy. Practical beauty.

Palm Desert, Country, or **Traditional Designer Boxes,** $125 + UPS S&H
Optional Privacy Cloth Canopy, $35
(Calif. res. add 7.5% sales tax)

PacifiCrafts
121 A Reservoir Rd.
San Rafael, CA 94901
(415) 459-3848

The Smell Cats Hate ®

Cats have an extremely sharp sense of smell and will avoid areas that smell bad. Sometimes you just have to keep the cat out of your plants, and the smell of Plantabbs Scent-Off is very effective at preventing your cat from nibbling poisonous houseplants, or rooting around near the trash, or going where you don't want him. Plantabbs pellets can be sprinkled outdoors to discourage your cat, and the manufacturer claims they won't wash away with the rain. The Twist-Ons can be easily attached—indoors or out—to plants, furniture, and other locations you want the cat to avoid. This product has been protecting shrubs, trees, plants, patios, and play areas for more than 20 years and is an excellent training aid that should drive the message home to your feline buddy. Safe and harmless, but keep out of the reach of children.

Plantabbs Scent-Off Pellets, $3.19 (3 oz.)
Plantabbs Scent-Off Twist-Ons, $3.19 (12)

Information:
Plantabbs Products
P.O. Box 397
Timonium, MD 21094
(301) 252-4620

First Aid for Cats: The Essential Quick-Reference Guide ®

Most people haven't a clue what to do if their cat is suddenly injured. This book addresses some of our worst fears about what can happen to our beloved pets. Virtually every conceivable feline medical condition is briefly and succinctly explained, along with photos of what to do in emergency situations. This is a quick-reference guide, something you grab and read fast when an accident or some mishap has occurred, and you need to act fast. Smart, to-the-point facts that might save your cat's life. View this paperback as an investment in something you hope you'll never need. But if you need it, you'll *really* need it. Buy one and keep it in the medicine chest.

By Tim Hawcroft, 1994, 96 pp., $10

Macmillan Publishing USA
201 W. 103d St.
Indianapolis, IN 46290
(800) 858-7674

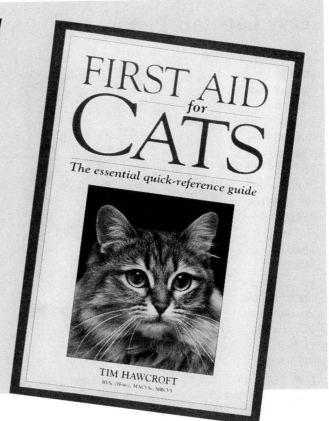

Keeping Your Cat Safe

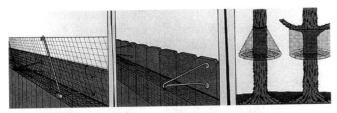

Cats can scale almost any wall you erect, up to 6 to 8 feet. They can also climb chain-link fences. In an ideal world, your cat could roam the yard freely—if there were only some way to keep her from bounding over the fence and into a dangerous universe of speeding cars, irritated neighbors, dogs, and raccoons.

Now here's a way to keep your cat from scaling wood, masonry, wire, or chain-link fences, and it's almost invisible. It's a fine-mesh polypropylene netting barrier that you attach to your fence using simple hand tools. Once installed, it projects into your yard at the top of the fence, preventing cats from going over the top. It's quite amazing, and it sure looks catproof to me. Combination or Strato systems available. Combination system will keep stray cats out of your yard, too. There's also a system called Tree Guard to keep all cats out of your trees.

Protecting cats is near and dear to my heart. I once had a wonderful cat named Caesar—a white Persian with the bearing of a benevolent king. He loved to sleep under one particular tree in my yard. Leaves would fall all around him, as a gentle breeze moved through the tree. It all ended one day

outside my yard with a vicious raccoon. It was a nightmare. So keep your cats safe in the yard, or if you can't do that—keep them inside.

TRUE CAT FACT

Japanese Scientists Construct "Kitten Brain"

A team of Japanese scientists is working on an artificial brain that can match the thinking ability of a kitten—or how they *think* a kitten thinks. The brain cells will actually be computer-software simulations, using a computer developed by MIT to run software that is programmed to evolve brain networks physically linked with software synapses that connect each cell. By the year 2001, the team expects to have a three-dimensional software brain of more than a billion neurons—a kitty-sized brain, but with no fur, or meows, or personality. Personally, I think they should forget the whole thing and adopt a few kittens.

Easy Cat-Hair Pickup

Anybody with a longhaired cat faces the same problem: tons of hair, all the time, all over the place, from your adorable one. What to do? For small jobs (pants, sweaters), a sticky roller lint brush will do. For big jobs, try one of these. Miraculous! Faster and better than a vacuum, and no noise to frighten the cat. Picks up hair like crazy from rugs, furniture, car interiors, everywhere. Loaded with 30 feet of sticky tape. Toss the old roll when it's full of hair and peel off a new one. Replacement rolls available. It's a rolling delight: lightweight, sturdy handle,

almost fun to use. I have two Himalayans. Trust me—this thing works.

Purr Fect PicUP (incl. 3 rolls), $23.85 + $4 S&H (Mo. res. add $1.54 sales tax)

Virlib Development Corporation
410 Union St.
Leadington, MO 63601
(314) 431-1320

How to Raise a Sane and Healthy Cat ®

In an engaging question-and-answer format, this hardcover covers almost every aspect of owning, enjoying, and caring for one cat, or a houseful. Chapters cover everything you need to know to intelligently raise your cat and develop a relationship you can maintain throughout her long, healthy life.

By Sean Hammond and Carolyn Usrey, 1994, 276 pp., $22.95

Random House
Outlet Books, Inc.
40 Engelhard Ave.
Avenel, NJ 07001
(800) 733-3000

After a Big Meal

Certain enzymes help cats digest meals and absorb nutrients. Made exclusively from plant sources, Dr. Goodpet's Feline Digestive Enzymes (powder, 4 oz.) is specially formulated for cats, with concentrations of protease, amylase, lipase, and cellulase, made from Aspergillus oryzae. Includes Lactobacillus acidophilus.

Dr. Goodpet's Feline Formula Digestive Enzymes, $10.95 + S&H

Dr. Goodpet
P.O. Box 4489
Inglewood, CA 90309
(800) 222-9932

Natural Herbal-Oils Bath

Many natural dips and shampoos are available for your cat. Try some out, and see which cleans best, smells best, and which your cat tolerates best. Whatever you choose, go "natural." A good choice: Cloud-Nine Herbal Dip, which uses aromatic herbal oils to keep your pet clean and to soothe irritated skin. A little goes a long way—½ oz. makes 4 gal. of shampoo or spray.

Cloud-Nine Herbal Dip
(½ oz. concentrate), $10.98 + $4.50 S&H
(Fla. res. add 7% sales tax)

Halo, Purely for Pets
3438 East Lake Rd., #14
Palm Harbor, FL 34685
(800) 426-4256

Tasty Remedy!

This is clever. The tasty Remedystick helps eliminate hair balls that may form when cats groom and swallow hair. Allow your cat to lick from the yummy malt-flavored stick or eat from your fingers.

Remedystick, $6.95 + $3.95 S&H
(Ark. res. add 7.5% sales tax)

Cat Claws, Inc.
1004 W. Broadway
P.O. Box 1001
Morrilton, AR 72110
(800) 783-0977

Debugging Kitty ®

Bugs love a free ride into your house on the cat. The problem with some insect sprays is that they contain chemicals that could be poisonous to both you and the cat. When you spray that stuff on your cat and then pet her, the chemical poisons are being absorbed into your skin. Not good. Bug Out uses natural extracts to effectively repel insects such as fleas, ticks, lice, mosquitoes, flies, gnats, chiggers, deer flies, and any other bug that hitchhikes on your cat.

Bug Out, $11.99 (Mass. res. add 5% sales tax)

Information or to order:
Biochemics, Inc.
7 Faneuil Hall Marketplace
Boston, MA 02109
(617) 367-4847

TRUE CAT FACT

Mealtime Nibbles

Cats never forget their wild past. Way back when, their biggest meal was generally a bird or a mouse. So, in other words, they ate small meals. But in modern times, many owners put the equivalent of that big Thanksgiving turkey platter out there for Kitty, and it's just too, too much. It'd be like you eating a couple of banana-cream pies—you can't do it. Small portions work best. And cats also know what they like. Some want the same thing, over and over and over. Go with the flow, as long as it's healthy!

The Cheetah: Animal Close-Ups ®

Cheetah kittens and their families are very photogenic. They have a special grace, and, as the fastest land mammal in the world, they have a unique appeal to children, who are always curious about the fastest, biggest, or slowest animals. A good children's book with plenty of great color photos, like those of four cute cubs growing to adulthood. Helpful in establishing the connection in young minds between wild cats and your cats.

By Philipe Dupont and Valerie Tracqui, 1992, 28 pp., $6.95

Charlesbridge Publishing
85 Main St.
Watertown, MA 02172
(617) 926-0329

· Animal Close-Ups ·
THE CHEETAH

Rechargeable Cat Collar!

Many natural products exist to help control fleas and other pests. The old poisonous flea collars made out of nasty chemicals just aren't necessary anymore. Imagine walking around, sleeping and breathing with that stuff around your neck. Ugh. Here are smart products which offer that safe, natural alternatives for pets, people, and the planet. The Herbal Collar provides protection against fleas and ticks for a full season, and it comes with

½ oz. of recharging solution. Also try the Herbal Cat Powder between shampoos. It's a natural deodorant that provides protection against pests and also helps give your cat a healthy coat and skin.

Rechargeable Cat Collar, $5.95 + $3.50 S&H
Herbal Cat Powder, $4.50 + $3.50 S&H
(Fla. res. add 6% sales tax)

Natural Animal
7000 U.S. 1, North
St. Augustine, FL 32095
(800) 274-7387

100% PURE SHARK CARTILAGE

Introducing "possibly the most important bone and joint product for your pet in this century!"

Eat Shark!

Just when you think you've heard of everything, along comes shark cartilage, which some people take as a dietary supplement. Now cats can use it as a good source of calcium and phosphorus for bones and joints. Note: This product comes

only from sharks that have already been harvested for food. Ask your vet if it might be helpful to your pet.

CartiVet, 42 capsules, $16; 180 capsules, $60; 200 grams, powder, $58

Cartilage USA, Inc.
200 Clearbrook Rd.
Elmsford, NY 10523
(914) 592-7111

Toss That Litter Scooper! ®

No more scooping out the litter box? That would be nice. Unbelievable, but nice. Now, notice the little handle on the right side of this litter box? Tilt the litter box over, and the clumped litter falls into a special tray. Put the litter box down and pull that little handle. Out comes the tray with the soiled litter. Flush it and you're done. Uses clumping litter, and the covered lid helps reduce odors and dust. Suitable for cats up to 15 lbs. Available in neutral, teal, or rose.

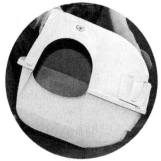

Measures
19" × 17" × 17".

Omega Paw, Self-Cleaning Litter Box, $32.95

Information:
Omega Paw, Inc.
P.O. Box 2979
St. Mary's, Ontario N4X 1A6
Canada
(519) 284-0513

The Cat Owner's Manual ®

This illustrated hardcover reviews cat medical conditions in easy-to-understand language. There's also a helpful, quick-scanning guide that's the best I've seen on what to do, *in a hurry,* if your cat is acting strangely and you suspect poisoning.

By Eric Allan and Lynda Bonning, 1994, 272 pp., $9.99

Random House
Gramercy Books
40 Engelhard Ave.
Avenel, NJ 07001
(800) 733-3000

Maximum Cat Restraint

If the thought of your cat's next trip to the vet is keeping you awake at night, you might want to consider the Cat Sack. This bag zips up the back and down the front. Includes a Velcro holder. Four sizes. A slightly more expensive model (not shown) features an added underside zipper. Maximum restraint for ferocious felines.

The Cat Sack, (medium size) $30 + $2 S&H
(Minn. res. add 6.5% sales tax)

Four Flags Over Aspen, Inc.
34402 15th St.
Janesville, MN 56048
(800) 222-9263

TRUE CAT FACT

A Growing Hazard to Your Cat

Many common household plants are poisonous to cats. Most cats, especially kittens, will nibble on anything green, which is why you should consider planting an oat garden for your cat's fresh salad (see pages 171 and 176). Here's a brief list of plants that you should not have in your house if you have cats: mistletoe, cherry or common laurel, poinsettia, true ivies, oleander, rhododendrons and azaleas, elephant's ears, tree lovers, dumb canes, false Jerusalem cherry, iris, amaryllis, rubber plants, and lilies. The list goes on: There are more than 150 houseplants that are poisonous to cats. Before you decorate, consult your vet!

How to Toilet-Train Your Cat: 21 Days to a Litter-Free Home

I suspect that many people have thought about doing this. All the fuss of a litter box and scoopers and litter and smell and bits of litter here and there . . . well, you know what I mean.

I won't tell you all the clues to training your cat to use the toilet, but it includes very, very slowly raising your litter box on magazines until it's at the height of your toilet, then placing it next to the toilet (lid up, seat down), then partly on the seat, or one of several variations thereof. The odd thing is that it's so easy, but you will need plenty of patience. Once accomplished, you will laugh all the way to the bank when you think of how much you'll save on cat litter. And you might do it in 21 short days. Almost any cat can learn at any age. Isn't it worth a try? Won't you benefit for years? Best paperback ever on getting the cat out of the box and on the can. Hilarious cartoons!

By Paul Kunkel, 1991, 124 pp., $5.95 + $2.50 S&H

Workman Publishing
708 Broadway
New York, NY 10003
(800) 722-7202

The Natural Remedy Book for Dogs & Cats

The trend in health for cats is toward "natural" treatments whenever possible. In this paperback, Diane Stein, author of *The Natural Remedy Book for Women,* applies to family pets her knowledge of nutrition, vitamins, homeopathy, minerals, massage, and herbs. Solid advice for the "holistic" cat and owner. Looking for a holistic vet in your area? Contact the American Holistic Veterinary Medical Association, 2214 Old Emmorton Rd., Bel Air, MD 21014; (410) 569-0795.

By Diane Stein, 1995, 332 pp., $16.95

The Crossing Press
P.O. Box 1048
Freedom, CA 95019
(408) 722-0711

What a Vet Needs to Know

We all pray it never happens, but what if your cat was injured and taken to a new vet by a neighbor or stranger? These handy tags, made of durable stainless steel, identify your cat's pertinent medical condition(s), including: diabetes, kidney disease, vaccine reactor, autoimmune disease, breathing disorder, cardiac arrhythmia, bleeding disorder, hearing impairment, heart disease, hyperthyroid, inflammatory bowel disease, seizure disorder, spinal disease, and vision impairment. An emergency vet will need to know your cat's medical status.

Pet Alert Tag (specify medical condition), $5.95 + 95¢ S&H (Fla. res. add 6% sales tax)

Florida Pet Products, Inc.
P.O. Box 8631
Coral Springs, FL 33075
(800) 838-8247

TRUE CAT FACT

Vegetarian Cats

Despite the well-meaning advice of your friend at the health-food store, cats cannot be vegetarians, for a couple of reasons. One, they need the substance taurine, which is derived from the amino acid cysteine, found only in meat. Cats without taurine in their diets can go blind. Two, their digestive system is not set up to digest large quantities of vegetable matter. That's not to say that cats won't nibble on salad greens, or an oat garden; they do enjoy munching on healthy greens. Just don't expect them to live as vegetarians. No matter what you do, nature always wins.

The Magic of Flower Essences

Flower essences have been popular for years. Now Gail Colombo and her crew of six cats have come up with a delightful Catnip Flower Essence that can be gently rubbed into Kitty's fur or put in food or drinking water. Cats need only one to three drops at a time. Humans may place a few drops under their tongue, or in a glass of water. Other flower essences—Fairy Rose, Lavender, Blue Pansy, Celebration, Marshmallow, White Hollyhock, Bind Weed, and Hyssop—also available. Meow Mist is a catnip floral water made of fresh dried, organically grown catnip. Spray it on your cat's toys or scratching post. According to Gail . . .

"Catnip Flower Essence provides emotional light in the darkness that can accompany change or upheaval. Anxious hearts and minds feel quiet, steady, and calm. Be reminded of how a cat's eyes effortlessly adjust to variations of light, never letting these changes interfere with concentration. When a cat friend is going through an upheaval or illness, Catnip Flower Essence 'holds the cat's paw.' Helpful for new kitties. Our infusion began in sunlight, followed by moonlight and starlight, and completed its cycle in the sunlight of a new day."

Catnip Flower Essence,
1 oz. bottle, $7 + $4.50 S&H
Meow Mist, 4 oz. bottle,
$9.95 + $4.50 S&H
(Calif. res. add sales tax)

Cat Faeries
260 Hazelwood Ave.
San Francisco, CA 94127
(415) 585-6400
E-mail: betty@catfaeries.com

Brushing Your Cat's Teeth

How many people do you know who brush their cat's teeth? Probably not many. Most people feel that cats in the wild do just fine without a toothbrush. But there's a flaw to that argument: Most cats in the wild don't live long enough to get cavities. Since domestic cats live much longer, brushing is a necessity in order to prevent cavities and damaged teeth. Low-grade dental pain can cause your cat to become ill and feel miserable. Can you imagine never seeing a dentist in your entire life? Same for your cat. You can do the brushing yourself—most vets recommend three times a week. Take the cat to the vet, watch, buy the supplies, and learn how to do it at home. You can also get excellent advice on this subject in many of the health books reviewed in *The Whole Kitty CATalog*.

How to Talk to Your Cat ®

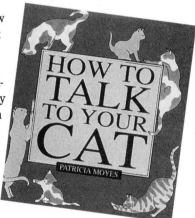

This paperback shows how you can develop a call that will bring your cat to you instantly. Nice section on lifestyles and travel, a challenge when you bring Kitty on the road. Useful tips on the dialogue between you and you know who.

By Patricia Moyes, 1993,
188 pp., $5.99

Random House
Wings Books
40 Engelhard Ave.
Avenel, NJ 07001
(800) 733-3000

Tapeless Clothes Saver ®

Anyone with a longhaired cat and dark clothes will need at least one of these. Saves you looking as though you went through a cat-hair hurricane when you show up in your black suit. Plus, there's no sticky tape to remove. When the roller is covered with fur, rinse in water to clean and restore the adhesion. Lasts much longer than standard tape-peel rollers, and will remove hair, dust, lint, dandruff, and practically anything else that clings to clothing or furniture. Pretty cool!

Tacky Pick-Up, $9.95

Information:
Classic Products
1451 Vanguard Dr.
Oxnard, CA 93033
(805) 487-6227

Microwave Pet Stains Away

It sounds incredible. The makers of this pet-stain remover direct you to pop open the lid, then put the plastic bottle in your microwave for 30 seconds before using. Microwaving energizes this environmentally safe, nontoxic, biodegradable, and noncaustic cleaner to help lift out stains and odors. Even removes pet-stain yellowing on light-color carpet, including old stains you've treated with other products. Apply, rub, blot, and that's it. Best of all, it's nonenzymatic, which means there is nothing left in your carpet to cause mildew, mold, and mold spores that can be inhaled by pets and children.

Get Serious Pet Stain Remover, pt., $6.95; qt., $9.95; gal., $29.95; + $4 S&H (Calif. res. add 7.75% sales tax)

Van Charles Laboratories
633 West Katella, Unit I
Orange, CA 92667
(800) 844-7967

Pregnancy and Kitty Litter Don't Mix

Most pregnant women know that handling kitty litter opens up the possibility of their developing toxoplasmosis, which can cause serious complications to their pregnancy. It's so serious that some pregnant women get rid of their cats. One less-drastic solution is these disposable litter trays. Made of durable plastic, they come nested four to a bunch. Fill the tray with litter, then throw it away instead of cleaning. There's another one ready right underneath the one you tossed. Shipped by the case (48 trays per case), it works out to about 50¢ a tray. A bargain solution to a health hazard for pregnant women, and easy relief for people who just don't like to clean litter boxes.

Kitty Lounge Disposable Litter Trays, $23.53 per case (48 trays) + $7.50 UPS

Argee Corporation
9550 Pathway St.
Santee, CA 92071
(619) 449-5050

Hair-Ball Tales

Some cats —especially longhairs— consume incredible amounts of hair as they groom each day, which can cause vomiting and constipation. Malt helps prevent and treat hair balls by eliminating accumulated hair. Gentle and effective.

Four Paws Miracle Malt for Cats and Kittens, $4.99

Information:
Four Paws Products, Ltd.
50 Wireless Blvd.
Hauppauge, NY 11788
(516) 434-1100

Twisted Litter Story

We return once again to the litter box . . . because it just won't go away. Here's yet another approach to the litter dilemma. Fill the bottom litter tray with the usual amount of litter. When it's soiled, snap on a grate that fits over the lid, install another clean tray, twist and turn it over and—ta da! All the waste is caught in the grate and you're left with a clean litter box—and a dirty one to hose out. However, you will have avoided the daily experience of holding your nose as you dig around with a pooper-scooper, so it just might be worth it.

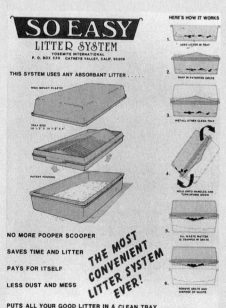

So Easy Litter System, $19.95 + $5 S&H per order Extra trays, $6 each (Calif. res. add 7.75% sales tax)

Yosemite International
P.O. Box 235
Catheys Valley, CA 95306
(209) 742-7245

Sasha's Tail: Lessons from a Life with Cats ®

So often the recurring theme in cat books is what we can learn about life through observing our cats. These days, it seems like everybody's in a hurry. We need books like this to slow us down so we can pause to reflect on the meaning of life, which goes by far too quickly. Herein are the stories of Sasha and many other cats and the interpretation of cat life—and human life—by the talented, highly observant author, who delves deeply into the force that sustains all of us.

By Jaqueline Damian, 1995, 192 pp., $19.95

W.W. Norton & Company
500 Fifth Ave.
New York, NY 10110
(212) 354-5500

TRUE CAT FACT

Tongue Talk

Your cat's tongue is rough because, in the wild, it's used for licking the bones of its prey. That same rough texture makes it perfect for grooming, and cats often accumulate so much hair in their stomach from grooming that they become uncomfortable. Cats in the wild eat grass to cough up this extra hair, so you might consider either an oat garden or some of the hair-ball remedies in this book to help your indoor kitty relieve this very common problem.

Try Cedar for a Change

Maybe it's time to try something new in the litter box. Most people use clay litter, but this cedar stuff is an interesting idea. It's made of soft woods, hardwoods, and specially ground aromatic cedar that actually becomes more aromatic when wet. It's all-natural, no chemicals added, biodegradable, and makes a superb natural mulch for the garden. Since it's easily tracked by kitty paws, use a litter mat near the box. Smells great!

Cedar Lite Cedarized Cat Litter, 3,000 cu. in. box, $12.88 + UPS (Calif. res. add 7.25% sales tax)

Cedrus International
4125 Market St., #1
Ventura, CA 93003
(800) 922-3327

Old Cat

This delightful paperback for young children recounts a cat's life in his own words: growing up from a kitten to old age, and sharing experiences with a loving family and children.

By Barbara Libby, 1993, 44 pp., $5.99

Random House Value Publishing
Gramercy Books
40 Engelhard Ave.
Avenel, NJ 07001
(800) 733-3000

The Holistic Cat

Homeopathy offers your cat a health-care alternative. Long recognized as a viable treatment alternative for many maladies, including anxiety, arthritis, cough, flea dermatitis, gastroenteritis, hot-spot dermatitis, miliary eczema, sinusitis, seborrhea, trauma, and urinary incontinence, homeopathy might be your solution. Products sold by HomeoPet are FDA-registered, cruelty-free, have no chemical residue, are 100% natural, easy to administer, are used by holistic vets, and have no side effects. This is your opportunity to explore treatments and educate yourself about alternative medicine for your cat.

HomeoPet
P.O. Box 147
Westhampton Beach, NY 11978
(800) 555-4461

Neater Floor Mat

Tired of those little crunching sounds as you walk around in your slippers? Cat litter often sticks to paws, and it winds up on your floor. Here's a bright green idea. This mat has a special surface that collects the litter off Kitty's paws as he leaves the box. Cleans easily. Measures 30″ × 36″.

Litter and Track Mat, $16.99 + $5.29 S&H (N.Y. res. add sales tax)

Pedigrees
1989 Transit Way
Brockport, NY 14420
(800) 548-4786

Kitty-Odor Candles ®

Keep this in the room with the litter box. The Pet Candle is made of a blend of citrus and wood oils, which naturally neutralize unwanted pet odors. It's an effective air freshener, and the candle burns up to 50 hours, thanks to a special compression molding technique that slowly releases natural oils into the air as it burns. Light it, and when the odor's gone, blow it out. It works. Lots of other interesting candles, too.

The Pet Candle, $4.99

Information:
Crystal Candles
2525 E. Beardsley Rd.
Phoenix, AZ 85024
(602) 569-0090

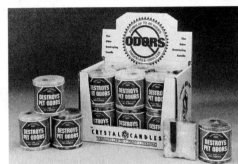

KITTEN CARE AND CRITTERS, TOO!

Judy Petersen-Fleming and Bill Fleming

Photographs by Debra Reingold-Reiss

Kitten Care and Critters, Too! ®

The innocent world of kittens and baby animals always appeals to young children. Here's a sweet hardcover with kittens and baby cheetahs and baby tigers, a very cool sea otter, an orangutan, a baby penguin, a koala bear, a gazelle, a baby giraffe, and many more adorable animals, some of them being fed with bottles. Lots of kittens in the arms of smiling young children. Plenty of hugs, too!

By Judy Petersen-Fleming and Bill Fleming, 1994, 40 pp., $15

William Morrow and Co.
Tambourine Books
1350 Avenue of the Americas

New York, NY 10019
(212) 261-6661

Litter-Box Solution #1001

Scooping out the litter box every day is a monotonous task. This box works by lifting a top tray, shaking out the litter into another tray, then dumping the debris. Saves you getting out the scooper. It's good enough to be patented. We need every litter-box option we can get.

Lift 'N Sift Litter Box, $19.99 + 5.75 S&H
(Calif. res. add $1.65 sales tax)

PurrCo Products
1155 Chess Dr., Suite 105
Foster City, CA 94404
(415) 571-7071

Healthy Cat, Happy Cat

A Complete Guide to Cat Diseases and Their Treatments

Ulrike Müller and H. Alfred Müller

Keeping your cat happy means keeping it in good health, recognizing disease symptoms, protecting against parasites, and learning which treatments you can give and when you need to see your vet.

Advice from expert veterinarians
• 60 full-color photos
• 50 helpful drawings
• Tables, checklists, and more

Healthy Cat, Happy Cat ®

Sixty full-color photographs and 50 line drawings help to describe, in everyday language, almost everything you'll ever need to know about feline good health and protection from diseases, parasites, and pests. Advice on accident prevention and treatment for scary moments, plus a complete explanation of cat physiology from birth to old age.

By Ulrike Muller and Alfred Muller, 1995, 128 pp., $8.95

Barron's Educational Series
250 Wireless Blvd.
Hauppauge, NY 11788
(516) 434-3311

TRUE CAT FACT

Tail Tales

The Manx cat, like the Japanese Bobtail, has no tail. It's a genetic deformity that is encouraged by breeders, a deformity so strong that a tailless Manx bred to another tailless Manx will not produce a viable litter. Instead, a tailless Manx is bred to a tailed one, yielding kittens with no tails (rumpies), a stump of a tail (rumpy-risers), stubbies (a short tail), and longies (a regular-length tail).

Kitty Vitamins & Minerals

Is your cat getting enough vitamins and minerals? Dr. Goodpet's Maximum Protection Formula restores and maintains healthy skin, coat, bones, and overall health, and provides nutritional support for the immune system. Contains vitamins A, B_1, B_2, niacin, pantothenic acid, B_6, B_{12}, folic acid, biotin, C, D, E, bioflavonoids, zinc, calcium, lecithin, taurine, and trace minerals. All-natural chicken flavoring. Hypoallergenic. Boosts resistance to fleas and allergies, and can help correct imbalances and deficiencies in Kitty's diet.

Dr. Goodpet Maximum Protection Formula, $9.95 (8 oz. powder); $29.95 (32 oz. powder) + S&H

Dr. Goodpet
P.O. Box 4489
Inglewood, CA 90309
(800) 222-9932

The Nose Knows ®

Offensive odors from spraying are why many cats wind up at the animal shelter. Consider using a safe, nontoxic cleaning product such as Cat-Off, which chemically eliminates cat odors from carpet and upholstery. It's not an enzyme, and it's non-irritating, noncarcinogenic, noncorrosive, nonflammable, and biodegradable. Ask your vet about it.

Cat-Off, $8.50

Thornell Corporation
160 Wheelock Rd.
Penfield, NY 14526
(716) 586-5147

TRUE CAT FACT

Cat Color Development

The seal point Siamese cat doesn't look that way as a kitten. In the womb, a kitten maintains a constant temperature. After its birth, colors begin to appear on the coldest parts of its body—its extremities, which include the face "mask," ears, feet, and tail. The warmer parts of its body do not change significantly in color after birth. A cat's colors—from eyes to fur—are all created by a natural chemical called melanin, also found in humans.

Ultrasonic Training Device ®

How's this work? A passive infrared motion detector senses when the cat nears a restricted area. If your cat jumps on the area, it gets blasted for four seconds with ultrasonic waves that are inaudible to humans. This repels the cat and trains him to stay away. It will work almost anywhere you declare off-limits, guarding a six-foot range on the floor or flat surfaces, or up to 15 feet when elevated or tilted. "Off-limits" could include dangerous balconies, windows or ledges, poisonous plants, hot stovetops, dangerous machinery. Small, portable, uses a replaceable 9-volt alkaline battery or a 9-volt electrical adapter you plug in the wall. An effective, harmless training aid that works.

Cat Scat—Ultrasonic Training Device, $39.95

Information:
Variety International
18 Technology Dr.
Suite 149
Irvine, CA 92718
(714) 727-3646

Mommy-to-Be ®

Pregnant kitties need extra nutritional supplements. Prenatl contains dicalcium phosphate and vitamin D_3 for strong bones, soluble oat fiber to minimize gestation complications such as constipation, hair-ball impaction, and gestational diabetes, and maltodextrin, a complex carbohydrate which promotes the unique storage of calcium during rapid fetal growth, labor, and lactation. One canister will carry Kitty through a full term of pregnancy. Also ask your vet or pet store about Kittylac, a feed supplement for kittens and lactating cats.

Prenatl, $16.50

Information:
Lander Corporation
P.O. Box 1878
Post Falls, ID 83854
(800) 356-4029

The Safety of Light ®

If your cats must go out at night, consider this unusual cat collar that flashes bright red. Good-looking and adjustable. With the push of a button, the lights start blinking. Up to 70 hours of continuous operation with four small cell batteries. Flashes even when wet.

Protect-A-Pet Flashing Collar, $19.95

Information:
Protect-A-Pet, Inc.
P.O. Box 7547
Beverly Hills, CA 90212
(800) 835-9899

Pet Allergies: Remedies for an Epidemic

Allergies in cats and people are very common. Almost everyone is allergic to something, and as you might have guessed, some of the potential solution to this epidemic is found in natural products and sensible thinking about what's really causing it. Makes sense that if you eat junk—fatty foods, artificial products with poor nutritional elements— sooner or later you're going to get sick. If you are genetically predisposed to certain types of illness, a poor diet certainly isn't going to help. It's very similar with your cats. If you treat them as individuals—with their own unique genetic heritage— you can carefully explore alternatives to lessen and even eliminate their allergic reactions.

This is an interesting book by a vet who discusses allergy-provoking foods; the impact of improper breeding practices, which have resulted in genetically crippled animals and rampant disease; and many new ideas on common cat illnesses. Consider buying this paperback if your cat is not well or if you are contemplating the purchase of a purebred cat.

By Alfred Plechner, D.V.M., and Martin Zucker, 1986, 134 pp., $8 + $2 S&H

Dr. Goodpet
P.O. Box 4489
Inglewood, CA 90309
(800) 222-9932

Mooore Moortser, Please

Where do you keep your litter scooper? Under the sink? Here's a more dignified approach: a hand-painted ceramic scooper and holder with a pewter look designed by American artist Donna Wood. Kitten measures 9″ × 9″ with 4″ opening. Speaking of litter, what's this outrageous product? An aquarium on a pedestal, with a built-in bed and litter box below. Nothing else like this exists on earth! Get the catalog.

Kitten Ceramic Scooper and Holder, $30 + $4.95 S&H
Aquarium Bed & Litter Box, $595 + S&H
(Fla. res. add sales tax)

Moortser, Inc.
2620 N.
Miami Ave.
Miami, FL
33127
(800) 557-4228

A Brush a Day Keeps the Tooth Vet Away!

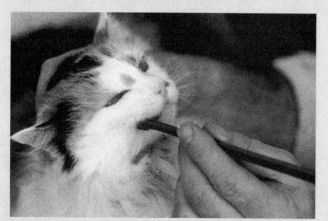

Great news! Cats are living longer than ever. Much longer than cats in the wild, who generally don't live long enough to have teeth problems. But since our house kitties live so long, their teeth need special attention. Here's a fabulous product from folks who care about your kitty's teeth. Please think about this. It's easy to do, and just imagine how your teeth and mouth would feel if you didn't go to a dentist for 15 or more years!

"How to begin: For a few days prior to starting your home dental-care program, merely stroke the outside of your cat's cheeks with your fingers. This will accustom Kitty to having your hand near his mouth. Your pet may also accept this as an extension of petting. When you are both comfortable with the massaging of the mouth, place a small amount of Petrodex toothpaste on your finger and allow your cat to taste it. When your cat becomes comfortable with the procedure and the toothpaste, moisten the brush, apply a small dab of paste, and begin brushing."

Petrodex Dental-Care Kit for Cats, $6.99 to $7.89

Information:
St. Jon Pet Care Products
1656 W. 240th St.
Harbor City, CA 90710
(310) 326-2720

Capture the Smell

This is amazing. Imagine attaching an odor-absorbing rod to the litter box, reducing odors, then using it for another month (after leaving it in sunlight for a day or two). Sound simple? It is. The De-Odor Rod contains natural mineral crystals that attract airborne ammonia and hydrogen-sulfide gases that float up from the litter box. Just use it, refresh it, and use it again. Handy Velcro-strip fasteners attach to virtually all litter boxes, or use special ties to hang it in your cat's living area. It works.

De-Odor Rod, $7.95 (small, 6"); $15 (large, 15"); + UPS. COD: $4.75 (Md. res. add 5% sales tax)

Environmental Care Center
10214 Old Ocean City Blvd.
Berlin, MD 21811
Information: (410) 641-1988
Orders: (800) 322-1988

The Complete Book of Flea Control

That's all this paperback talks about: fleas, and how to control them. If your cats have fleas, you have fleas. All over the house. They will not go away unless you do something about it. They will get worse. The author's emphasis is toward natural control, though discussion of insecticides—with an eye toward maximum effectiveness and minimal exposure—is included. Probably the greatest collection of every known method, chemical, and technique for controlling these monsters, by an author who's been studying them for years. An intelligent alternative to dousing your cat—and home—with harmful chemicals.

By Ted Kuepper, 3d ed., 1995, 78 pp., $5.95 + $2 S&H

TK Enterprises
4907 Marlin Way
Oxnard, CA 93035
(805) 985-3057

Vacuum the Cat? ®

Most cats like to be brushed, but for those who don't, you do have another choice when it comes to keeping Kitty presentable. The hand-held Pet-Vac II picks up loose hair and fleas and helps keep Kitty's coat clean. As you hold your cat, it vacuums the fur. It's quiet, lightweight (7 oz.), has a nonabrasive nylon brush with rounded tips, and operates on two C cell batteries. Powerful motor provides plenty of suction. Ease into this slowly with your cat. It takes some getting used to.

Pet-Vac II, $39.95

Information:
Variety International
18 Technology Dr.
Suite 149
Irvine, CA 92718
(714) 727-3646

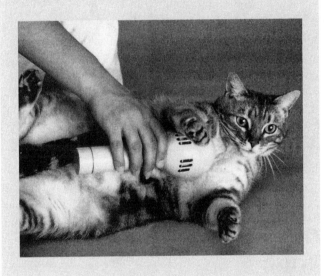

TRUE CAT FACT

North American Cats

The great Ice Age three million years ago wiped out many species of wild cats, and forced others to move. The cats found in North America got here by migrating across the Bering Sea and a great land bridge that connected Russia with Alaska. When that bridge eventually submerged, the cats that made it across gradually evolved to the indigenous domestic cats we see today. It took more than a million years for cats to arrive in South America from the North. And Antarctica and Australia never had indigenous cats at all!

Dr. Pitcairn's Complete Guide to Natural Health for Dogs & Cats ®

I don't have to tell you that natural products are best for cats. Too many products sold today are laden with chemicals, artificial colors, and preservatives. And when it comes to flea control, some products use poisons you certainly wouldn't use on yourself. This helpful paperback is a best-seller (more than 200,000 sold) from the folks at Rodale Press, publishers of *Prevention* magazine for people. Helpful tips on all aspects of cat life—from creating a healthier environment for your cat to special natural diets and holistic/alternative medical treatments. Lots of simple, practical tips that just might make a difference in your cat's quality of life.

By Richard H. Pitcairn, D.V.M., and Susan Pitcairn, 1995, 384 pp., $16.95

Rodale Press
33 E. Minor St.
Emmaus, PA 18098
(610) 967-5171

Electrostatic Grooming Brush ®

The plastic bristles of this professional grooming tool are safe to use with Kitty's delicate skin, especially on shorthaired cats. Double-faced grooming blade features teeth that reach deep down into the fur, and the electrostatic action helps lift dirt out of the coat, onto the brush. Used by professional groomers, includes lanyard for hanging and easy storage. Available in red, orange, lime, or pink.

Sheds-All Grooming Tool, $5.69 (N.Y. res. add 8.5% sales tax)

Information or to order:
Real Animal Friends
101 Albany Ave.
Freeport, NY 11520
(800) 654-PETS

Wipe Those Fleas Away ®

There's a new way to eliminate fleas. You already know the old methods: dusting and spraying, the dreaded flea bath. Each is a big deal, especially the bath! Here's a simpler solution. Wipe the cat with these nontoxic organic Pet Wipes. Each box contains enough wipes for eight applications. Safe for cats and kittens; veterinarian-approved.

Pet Wipes, $14.95 + $3 S&H (24 wipes); $27.90 + $5 S&H (48 wipes)

Information:
United Pet Supply
19785 W. 12 Mile Rd., Suite 179
Southfield, MI 48076
(810) 569-6040

The Re-Viv-Al Catalog

Re-Viv-Al's eclectic collection includes many health items for cats; grooming products, many shampoos, and special blacklight lamps (called Woods Lamps) that help you spot ringworm on your cats. Large variety of very practical products for the cat fancier who likes to take health-and-grooming matters into her own hands.

Re-Viv-Al, Inc.
913 8th Street, SW
Orange City, IA 51041
(800) 786-4751

Knock Out Fleas! ®

Natural solutions exist for getting rid of fleas. Flea Patrol Coat Spray and Flea Patrol Shampoo both use pH-balanced ingredients and fine oils with the finest natural anti-inflammatories and palliatives. Both kill fleas and also work just fine for general grooming. The Flea Patrol Collar/Bandanna is made from 100% pure cotton, and all five herbs contained in the collar are organically grown in the good ole U.S. These are the same herbs that controlled fleas for more than 100 years, before the chemicals came along. Sometimes going back to the old ways of doing things is actually a step forward.

Flea Patrol Coat Spray, $7.69 + $2.50 S&H
Flea Patrol Shampoo, $7.69 + $2.50 S&H
Flea Patrol Collar Bandanna, $5.99 + $2.50 S&H

Information:
Danklied Laboratories, Ltd.
P.O. Box 436
Cazenovia, NY 13035
(800) 497-4757

Electric Flea Remover ®

Now there's an alternative to dousing your cat in chemicals to get rid of fleas. The Flea-Zapper Electronic Flea Comb works in a very unusual way: It emits an extremely low electronic charge through the metal teeth of the combing unit—enough to kill or stun adult fleas on contact, but not enough for most pets to feel. Every time it detects a flea, the motor automatically stops for the flea to be removed with a special enclosed brush. Drop the dead and stunned fleas into a self-sealing plastic bag and discard. That's it. Battery-operated; available in many mail-order catalogs and through selected retailers.

The Flea Zapper, $49.95

Information:
The Kensington Marketing Group, Inc.
P.O. Box 1651
New Rochelle, NY 10802
(914) 235-9300

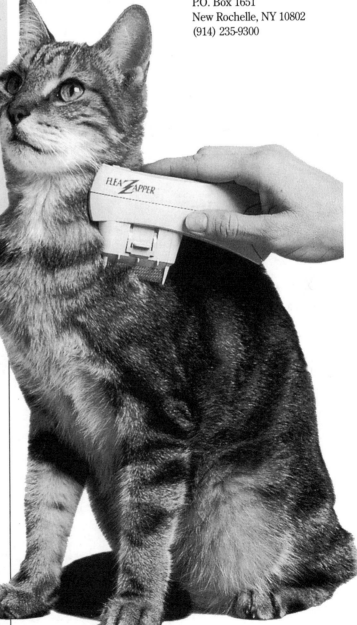

TRUE CAT FACT

Cats, Classified

There are 38 recognized species of cats, though that changes as new breeds evolve. They all belong to the *Felidae* family. Cats that cannot roar (due to a rigid hyoid bone at the base of the tongue) are small cats, like our domestic cats, in the family *Felis Catus.* The cheetah is in a family of its own, because its claws do not retract. Domestic cats obviously interbreed among one another, perhaps too successfully, but wild cats of different breeds cannot successfully breed and produce fertile kittens. That's why you don't see a cross between a tiger and a lion.

Organic Solutions to Kitty Problems

With natural products like these, why bother with artifical chemical junk? Anti-Itch Spray with citrus fragrance helps relieve itching while making Kitty smell great; Catnip Spray is a specially formulated herbal-and-catnip blend that Kitty will appreciate when sprayed on toys, scratching posts, and cat furniture. Herbal Collar has all-natural ingredients, including oils of pennyroyal, eucalyptus, cedarwood, citronella, and rue. Herbal Skin & Coat Rub helps relieve itching with a special blend of pure pennyroyal and comfrey oils. For bath day, try Kleen Pet Natural Herbal Shampoo with natural oils to clean, soothe, and relieve skin irritation.

Anti-Itch Spray, $9.99
Catnip Spray, $4.99
Herbal Collar, $4.49
Herbal Skin & Coat Rub, $8.99
Kleen Pet Natural Herbal Shampoo, $8.99

Information:
Nala Barry Laboratories
P.O. Box 151
Palm Desert, CA 92261
(619) 568-9446

100% Wheat Litter

Wheat husks and all-natural bonding ingredients make this a really unusual cat litter. No clay. Wheat husks clump the waste, control odor, and can be flushed away with no qualms. Good idea.

Heartland Wheat Litter, $6.95 (12 lb. box) + UPS (average: $4.84)

Information or to order:
Heartland Products
P.O. Box 777
Valley City, ND 58072
(800) 437-4780

Mr. Fuzzy's Bag

Consider this product if Mr. Fuzzy is in an ornery mood on bath day. It's pretty simple. You put the cat in the bag, put them both in the washbasin, squirt shampoo through the nylon mesh of the bag, scrub Kitty until he's squeaky-clean, lift him out, blow-dry him while he's still in the bag, and—with a bit of luck—you won't have a single bite or scratch mark. Also pretty good for controlling the cat during nail clipping, another dreaded event.

The Grooming Bag, $14.95 (Wash. res. add sales tax)

Kelorna Products, Ltd.
P.O. Box 2606
Blaine, WA 98231
(604) 460-0141

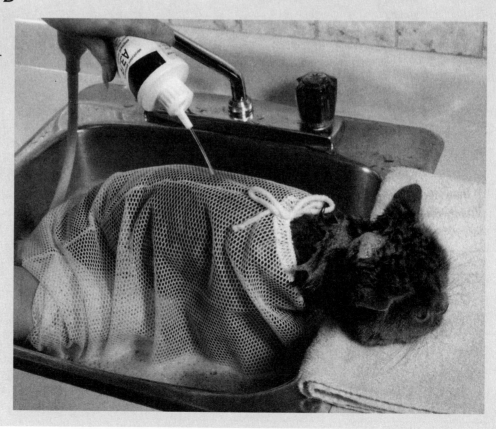

A Major Social Advance for Some Cats ®

Many cat foods contain soy, wheat, corn, oats, and other whole grains. Only problem is, it can turn Fluffy into a "little stinker" in whose company even the most polite people raise their eyebrows. CurTail contains a natural-source food enzyme that aids in the digestion of the complex sugars found in many cat foods. You place 4–6 drops (for a cat under 15 lbs.) onto your cat's food,

and that's it. Available in dropper bottles of 12 and 75 feedings.

CurTail, $2.19 (12 feedings); $9.95 (75 feedings)

Information:
AkPharma, Inc.
6840 Old Egg Harbor Rd.
Pleasantville, NJ 08232
(800) 257-8650

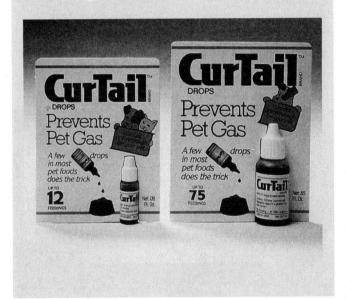

Deluxe Kitty Dryer

If you have one or more cats, and you bathe them, you might want to consider this rather impressive grooming dryer. Built for professionals and available in three models, it's the top-of-the-line model for your in-home grooming needs. I like the wheeled base—it's a big step up from a handheld dryer—and the heavy-duty motor will last for years and years. Two-speed powerful performance; 900-watt unbreakable "incoloy" tubular heating element; solid-state variable temperature control; temperature range from 80° to 120°; antitip 5-leg (23″ dia.) base with wheels; nozzle swivels 360°; many other features.

Metro Top Gun with Optional Hose, TG-1 (1.17 hp.), $360; TG-2 (1.7 hp.), $395; TG-3 (4 hp.), $439.50; + UPS

Metropolitan Vacuum Cleaner
P.O. Box 149
Suffern, NY 10901
(800) VAC-1602

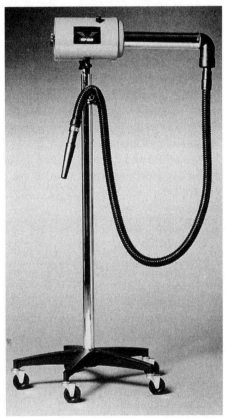

Odor Stomper!

Fresh Again does more than just block odors. It chemically interferes with the process by which substances, such as cat urine in your carpet, change from a liquid to a gas. Does it work? Absolutely, and it's harmless to cats. Safe to use with any fabric that's unaffected by water, including carpeting, upholstery, and clothing (best to

try it on a small sample piece that's hidden from view). You might try a squirt or two in the litter box, too. Depending upon the size of your problem, you can buy the stuff in amounts ranging from 8 oz. to a 55-gal. drum. If you need the drum size for your home, I'd suggest you contact an animal behaviorist as well.

Fresh Again, $6.75 (8 oz.); $20.25 (32 oz.); + UPS + $2 S&H; $1,650 (55 gal.) + $25 for the drum container + UPS (Minn. res. add 6.5% sales tax)

Uncommon Conglomerates
287 E. 6th St.
St. Paul, MN 55101
(800) 323-4545

Add Some Color! ®

That plain old gray stuff in the litter box is pretty drab. Kitty Kolors to the rescue! Yes, it's colored, all-natural, clumping litter and it comes in your choice of four pastels: sea green, sky blue, fuchsia, and violet, in a clear plastic five-quart container. Bright stuff!

Kitty Kolors, $3.99 + UPS (Calif. res. add 7.75% sales tax)

Information or to order:
Kat Company
35541 Camino Capistrano
San Clemente, CA 92672
(714) 493-7926

Use It, Then Toss It

If you absolutely can't stand cleaning the litter box, or you're traveling, or you just want a break for a while, consider this totally self-contained, disposable litter box. Set it up and that's it. Fully enclosed, folds flat for convenient traveling. Disposable, biodegradable litter included. Shipped with 6 complete boxes per pack, and each box lasts 3 to 5 weeks. You never handle the litter.

Fussy Cat, with litter, $58.60

Fussy Cat
465 Arapahoe Ave., Suite A
Boulder, CO 80302
(800) 484-3848

PetSage Goodies

Committed to quality all-natural products, PetSage has a catalog full of the best cat goodies by mail order. Here's a sampling: a cozy Heated Bed that's especially nice for an older or recovering cat, natural dietary supplements, kitty litter, and many books.

Heated Kitty Bed, $49.95 + $5.95 S&H (Va. res. add 4.5% sales tax)

PetSage
4313 Wheeler Ave.
Alexandria, VA 22304
(703) 823-9711
http://www.petsage.com

Protecting Your Cat & Your Wallet

Visits to the vet can be incredibly expensive. Add in the cost of continuing care, or an accident, and it can easily climb into the hundreds of dollars. Veterinary Pet Insurance (VPI) is the largest and oldest pet health provider in America, having sold more than a half-million pet policies designed to cover accidents and illness since 1982. Coverage is currently available in 39 states and the District of Columbia, and VPI is exclusively endorsed by the American Humane Association. Benefits include: no age limit, multiple-pet discounts, substantially discounted two-year premiums, and easy payment plans. They have five different accident and illness plans, with varying premiums and deductibles. Best way to find out more is by calling their toll-free telephone number and requesting their brochure. Is this worthy of your consideration? Unfortunately, many cats are euthanized because looming vet bills put expensive treatment out of reach for their owners. Health and accident insurance can really help when you need it.

Cat Health & Accident Insurance

Veterinary Pet Insurance
4175 E. La Palma Ave.
Suite 100
Anaheim, CA 92807
(800) USA-PETS (872-7387)

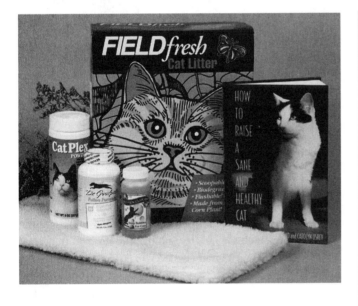

TRUE CAT FACT

Gene Control

Because of rigorous show standards, it's possible that some purebred cats will become extinct over time because of relentless inbreeding. The feline gene pool for some breeds—the shared genetic knowledge inherent in cells and DNA—is small. Strict standards for certain breeds prohibit diluting that gene pool with related cat species. The upshot is that inbreeding can produce cats with undesirable, even fatally flawed, genetic characteristics. The healthiest, toughest, most resilient domestic cat is the common interbred house cat.

Glue Those Fleas!

Forget the insecticides. The Zema Flea Trap is easy to assemble, and works on regular 120V household current. Plug it in, and turn off the lights. In a dark room, fleas are drawn to the lighted traps and instantly glued forever to the sticky, gummy surface. Smart idea. Five-pack refills also available.

Zema Flea Trap, $14.95 + $5.95 S&H (Penn. res. add 6% sales tax)

Discount Master Animal Care Catalog
P.O. Box 3333
Mountaintop, PA 18707
(800) 346-0749

Home-Grooming Clipper

Clipping can be a necessity with longhaired cats. They get these clumps and lumps that just can't be brushed out. You can take the cat to a groomer, or, if you do it yourself, these quality Laube clippers are the lightest and most powerful you can find. They operate quietly with a sealed motor, and have a two-year warranty and two-speed operation. You can switch quickly from cord to cordless operation, blades stay sharp longer, and, you can choose your clipper in pink, blue, yellow, white, purple, black, or red.

Laube 503 Cordpack Clipper, $99 to $200, depending upon accessories

Kelco Industries
16842 Saticoy St.
Van Nuys, CA 91406
(800) 451-1355

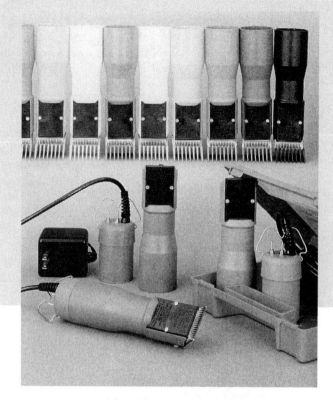

A Rich Cat's Shower

If you want the best grooming equipment available anywhere and money is no object, look no further. The Du-Zee Hydraulic Pet Shower saves your back because the hydraulic tub raises and lowers to meet your needs. Comes with either right- or left-hand plumbing ready to hook up, has cat retaining bath-time holders, includes 60″ stainless supply hose, a dip reclaim system, a grate to keep Kitty's paws out of the drain, and many other features. After Kitty's bath is over, you can blow-dry her and brush her on the Du-Zee Hydraulic Table (below), which will raise or lower to accommodate your standing or seated grooming needs. Choose a round, rectangular, or oval table top. And give some thought to picking up a Groomer's Chair to make the task a bit easier on you.

Du-Zee Hydraulic Pet Shower, $1,999 + UPS
Du-Zee Hydraulic Table, $999 + UPS
Groomer's Chair, with back, $199 + UPS
(Ohio res. add sales tax)

Du-Zee Products
P.O. Box 1164
Kent, OH 44240
(800) 470-4004

TRUE CAT FACT

Boarding and Health

Be extremely careful where you board your cats. Taking your cat into most (but not all) boarding environments is just asking for a flea problem, or worse, a serious illness.

Think about this: If you're in a crowded movie theater, and somebody behind you has the flu, and they're coughing, there's a good chance you might get sick, too. Like human ailments, many cat diseases are transmitted by other cats. Does it make sense to put your cat into a packed boarding situation dense with other, potentially unhealthy, cats?

Better to try one of the many pet-sitting businesses available in most areas of the country. Many pet-sitters are bonded. They come to your house daily, feed the kitties, give them some nice attention. Also, it's much healthier and easier psychologically on your cats. They stay in their home environment instead of languishing in a cage until you return. Pet-sitters are a great idea. To find one, ask your friends whom they use and check the telephone yellow pages and local community bulletin boards. The cost should be comparable to boarding your cat, or less.

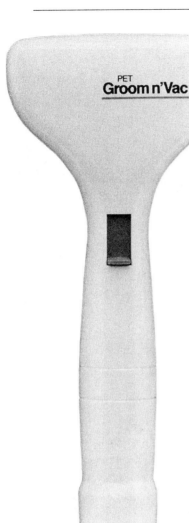

PET
Groom n'Vac

Air Fur Control ®

Both of my cats are very calm. Not freaky or spooky, just sweet-tempered and very affectionate. But things change immediately as soon as I drag out the vacuum cleaner. One look at that noisy, belching monster and they head out of the room at a hundred miles an hour. They reemerge from someplace a few hours later, long after the monster is back in the closet. This contraption is useful, but if you plan to use it, you'll have to have cats who are free of "vacuum terror." You attach the handle to your 1¼″ vacuum-cleaner hose and the retractable beaded-bristle brush allows Kitty's loose hair to be pulled directly into the vacuum without irritating the skin. Makes lots of sense if those furry characters in your life don't have a big hang-up about vacuum cleaners.

Groom n'Vac, $12.95 + UPS S&H (N.Y. res. add 7.25% sales tax)

Information or to order:
Metropolitan Vacuum Cleaner
P.O. Box 149
Suffern, NY 10901
(800) VAC-1602

The Outdoor Litter Box

Some smart people install a cat door and let the cat use the litter box on their deck or patio. Good idea. Here's how your cat can get in and out: The Plexidor is a spring-loaded four-way cat door with a lock that you can set to In Only, Out Only, In and Out, or Locked. Small is the best size for an average cat. Made in the U.S., guaranteed.

Plexidor, $86 + $6.25 S&H (Fla. res. add 6% sales tax)

Pet Doors USA, Inc.
4523 30th St., W.
Bradenton, FL 34207
(941) 758-0274

Pine in the Box ®

Here's a fresh alternative to clay litters. There's been some grumbling lately about the potential health hazards of silica, found in clay litter. Bentonite, also found in clumping clay litter, might be harmful to the feline urinary tract. This litter, however, is made of compressed pellets of pine sawdust. It has almost no smell, can be composted or used as garden mulch, has excellent absorbency, and, best of all, cats don't track it around when they leave the litter box. Cats really will try new litter-box materials.

Nature's Way Feline Pine, $3.89

Information:
Nature's Way Earth Products
1260 S. Federal Highway
Suite 201
Boynton Beach, FL 33435
(407) 732-8686

A Sweeter Smell

Freshen up the litter-box room with the Worldwind Fan Dispenser. A compact (3½″ × 4¾″) and attractive device, it continuously distributes natural fragrances for 60 days with a battery-operated fan. Refill scent cartridges contain pure essential oils of flowers, fruits, and organic plants. Specify apple/spice or rose. The battery is included, and it lasts about two months. J-B has a minimum order of $25, but you get what you pay for.

Fan Dispenser
(cartridges sold separately),
$11.95 + UPS
Cartridge, $5.85 (each)
+ UPS
(N.J. res. add 6% sales tax)

J-B Wholesale Pet Supplies
5 Raritan Rd.
Oakland, NJ 07436
(800) 526-0388

In the Spotlight: A Guide to Showing Pedigreed and Household Pet Cats ®

One of the premier handbooks to guide you through the world of cat shows. Twelve chapters provide an analysis of the major registries and show-giving federations, information on how to register both pedigreed and household pet cats, as well as pointers on grooming, showing your cat, and the entire judging process.

There's a bit more to it than just putting Mr. Whiskers in the cat carrier and driving to the show: The necessary preparation is really staggering. Is your pretty kitty the Cindy Crawford of the neighborhood? Today's companion may be tomorrow's star.

By Carolyn Vella and John McGonagle, Jr., 1990, 224 pp., $22.95

Macmillan Publishing USA
201 W. 103d St.
Indianapolis, IN 46290
(800) 858-7674

Smell 'B Gon

If the smell is getting to you—on carpets and clothing—give some thought to this all-natural cleaner that works to eliminate organic odors at their source. Made from the extract of the agave plant, which breaks down and neutralizes odors without a heavy perfume residue. Safe to use on almost anything; great for cat odors, skunk reek, even onion smell on your hands. Slight herbal scent evaporates quickly. Just spray it on!

Smell Guard, $12 (28 oz. bottle) + $4 S&H (Calif. res. add 7% sales tax)

Tomahawk
12255 Kirkham Rd., #100
Poway, CA 92064
(800) 336-4295
(619) 748-9001

My First Kitten ®

Wonderful hardcover children's book (ages 5 to 8 or so) that helps to prepare little ones for the new kitten who will shortly arrive in their lives. Lots of fun facts and how-to's about cats, written to be understood by children. Gentle, practical advice, relaxed with a sense of humor, *plus* there's a free purple cat tag shrink-wrapped onto the cover, so you and your child can write Kitty's name and address on her collar. An endearing book.

By Karla Olson, 1994, 36 pp., $9.95, + $2 S&H

Andrews and McMeel
4520 Main St.
Kansas City, MO 64112
(800) 826-4216

By Karla Olson ❧ Illustrated by Diane Blasius

Working with Nature ®

Pyrethrin is a natural product for controlling fleas, derived from the African chrysanthemum. The Natura Flea & Tick Collar contains man-made permethrin, which provides longer-lasting protection than the natural variety. Flea & Tick Shampoo contains pyrethrin, has a fresh fragrance and rich lather, and is gentle enough for kittens. Microencapsulated Mousse for flea-and-tick control does a quick pest knockdown, then lasts eight days. Ear Mite Drops provide a quick, natural pyrethrin formula to knock out mites in kittens and cats.

Natural Flea & Tick Collar, $6.79
Flea & Tick Shampoo, $7.39
Flea & Tick Mousse, $11.99
Ear Mite Drops, $5.39

Information:
Francodex Laboratories
3200 Meacham Blvd.
Ft. Worth, TX 76137
(800) 628-7003

Litter-Box Diaper Pads ®

There are times—late at night, with the clock ticking—when I think I will go quietly mad reviewing litter-box products. It's mind-boggling considering the sheer amount of thought and energy that goes into dealing with this problem. There are people sitting around, right now, getting paid *serious money* to come up with new litter-box ideas. It's all rather fascinating. This amazing product, for example, is like a diaper that fits on your litter box. You tape it lightly in place, pour in the litter, and you're both in business. The clawproof top sheet allows moisture to pass through to the absorbent pad below. A waterproof underliner keeps the litter box clean and dry. To dispose, you just lift it off, placing a new pad and litter in the box. Standard and jumbo sizes.

All natural, contains no chemicals or preservatives.

Fresh Feliners, $2.79

Information:
Feliners International
P.O. Box 458
Manasquan, NJ 08736
(908) 528-2287

First Aid Kitty Kit ®

Nasty tick stuck on your kitty? Just one drop and the tick backs out instantly. Contains tea-tree oil, recognized for centuries for its healing properties, especially for skin irritations due to fleas, allergies, hot spots, and any type of wound or abrasion. Has anesthetic, antiseptic, and insect-repellent benefits. Good to have around just in case.

First Aid Kit in a Bottle,
$5.99 + $2.50 S&H

Danklied Laboratories, Ltd.
P.O. Box 436
Cazenovia, NY 13035
(800) 497-4757

Those Smiling Persian Eyes ®

Some cats, especially Persians, secrete almost constantly from their eyes. You could take a good, close look at your cat's face and swear he's been up gambling, with no sleep or a shower, for a week. Eye Scrub is a nonirritating hypoallergenic solution paired with 80 low-lint cleansing pads. Used together, they help remove environmental debris (dust and dirt) and crusted natural secretions from Kitty's eyelids. For external use only.

Eye Pet Scrub, $12.95

Information:
Eye Pet, Inc.
372 S. Milwaukee Ave.
Wheeling, IL 60090
(708) 215-3933

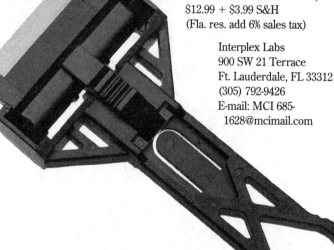

A New Angle on Grooming

Brush this comb through your kitty's fur to remove fleas instantly. There's a precise gap of four microns between comb teeth, which makes the comb incredibly effective at catching and removing fleas. The three different settings allow you to lock the head in whatever position you like for maximum grooming effectiveness.

Groom 'N Flea Pet Comb,
$12.99 + $3.99 S&H
(Fla. res. add 6% sales tax)

Interplex Labs
900 SW 21 Terrace
Ft. Lauderdale, FL 33312
(305) 792-9426
E-mail: MCI 685-
1628@mcimail.com

Professional Nail Trimmer

If you're going to trim the cat's claws yourself, get the right tool for the job. This is it. The Resco Cat Nail Trimmer is a solid, long-lasting professional grooming tool. The people you pay to trim your cat's nails use quality tools just like this one. It's not rocket science, and you can do it yourself. Just read up on how to do it and be careful not to trim too deep.

Resco Cat Nail Trimmer,
$11.40 + shipping
(Mich. res. add sales tax)

Information or to order:
Tecla Company, Inc.
2455 E. West Maple Rd.
Walled Lake, MI 48390
(810) 624-8200

Carpet Fleas

If your cat has fleas and you don't treat the carpet, you will never get rid of the little monsters. No sooner do you de-flea the cat than a new crop hatches under your feet. Boric acid helps get rid of them. The application is simple: Vacuum your carpet, pour Fleabusters lightly onto the carpet, and work it in until it's no longer visible. It dehydrates/desiccates the flea eggs, and it really does work. Safe on carpets and fabrics; odorless; it's not necessary to vacate your home while applying. Enough to treat five average-size rooms. Treatment lasts for one year.

Fleabusters RX for Fleas,
$39.95 (3 lbs.)

Information or to order:
Fleabusters RX for Fleas
6555 NW 9th Ave., Suite 412
Ft. Lauderdale, FL 33309
(800) 6NO-FLEA

Supercat: Raising the Perfect Feline Companion

Author Michael Fox is a well-respected veterinarian with great insights on what makes cats tick. Much of his book is devoted to an analysis and explanation of feline psychology; how cats relate to their constantly changing environment, and how they communicate with you. If you know what your cats are trying to tell you, you'll both get along better. Great question-and-answer section with many helpful tips. Major attention is paid to what affects a cat's life in your home, including changes such as bringing a baby into the house—a major concern of parents of newborns. IQ tests for cats, including advanced questions and exercises.

By Michael W. Fox, D.V.M., 1990, 212 pp., $19.95

Macmillan Publishing USA
201 W. 103d St.
Indianapolis, IN 46290
(800) 858-7674

When the Scratching Strikes

Help eliminate scratching and itching from fleas with Pet Wipes. They don't kill fleas, because they contain no toxins or poisons, but they will make your kitty feel much better, with natural oils of eucalyptus, cedar wood, citronella, and lavender. Hawaiian white ginger, lanolin, and vitamin E also help build a fuller, shiny coat.

K.O.S. Pet Wipes (25 individually wrapped), $12.95 + $2.50 S&H

Information or to order:
K.O.S. Industries, Inc.
7335 E. Acoma Dr., Suite 204
Scottsdale, AZ 85260
(602) 905-7117

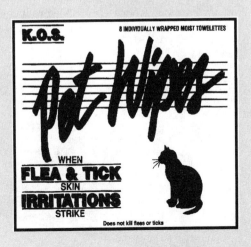

No-Contact Litter Cleaning ®

Everybody's worst job just got easier. The LitterMitt is a degradable plastic glove you place over your hand. Reach into the litter box, remove the solids, then reverse the glove, seal it, and toss it in the trash. For pregnant women, it's a natural protection against dangerous toxoplasmosis. It protects you from contact with the litter. Each package contains 10 gloves.

LitterMitt, $1.99 to $3.99

Information:
Intelligent Products, Inc.
P.O. Box 626
Burlington, KY 41005
(606) 689-7200

Jon, Flora, and the Odd-eyed Cat ®

This hardcover mystery for preteen readers combines mysticism, preadolescent love, a mysterious white cat that smells like flowers, and an unusual friendship between a boy recovering from a long illness and an ethereal girl named Flora. Helpful messages about young love and the passage of time, the strong, emotions young people share with others who come into their lives, and the way we feel when those we love move away. We all remember our first love.

Houghton Mifflin
Clarion Books
215 Park Ave. S.
New York, NY 10003
(212) 420-5889

By Stella Pevsner, 1994, 188 pp., $13.95

Feline Restraint or Wrestling Lessons?

Judging by the sheer number of cat-restraint products, there must be some serious wrestling going on in cat-owning American homes. Seems like you can use a product like The Kitty Bag, or sign up for cat judo lessons. The bag seems easier. This is a smart, well-made product that will loosely hold your cat while you apply flea products, transport or groom Kitty, or during medical procedures. It has zippers in the front and back of the bag for clipping those claws, and an adjustable collar so Kitty can stick out his head and see what's going on. Solidly made of a thick, nonrip, scratchproof fabric in an attractive teal color, with a Velcro collar closure.

The Kitty Bag, $24.95 + $5 S&H (Maine res. add sales tax)

B. Nelson Enterprises, Inc.
P.O. Box 1084
Damariscotta, ME 04543
(800) CAT-B-SAFE

Flea Powder

Nontoxic Odor Eliminator ®

Get rid of kitty odors fast with this spray-on odor eliminator. Use on bedding and cages, spray it on litter in the box; eliminates skunk spray smell, cleans up all odors from messy kitties.

Odorless Pet Odor Eliminator, $13.99 (8 oz. bottle) + $4.50 S&H

Information:
K.O.S. Industries, Inc.
7335 E. Acoma Dr., Suite 204
Scottsdale, AZ 85260
(602) 905-7117

Fruity Shampoo ®

Plum White is a natural, bright-white cleansing shampoo that includes plum, aloe, avocado, banana, jojoba, coconut, and cranberry. It's great for cleansing and getting out stains, and it's organic and nontoxic. Safe for cats and kittens, and you, too! Very concentrated;

dilute 15 parts water to 1 part shampoo. Smells great.

Plum White Shampoo, $35 (1 gal.); $11 (16 oz.); $8 (8 oz.)

Information:
Kelco Industries
16842 Saticoy St.
Van Nuys, CA 91406
(800) 451-1355

The Natural Cat

Slowly but surely the cat industry is switching over to natural products. This company, which bills itself as "The Health-Food Store For Pets," is conscious of natural, holistic approaches to food and diet and fleas and all the best natural products. It's not the only one, but Chip Sammons, the "owner and janitor," puts out a smart catalog of good natural stuff—from cat foods to supplements, toys, and flea control—and

he chooses products very carefully. This natural product called Fleago uses orthoboric acid, which destroys flea larvae and disrupts the flea life cycle in your carpets. Sprinkle it on, sweep it in, and leave it. The 5-lb. container shown covers about 2,000 square feet.

Fleago, $39.99 + $5.99 S&H

Holistic Pet Center
P.O. Box 1166
Clackamas, OR 97015
(800) 788-PETS

Persian Cats and Other Longhairs ®

Persians are the most popular breed in America. They come in all shapes, sizes, and colors. There's a reason for their popularity: They look beautiful, and they like people. They're one of the most personable, lovely cats you could ever have the pleasure of knowing. This hardcover provides much practical advice, including information for cat fanciers who enjoy hard-core breeding details. With 147 photos, it's sure to be of use to anyone with a serious interest in Persians.

By Jeanne Ramsdale, 1976, 271 pp., $23.95

TFH Publications, Inc.
One TFH Plaza
Third and Union Aves.
Neptune City, NJ 07753
(908) 988-8400

A Glove for All Seasons

You could buy two of these and wear them during winter, but it would look dumb. Instead, get one and rub it gently on any soft surface covered with cat hair. Away comes loose hair and dander, even light soil. Works by producing static electricity and friction. Super for furniture and clothing. Just peel the fur off the glove, toss, and keep the glove handy for the next cleanup. Not for use on your kitty.

FurFetcher, $11.99 + $4.95 S&H (Calif. res. add sales tax)

Allie Cats
P.O. Box 2474
Martinez, CA 94553
(800) 444-5917

Super-Quality Cat Comb ®

If you need a cat comb, buy the best. It'll last for years, and save on grooming costs in the long run. If you have a longhaired cat, you absolutely need one of these. There's really no other way—except clipping —to get out those lumpy, matted clumps. And once you get them out, this superior cat comb will help keep them away. Red handle, medium size, solid made-in-the-U.S. quality.

Resco Professional Cat Comb, $10.50 + shipping (Mich. res. add sales tax)

Information or to order:
Tecla Company, Inc.
2455 E. West Maple Rd.
Walled Lake, MI 48390
(810) 624-8200

Chapter Six

The Gourmet Cat's Food and Drink

Real Cats Drink Milk

CatSip is real Grade A 1% low-fat ultrapasteurized milk, conveniently packaged in 12 fl. oz. containers for ease of use. Some cats can't digest ordinary milk because it contains lactose (milk sugar), which can cause loose bowels. CatSip is lactose-free and contains taurine, a nutrient needed for healthy kitty hearts and eyes. Once opened, CatSip will last 7 to 10 days in your refrigerator. Call for availability in your area and direct orders.

CatSip 12 oz., $1.19

Information:
AkPharma, Inc.
6840 Old Egg Harbor Rd.
Pleasantville, NJ 08232
(800) CATSIP-9

Maine Pet Diner

One of the best custom pet bowls you'll ever see. Handcrafted of solid pine; your choice of golden oak, natural, ebony, mahogany, cherry, or walnut stain. Engraved with your pet's name. Stainless-steel inner bowl removes for easy cleaning and refilling. Rubber floor pads protect floor finishes and keep the dish from sliding around the floor like a hockey puck.

Bowl sizes vary from ½ pt. (nibblers) to 2 qt. (gobblers). Solid no-nonsense Yankee quality.

Maine Pet Diner, $42–$62
(Maine res. add 6% sales tax)

Maine Pet Products
907 College Rd.
Lewiston, ME 04240
(800) 872-4502

Real Protection Against Ants

You've been there: The cat comes in, gives you a weird look, and you just know something is wrong. I always head to the food dish first, and the cat and I stare at it together. Either it's empty (not good), he's out of water (also not good), or there are ants in the dish, and he's not eating ants today or any day, thank you. He looks me straight in the eye and meows, "Fix it." This antless pet dish will protect your pet's food and health, and its futuristic design looks great for the indoor pet. Holds up to four regular-size cans of food. Recommended by vets, non-toxic, microwave and dishwasher safe.

Available in Glow in the Dark, Mauve, and Black.

Antless Pet Dish, $20 + $4.95 S&H (Tex. res. add 7.25% sales tax)

Accessory Pet
5836 Pathfinder Trail
Plano, TX 75093
(800) 558-7387

Calling All Cats: Food Alert! Food Alert!

This is great. Not only does it dispense food to your cat when you're not around, but it records and plays back your message. So . . . meal-time rolls around. The tape comes on and, not once, but twice, the cats hear your voice saying, "Okay, kitties, dinner is served" (or whatever you say when that big event rolls around). You can program the number of feeding times (up to three per day) and the amount of food in each meal, and a motor will lower the food dish to your cat and play your message. Capacity of about 4 lbs. of dry food. A backup battery is included. Farout design, looks like a *Star Wars* droid. The future is here!

Petjoy Automated Feeder, $149 + $15 S&H (Calif. res. add 7% sales tax)

REON
7486 La Jolla Blvd., Suite 555
La Jolla, CA 92037
(800) 776-REON (7366)

Cats: A Feline Potpourri ®

The history of writing is replete with references to cats in virtually every culture worldwide. Some of the best kitty quotes are found in this very small book that will make a thoughtful gift—for absolutely no reason—to brighten the day of someone you love.

By Armand Eisen, 1992, 70 pp., $4.95 + $2 S&H

Information:
Andrews & McMeel
4520 Main St.
Kansas City, MO 64112
(816) 932-6700
(800) 826-4216

· A Feline Potpourri ·

Cats with Style

You have a right to cool cat stuff. Not boring, ho-hum stuff, but beautiful things you'll enjoy looking at every day. Check out these great bowls and treat jar by Art Itself, a lively, progressive company from the Mile High City. Large stoneware cat dishes hold 1½ cups, and can be custom-painted. Dishwasher- and microwave-safe. Get two—one for food, complementary "yang" for water. Great-looking Treat Jar is approx. 9″ tall. You can match it to your kitty's bowl. Super products, bold colors in clean, modern designs. Bright, lively stuff that's fun to use.

Large Cat Dishes, $28 each
Treat Jar, $36

Art Itself
P.O. Box 12397
Denver, CO 80212
(303) 477-5423
E-mail: pcloyd@CSN.ORG

Working for Dinner

This is something else. You fill up the container —which holds up to seven days of dry food. Your cat scratches the feeder instead of the sofa. Food tumbles down (adjustable settings for hungry kittens and lazy, fat cats). The cat eats. The sofa is spared. Wall mount or free-standing design, replaceable scratch carpet, comes with a one-year warranty. Now there's Pavlov's Cat!

Cat Scratch Feeder, $39.95 + $8 S&H
(Calif. res. add 7% sales tax)

Del West Enterprises
9733 Caminito Doha
San Diego, CA 92131
(619) 689-9999
http://www.mkt
mkt.com/pavlovs
cat.html

International Treats for Your Cat

Wondering what to give the cat who has everything? How about a membership in the Cat-Treat-of-the-Month club? The Catnip Trading Company's agents roam the world seeking rare cat delicacies, and for $67 and change, they'll send your cat a different treat each month for a year. Rocky Mountain (high) catnip. Gourmet salmon snacks imported from the Netherlands. German Katzen-Muschein (little chewy snacks filled with fish and meat). Shrink-wrapped bags of small whole dried fish from England that cats *adore*. One incredible treat after another. Doesn't your cat *deserve* this?

"Your Cat-Treat-of-the-Month will be things you've never seen in a pet store, let alone a supermarket. All from major, respected food suppliers in Europe, Africa, Asia, and Down Under. And when we find something special on a small farm in Maine, or a small kitchen in Nebraska, you might get that, too!"
—Gene Kalb, owner

Cat-Treat-of-the-Month, one year for $67.20 ($43.20 + $24 S&H)

Catnip Trading Company
P.O. Box 451
Lexington, MA 02173
(800) 822-8647

The Cat-Lovers' Cookbook ℞

Your cat works hard for his keep. He's a constant source of love and companionship whom you can always count on to keep your favorite chair warm. And what does he get in return? Canned food, dry food, seven days a week. If you believe it's time to stop treating your cat like an animal and start treating him like a member of the family, here's the purr-fect way to show your appreciation. Dietary tips for the overweight cat, nursing cat, or cat with allergies; scrumptious recipes just for cats, like Kitty Jambalaya, Boogaloo Shrimp, Chicken Chow Mein, Gizzard Goulash, Kidney Stew, Kitty Pizza. Lots and lots of great recipes, intelligent food advice for every conceivable need. Reading these kitty recipes actually made me hungry!

By Tony Lawson, 1994, 131 pp., $6.99

Wings Books
Outlet Books
40 Engelhard Ave.
Avenel, NJ 07001
(800) 733-3000

Yahoo—Seaweed at Last!

Eureka! It exists! After years of fruitless searching, you have finally found seaweed for your cats. Actually, many people do swear by kelp as a marvelous natural dietary supplement; in one form or another, people eat it all over the world. Harvested in the Atlantic Ocean off the Canadian coast, these kelp products contain plenty of vitamins and minerals for your cat.

Nature's Own Feline Formula, $10 (6 oz.); $12 (1 lb.); $18 (3 lbs.) (Includes shipping; COD $4.75) (Calif. res. add 7.7% sales tax)

Nature's Own Kelp Products
3822 Kreuer Rd.
Phelan, CA 92371
(800) 821-8855

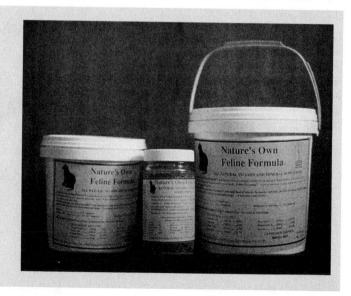

The Tiger in his Pocket ®

Delightful, imaginative book for young readers about a small boy and the tiger he keeps in his pocket. The boy doesn't like school much; bullies push him around, and sometimes it seems as if the only friend he has is the tiger, who totally transforms his life. Ultimately we see everyone happy, and—surprise of surprises—the boy and his tiger have joined the circus.

By Sandra Clayton, published by Allen & Unwin, Australia, 1994, 64 pp.

Independent Publishers Group
814 N. Franklin St.
Chicago, IL 60610
(312) 337-0747

Copycats

A small jewel of a book that captures the musings of five felines who escape from their humdrum cat lives by imagining themselves as other animals. Exquisite illustrations, wonderfully imaginative for cat lovers of all ages. Great for children!

By Nicola Bayley, 1984, 96 pp. $14.95

Candlewick Press
2067 Massachusetts Ave.
Cambridge, MA 02140
(617) 661-3330

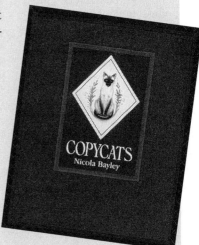

Fresh Water Fountain ®

A thirsty cat is an unhappy cat. Here's the simplest solution you'll find: Take a one- or two-liter bottle, wash it out, fill it up with fresh water (or, for special occasions, a bottle of your cat's favorite mineral water), and screw it into the base of this very economical waterer. You can't beat the price.

Cat Fountain, $2.99

Molor Products Company
1350-A Shore Rd.
Naperville, IL 60563
(708) 416-6840

On-the-Run Cat Bowl ®

In a hurry? No time to mess with washing the food dish? Now you don't have to. Toss out the liner that comes with this cat bowl, and there's a new liner below it. Toss that one tomorrow, and so on. A truly disposable dish, comes already packed with 20 plastic food-safe liners. Available in blue, mauve, and ivory, with disposable white liners. Replacement liners available in packs of 40. Feed and toss. It's that simple.

Kwik Kleen Bowl (includes 20 liners), $3.99

Replacement Liners (40 liners), $2.99

Information:
Sanitary Pet Products
170 Skipjack Rd.
Prince Frederick, MD 20678
(301) 855-1266

The Elegant Dinner

The beautiful grain of this natural cedar-wood feeder provides a lovely place setting for a stainless-steel food dish and water bowl. Comes in 1 pt. or 1 qt. sizes. Easily removable for cleaning. Ideal for placing anywhere indoors, and may be secured to the wall with heavy-duty hardware (free on request). Includes a clear Plexiglas splash guard. Dimensions: 4½″ h. × 20½″ w. × 14″ dia.

Cedar Wooden Feeder
With 1 pt. bowls (2), $100
With 1 qt. bowls (2), $120
Price includes free home delivery within the U.S., except Alaska and Hawaii. (Tex. res. add 6.75% sales tax)

House of Cats International
25011 Bell Mountain Dr.
San Antonio, TX 78255
(800) 889-7402

Parlor Cats: A Victorian Celebration ®

In Victorian England, the queen openly displayed her love of cats, and the entire population went cat-crazy. Nothing even remotely like it has happened since. In this hardcover you'll find an overview of the Victorian obsession with cats in full bloom, plus hundreds of pieces of cat artwork, all in color, with period writing celebrating cats in every conceivable manner. An exceptional introduction to the world of Victorian cats.

By Cynthia Hart, John Grossman, and Josephine Banks, 1991, 88 pp., $15.95

Workman Publishing
708 Broadway
New York, NY 10003
(800) 722-7202

A Fresh Mountain Stream!

Well, not quite, but this is a very cool kitty drinking fountain. Kitty Kreek is a miniature mountain that hides a pan of water and a pump. Water continuously runs down the mountain to the pool on the bottom. In the top pool there is a miniature "boulder" covering the water outlet. By turning this boulder, the flow of water can be increased or decreased. The electric pump is a high-performance submersible pump with a quiet miniaturized motor. It requires minimum maintenance, is rated for continuous operation, and uses very little power. Included with your Kitty Kreek is a small bag of smooth stones that you can use in different combinations to vary the

sound and velocity of the running water. Provides a soothing sound in your house and fresh water for your cat. Easy to clean, fascinating to cats (and people!).

Kitty Kreek, $59.95 + $6 S&H (Tenn. res. add sales tax)

Tranquility Enterprises
160 Sinking Creek Rd.
Petersburg, TN 37144
(800) 839-9059

Thomasina

I have a major weakness for Paul Gallico's writing. The late author produced 41 novels and numerous short stories, most of which are still in print. One of my favorites, *Thomasina*, is a lovely mystery about a cat and a murder. As in most of his books, you, the reader, participate in the conversations between his cat characters. Perhaps that is what makes his books so enjoyable. You get into feline minds and personalities, and it seems to make perfect sense that cats talk and think and feel just like us. One of the best cat writers of all time.

By Paul Gallico, 1957,
288 pp., $5.95 paperback

International Polygonics, Ltd.
Box 1563, Madison Sq. Station
New York, NY 10159
(212) 683-2914

Now You Can Kiss Me!

All sorts of goodies are now available to add to your cat's water. This all-natural aloe vera drink has been tested and approved by the FDA. It's tough to get cats to chew a vitamin, so it makes sense to add a supplement that provides vitamins, minerals, and amino acids to their water. Nice for the breath, too!

Aloe Vera Pet Drink, $13 + $4.95 S&H
Three-month supply, $35 + $5.95 S&H
(Tex. res. add 7.25% sales tax)

Accessory Pet
5836 Pathfinder Trail
Plano, TX 75093
(800) 558-7387

Easy Dinner Cleanup!

A handy, colorful place mat under Kitty's bowl assures easy cleanup after spills. Sure, the cat can have one too, but I want four on my table! Bright colors, four designs (tiger print, paw print, spotted/Dalmatian print, leopard print). Op art. Visual fun at mealtime.

Pet Buddies, $2.95 each + $3.95 S&H (Wash. res. add 8.2% sales tax)

Keller Design, Inc.
P.O. Box 3854
Seattle, WA 98124
(800) 683-1227

Three Little Kittens ®

A charming contemporary version of the classic Mother Goose rhyme about three rather careless little kittens who always manage to correct their mistakes. Fun book offers lessons for preschool children. Such a happy ending!

By Paul Galdone, 1986, 32 pp., $4.95

Houghton Mifflin
Clarion Books
215 Park Avenue S.
New York, NY 10003
(212) 420-5889

Get Out the White Gloves 'Cause We're Dining at the Ritz ®

How's your tap water these days? Do you drink it? Due to chemicals, impurities, and dissolved minerals, some tap water not only smells bad, it tastes bad, too. And if it's bad for you, it's worse for your cat. Her sense of smell is much, much more sensitive than your schnozz. Here's one rather elegant solution: vitamin-enriched Pawier, fresh out of the bottle, purified, perhaps chilled in your refrigerator. At a minimum, you should serve this on the cat's birthday and major holidays. Plus they sell a vitamin concentrate you can add to your own purified water. Ask Pawier about buying in bulk if not available at your pet store.

Pawier Water for Distinguished Pets, $2.79 (2 l. bottle); $1.79 (1 l. bottle)

Vitamin Concentrate, $11.69 (½ oz.) + $3.95 S&H (Calif. res. add 7.75% sales tax)

Pawier
P.O. Box 3397
Saratoga, CA 95070
(800) 367-7294

Atlanta Cats

Some of the hippest, brightest cat bowls and goody jars you'll find anywhere. The yellow-and-lime series and the purple cat bowls shown here vary in price from $19 up to $52 for the big yellow Treat Jar. Many, many fun designs.

Great Cat Bowls and Treat Jars

Morningside Design
1737 Meadowdale Ave.
Atlanta, GA 30306
(404) 872-1110

TRUE CAT FACT

Natural v. Un-Natural Cat Foods

Read your cat-food label lately? You've probably seen the words *meat by-products.* What's a meat by-product? Brace yourself. Technically, it's "tissue from dead, diseased, or disabled animals, including hair, hide, beaks, feathers, and hooves." Is that something you'd voluntarily feed your cat? I didn't think so. Fortunately, you have a choice.

Choosing natural foods for your cats means you're giving them no by-products, artificial preservatives, colors, or flavors; no sugar and no nitrates in their food. Natural cat food includes vitamins C and E as food preservatives (instead of the chemicals BHA, BHT, and benzoic acid). Commercially prepared cat foods often include sodium nitrite (a preservative found in treated meat like hot dogs and bacon) to give the product a meaty reddish tint. This is mostly for your sake, since cats appear to have limited color perception.

Feline Salad Garden

Wild oat greens are a natural source of chlorophyll for your cat and also an excellent hair-ball remedy. Picture an edible garden for your cat to nibble at leisure. Great for cats who stay inside, or to spice up those barren winter months. Kit includes wooden cat planter, liner, potting soil, and seeds. Replacement oat seeds available. Measures 10½" l. × 5" w. × 4½" h. Tasty, and healthy, too!

Wild Oat Garden Kit, $21.95 + $2.95 S&H (Ark. residents add 7.5% sales tax)

Cat Claws
1004 Broadway
Morrilton, AR 72110
(800) 783-0977

The Well-Versed Cat: Poems of Celebration ®

A teeny-tiny book with poems about cats by Yeats, Tolkien, Oscar Wilde, Marianne Moore, and 30 other poets. Slip it in your purse or pocket for reading on the bus or the beach.

Compiled by Running Press, 1993, 124 pp., $4.95 (+ $2.50 postage and handling)

Running Press
125 S. 22nd St.
Philadelphia, PA 19103
(800) 345-5359

Never-Ending Stream

Some cats love to drink out of faucets and other sources of freely running water. It's an instinct that must date back to their predomesticated days. The Drinkwell Pet Fountain provides a waterfall of drinking water that circulates into a custom-designed water dish through a purifying filter. Created by a veterinarian, the waterfall satisfies that feline urge for water on the move. Also aerates the water to keep it fresh. Dishwasher-safe. No need to connect to a water source: Add to the water level in the bowl as needed. Nice sound of trickling water.

Drinkwell Pet Fountain, $39.95 + $4 S&H (Nev. res. add 7% sales tax)

Veterinary Ventures
Mary Burns, D.V.M.
844 Bell St.
Reno, NV 89503
(800) 805-7532

Ring That Dinner Bell!

Remember those old movies where Mom would go out on the porch and ring a big bell with a wood handle until everyone came running in for dinner? Lifting the lid of this dishwasher-safe stoneware bowl rings a bell that Kitty will want to hear. Cats learn to associate the sound of the bell with food, and as we all know, there aren't too many things more important than food. The lid also keeps food fresh between meals.

Here Kitty Kitty, $19.99 + $5.29 S&H (N.Y. res. add sales tax)

Pedigrees
1989 Transit Way
Brockport, NY 14420
(800) 548-4786

While You're Away . . .

It's nice to know that Kitty won't go hungry if you're late. Set the timer on this automatic feeder to open the lid on the food dish at different times, so the cat gets adequately fed if you're not around, but doesn't go on a binge. Put a little food in each bowl—just enough for a nice dinner—and you're set. Runs on one AA battery (included). Serves two separate meals: Holds 1 lb. canned food or 2 c. dry. Includes ice pack for keeping foods fresh.

Automatic Pet Feeder,
$59.99 + $7.99 S&H
(N.Y. res. add sales tax)

Pedigrees
1989 Transit Way
Brockport, NY 14420
(800) 548-4786

Personalized Kitty Place Mats

One of my cats —Rollo, a big Himalayan with a sweet disposition— loves to push his dishes around the kitchen floor with his paws. He also likes three ice cubes in his water, but that's another story. Anyway, he's a pretty dignified eater, but Bella, the other one . . . she practically stands in the bowl. Here's a fun, nonskid place mat, which, personalized with your cat's name, helps keep things a bit neater. Place-mat image is of a shadow of a cat over a colorful meal of shrimp and canned sardines. Looks almost French to me! Nonskid backing, measures 17″ × 14″.

Personalized Cat Place Mat, $22 + $4.95 S&H
(Tex. res. add 7.25% sales tax)

Accessory Pet
5836 Pathfinder Trail
Plano, TX 75093
(800) 558-7387

Dinner Diner When You're Gone ®

Cats don't need a watch to know when it's mealtime. If you have to leave them alone for a day—or, two, or three, or four, or five—odds are they'll be sitting by their food dish—staring. The lightweight and durable 24-hour Automatic Pet Feeder is ideal for getaways of overnight or longer. Battery-operated with a quartz timing mechanism, it allows you to serve your pet in your absence at his *normal mealtime.* The 48-hour feeder allows you to feed him twice at normal mealtimes during a two-day period. An ice pack stored below the food dishes helps keep the food fresh. The 5-Day Automatic Pet Feeder allows you to serve your pet five meals during five days. Easy to disassemble for cleaning and maintenance. My suggestion: Try it at home first, while you're there, so you and the cat get used to it.

24-Hour Automatic Pet Feeder, $46.60; 48-hour, $53.55; 5-day, $112.45

Information:
Classic Products
1451 Vanguard Dr.
Oxnard, CA 93033
(805) 487-6227

Just One More Breakfast . . . Pretty Please?

Bella likes to eat. She's not compulsive or overweight—yet. In the morning, she's always first to the bowl. Rollo, on the other hand, strolls up to his bowl, says a nice "meow," and takes his time. If you have a chubby cat—and especially if you have more than one furry pet—this is a great product for you. How does it work? Simple. Your chubby or special-diet cat wears a collar that contains a magnet. The magnet will set off an alarm in the Smart Bowl. If you have two cats, feed the more slender cat in the Smart Bowl. When Chubby gets too close, thinking, "Oh, boy, a second breakfast," a high-pitched loud tone sounds. Scares the cat away from eating another cat's food. (Just watch out that the cat doesn't get near your computer disks. Magnets destroy data.) Eventually Chubby learns to stay away from the other cat's food bowl. No training required, safe and easy to use. Veterinarian-approved.

The Smart Bowl, $39.95 + $4.95 S&H
Extra collars, $5 each (Canadian residents add 7% GST. Ontario residents add 8% PST)

AQCON, Inc.
340 Kingswood Rd.
Toronto, Ontario
Canada M4E 3N9
(800) 891-BOWL (2695)

TRUE CAT FACT

Next, We Drink from Saucers

The following is a true story. A first-time guest was having breakfast with President Calvin Coolidge at the White House in the 1920s. Eager to make a good impression, the guest diligently followed his host's lead when he saw the president pour some milk into his coffee-cup saucer. But before the guest could drink it, Coolidge smiled, paused, and leaned down and offered the saucer to his cat.

The Quintessential Cat ®

In A-to-Z format, this attractive hardcover combines cat fact, folklore, and fiction with illustrations and full-color photos. It's almost everything you've ever wanted to know about cats, from Abyssinians to "Pets Are In," a pet-sitting network. Historical information is interspersed with intriguing feline mythology and superstitions, explanations of cat behaviors like purring, meowing, and caterwauling, and the origins behind such age-old expressions as "raining cats and dogs." Worth a look. Great trivia. Stump your cat friends.

By Roberta Altman, 1994, 288 pp. $27.50

Macmillan Publishing USA
201 W. 103d St.
Indianapolis, IN 46290
(800) 858-7674

Happy-Food-Face!

Food can be *the* big event of the day for your cat, and this ceramic bowl makes it even more special. Solidly made, it feels substantially weighty in your hand. Dishwasher-safe, painted gray and white with pink ears, nose, and tongue. Double bowl is great for a food/water combination, and this happy design is a pleasure to look at.

Ceramic Double Cat Bowl, $16.95 + $3.95 S&H
(Wash. res. add 8.2% sales tax)

Keller Design, Inc.
P.O. Box 3854
Seattle, WA 98124
(800) 683-1227

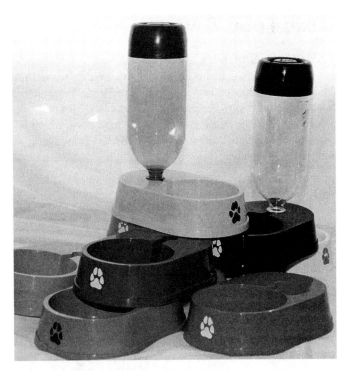

The Bowl That Never Runs Dry 📰

Here's an affordable pet bowl that makes sure your cats will always have fresh water. It also recycles emptied one- or two-liter soda bottles. Fill the old soda bottle with water, screw it into the bowl, and your cats will never go thirsty. You can also partially fill a soda bottle, pop it in the freezer, then attach it to the bowl for cold water all day. Available in dark and light blue, pink, red, hot pink, beige, black, white, teal, and raspberry. Gravity-fed, automatic shutoff.

Freedom Self-Watering Pet Bowl, $3.95 + $2.50 S&H

Information:
Freedom Distributing, Inc.
P.O. Box 11280
Denver, CO 80211
(303) 320-6449

Just Sprinkle It On

I've always thought dry food was incredibly tedious, day after day, so try this out if Kitty is balking at meals. Sprinkles is a natural flavor enhancer for your kitty's food. Directions are: sprinkle on food, and Kitty starts eating! Handy shaker lasts for months. You should also try to vary your cat's diet a bit so monotony doesn't set in.

Sprinkles, $3.95 + $1.95 S&H
(N.Y. res. add sales tax)

Nickerson International, Ltd.
12 Schubert St.
Staten Island, NY 10305
(800) NICKERS

Pets-R-Permitted—Travel & Pets Directory 📰

Thinking about taking the cat along on a trip? More and more hotels and motels allow pets, but you need to plan ahead. This guide has more than 10,000 listings of hotels and other locations that allow pets, plus some straightforward suggestions for traveling with a pet. Toll-free phone numbers of major hotel chains are included, as well as tips on moving with a pet, flying with your cat, and more. The number one rule when traveling with your cat? Call ahead, confirm that they will allow cats in the hotel, and record the name of the person with whom you spoke. That helps eliminate surprises when you show up, Kitty in carrier, exhausted from driving, and the check-in clerk gives you that dreaded blank stare. Excellent, practical guide to make traveling with a cat pleasant for both of you.

Compiled by Annenberg Communications, 1995, 308 pp., $11.95

Annenberg Communications Institute
P.O. Box 3930
Torrance, CA 90510
(800) 274-7297

You Remember Sprouts

No, he wasn't that weird neighborhood kid. He wasn't the dog, either. It was that stuff they used to put on sandwiches—alfalfa sprouts, bean sprouts, sunflower sprouts. *Sprouts*. The word itself sounds weird, but when you let sprouts grow, they turn into a tasty, healthy treat for your cat. Sproutsville's Cat Planter includes a basket grower and a greenhouse tent, plus ½ lb. of barley/wheatgrass, which cats love to nibble. Great growing suggestions and helpful hints from very nice folks. Much safer than eating the houseplants.

Plants for Pets Cat Planter, $7.95 + $3 S&H (Mass. res. add 5% sales tax)

Sproutsville! USA P.O. Box 539 Otis, MA 01253 (413) 269-7307

Basic Food & Water ®

Nothing fancy here, but it works. Just take any one-liter soda or mineral-water plastic bottle, fill it up with water, screw into the base of this feeder, and the cat is nourished. Water stays fresh in the bottle, trickling down as necessary. Elevated mount keeps water bottle away from the food bowl, which is removable for easy cleaning. Available in blue, brown, gray, and pink. Great price.

Mini Food 'N' Fountain, $3.99

Information:
Molor Products Company
1350-A Shore Rd.
Naperville, IL 60563
(708) 416-6840

Absorbent Cotton Cat Place Mats

The nice thing about cotton place mats is that you can toss them in the washer. Made of 100% batted cotton, they're a natural to keep Kitty's feeding area dry, clean, and attractive. Cotton has the added advantage over plastic place mats in soaking up spills. Large size (16½″ × 20″) and lively reversible cat print should work just fine for both the food and water bowls.

Cotton Cat Place Mats, $6.95 each

Palsie Wowsie, Inc.
P.O. Box 79
Narberth, PA 19072
(610) 853-2697

A Passion for Cats

The British are fanatics about cats, and you know what? You can't tell a British cat from an American cat, and this book proves it. Plenty of solid cat-raising advice from the Cats Protection League: living with a cat, basic care and feeding, amazing cat stories as only the British can tell them, breeding and showing, photographing cats, cats and the law, feline physiology, alternative medicine for cats, an A-to-Z listing of cat ailments and diseases, and just about everything you'll ever need to know from people who love, shelter, and cherish all cats. Distinctly British dry humor and marvelous short stories make this hardcover unique. It might take some looking, but you can find this volume. Ask your favorite bookstore for help.

By The Cats Protection League, 1987, 208 pp., $17.95, published by David & Charles, Devon, England

Distributed by:
Sterling Publishing Co.
387 Park Ave. S., 5th Floor
New York, NY 10016
(800) 367-9692

Personalized Kitty Bowl

The Kitty Bowl is made of colorful hand-painted ceramic, personalized with Kitty's name (up to 12 letters). Holds two cups of food, measures 5½″ l. × 3½″ h. Be sure to include your cat's name when ordering.

Kitty Bowl, $14.95 + $2 S&H (Minn. res. add 6.5% sales tax)

Chandler
Enterprises
Suite 2904
Galtier Plaza
168 E. Sixth St.
St. Paul, MN
55101
(612) 291-0498

Elegant Dining ®

This fine handcut Bavarian crystal dish will hold 8 oz. of your feline's favorite food or water. Elegant reflective crystal adds atmosphere and class to every meal. Crystal candleholders must be next!

Crystal Food & Water Bowl, $36

UltraMouse, Ltd.
123 Assembly Ct.
Cary, NC 27511
(800) 573-8869

The Atlas of Cats of the World ®

This massive coffee-table book is an atlas of world-wide cats with more than 350 color photographs, along with practical information covering the natural history of cats, domestication, the mind of the cat, feline anatomy, general care, nutrition, breeding theory, exhibition, cat registration, and exporting. A gorgeous, helpful hardcover that makes the "wish list" of every cat owner.

By Denise Kelsey-Wood, 1989, 384 pp., $69.95

Information:
TFH Publications, Inc.
One TFH Plaza
Third and Union Ave.
Neptune City, NJ
07753
    (908) 988-8400

Wheel of Kibble Fortune!

There's something mildly bizarre and interesting about a cat working for its dinner. This crazy, practical device doles out the kibble when Kitty turns the wheel. Looks like an "olde tyme" cherry red gumball machine, made from cast metal with a glass globe. Lest you think you'll never get the cat to use it, complete training instructions are included! And after your cat masters it, you receive a free Master of the Kitty Kitchen diploma—suitable for framing—in recognition of his achievement. Here's how to prove you have the smartest cat on the block.

Kitty Kitchen Treat Machine
(Regular Size), $29.95
+ $6 S&H

Lucky Yuppy Puppy Company
571 W. Golf Rd.
Arlington Heights, IL 60005
(800) 762-7836

Kitty Dinner Accessories ®

These sturdy Stainless-Steel Food Bowls have a nonslip rubber base. Each holds 16 oz., is dishwasher-safe, and is decorated with pewter charms like "Good Kitty," "Picky Eater," and the lovers' "XOX." Whimsical Treat Canister is decorated with "Good Kitty" and fish-shaped pewter charms. One-qt. capacity, dishwasher-safe. The fish-shaped canvas Place Mat is reversible, with maroon plaid on one side, silk-screened maroon hearts on the other.

Stainless-Steel Food Bowls,
$22 + $2.50 S&H
Treat Canister, $22
+ $2.50 S&H
Place Mat, $17 + $1.50 S&H
(Calif. res. add 8.3% sales tax)

Laid Back Enterprises
4020 Will Rogers Pkwy.
Oklahoma City, OK 73108
(800) 843-5242

Christmas-Tree Breakfast ®

Your cat will be immensely impressed (but don't expect a round of applause) when you remove this ornament from the tree on Christmas Day, open it, and serve a chewy beef treat. Hang it on a nice low spot near the floor so Kitty can keep an eye on it 'til the big day!

Kittypaws Christmas Ornaments, $3.99

Information:
Doca, USA
24461 Ridge Route Dr.
Suite 200
Laguna Hills, CA 92653
(800) 362-9812

Eat Your Way Down to the Kitty Picture!

These lovely round rim dishes are stoneware finished with a pleasing cream glaze. Pick your favorite silhouette—Shorthair, Persian, Stretching, Playing—in your choice of country teal, mauve, blue, or green. Rim color matches silhouette. Food- and water-safe, dishwasher-safe, too. Each is individually painted and signed by the artist.

Pretty Kitty Dish,
$10.95 (6 oz.);
$11.95 (10 oz.);
$12.95 (14 oz.)
(Fla. res. add 6% sales tax)

Marracini Studios
1010 E. Gaucho
Circle
Deltona, FL 32725
(407) 321-8897

Come the Terrible Tiger ®

In a child's imagination, anything is possible. From out of the sky comes Terrible Tiger, who can—and does—make the impossible a reality for a little boy sleeping in his bed. Soaring through space, atop the highest mountain, hearing the whales sing their songs—Terrible Tiger is a wonderful imaginary companion who will never let you down. This hardcover is beautifully illustrated by Kim Gamble, recipient of the 1992 Crichton Award for best new illustrator. For young children; not a scary moment in it.

By Rosalind Price, illustrated by Kim Gamble, published by Allen & Unwin, Australia, 1995, 32 pp., $14.95

Distributed by:
Independent Publishers Group
814 N. Franklin St.
Chicago, IL 60610
(800) 888-4741

Fun Feeding Time

For a change, consider switching from those two bowls down on the floor to this handcrafted wooden, food-and-water stand. It's cute! Keeps the bowls off the floor, looks great, nicely stained, all wood with a perky tail.

Handcrafted Wood Food & Water Stand, $29.95
(N.J. res. add 6% sales tax)

Kittytowne, USA
308 Duff Ave.
Wenonah, NJ 08090
(609) 468-3183

Handy Watering Fountain ®

Both Rollo and Bella use their own version of this goody. Fill it up, wash the bowl out every couple of days, and the cats always have a nice supply of H$_2$O. Holds 32 oz. Many colors, antitip and antispill base. They've never knocked it over. Indoor or outdoor use. As you know, cats can be very suspicious of anything new, even a food bowl. When somebody dropped and broke one of the cats' food bowls, I substituted a new plastic bowl a few weeks ago, which can be completely full of food, but Rollo won't touch it. He insists on eating out of the one remaining ceramic bowl. The bowl six inches from him is full. But as far as he's concerned, it's empty. Does the plastic smell bad? Noooooo. He walks around the house moaning and groaning until somebody fills up the remaining original bowl. Hope we don't break it.

Lixit Water Fount, $7.80

Information:
Lixit
P.O. Box 2580
Napa, CA 94558
(707) 252-1622

High-Tech Cat

There's something about the shine and the clean design of stainless steel that makes this bowl particularly attractive. A 21st-century bowl; embossed with cat prints; just right for food or water with a black rubber base to prevent sliding; easy to clean.

Cat Stainless-Steel Bowl, $12.95 + $3.95 S&H
(Wash. res. add 8.2% sales tax)

Keller Design, Inc.
P.O. Box 3854
Seattle, WA 98124
(800) 683-1227

The Valley Vet

Valley Vet Supply distributes a very careful selection of quality pet supplies, with an emphasis on cat dietary supplements, wormers, topical lotions, eye care, ear care, and general health products that many vets use.

Top-of-the-line grooming supplies, too.

Valley Vet Supply, free catalog

Valley Vet Supply
P.O. Box 504
Marysville, KS 66508
(800) 360-4838

Mice, Yarn, and Kitty Mat ®

This attractive white place mat comes decorated with little black mousies, colorful red and blue yarn twirls, and two dignified black cats with red collars. Place it under Kitty's dish; cleans up easily with a damp sponge or paper towel.

Laminated Cat-Design Place Mat, $3.75

Information:
Classic Products
1451 Vanguard Dr.
Oxnard, CA 93033
(805) 487-6227

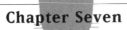
Glorious Gifts and Surprises

The Sherpa Pet Carrier

"Stop treating your pets like baggage." That's the message from Sherpa's Pet Trading Company, and it's a good one. This is the Mercedes of cat carriers. Zipper flaps. Plenty of ventilation. Soft comfort pad. Mesh in the back so Kitty can look out, and it unzips, so he can stick his head out! The Accessory Pouch allows you to bring along food, toys, and grooming supplies. Optional Biscuit Bag holds extra goodies.

Each bag comes with a free pet-travel brochure with smart pet traveling tips, and Sherpa Bags are approved on Air Canada, Alaska, America West, American Airlines, Continental, Delta, Northwest, TWA, United Airlines, and US Air. Need I say more?

Sherpa Bag, various sizes and prices

Sherpa's Pet Trading Company
357 E. 57th St.
New York, NY 10022
(800) 743-7723

A Passion for Kittens 🐾

Sweet, mischievous, cuddly, and full of energy, kittens are a wonderful reminder of the beauty of life and the preciousness of time. Illustrated with plenty of line drawings and duotone photos—some of movie stars with kittens from many years ago—this is a sweet little hardcover with lovely prose that celebrates the timeless attraction of rambunctious kittens. Cute!

A PASSION FOR KITTENS

J. C. SUARÉS

By J. C. Suares, 1995, 66 pp., $10.95

Information:
Andrews and McMeel
4520 Main St.
Kansas City, MO 64112
(800) 826-4216

Cleocatra

Monica Nelson of Jacksonville, Oregon, makes wonderful stained-glass cats. She doesn't have a fancy brochure, but she's glad to send you information about her products and a color photocopy. There's a stained-glass plant and candle holder, broaches, mirrors, night-lights, a jewelry box, and a ceiling cover light. She makes everything herself, and it's all well-crafted and looks good. Her night-light cheerfully beams in my bathroom, and I'd be proud to send anything she makes as a gift to my friends with cats.

Cleocatra, Night-Lights, $21.95 each + $4.25 S&H

Cleocatra
7980 Upper
Applegate Rd.
Jacksonville, OR 97530
(800) 480-0231

It's in the Stars

Curious about how astrology affects your cat? Dr. Gary Miller will do your cat's chart and personality analysis, along with a unique profile that depends on the location of Kitty's planets. The chart shown is for Calvin, Dr. Miller's cat (he'll tell you how to read it). Here's your chance to get in sync with your cat.

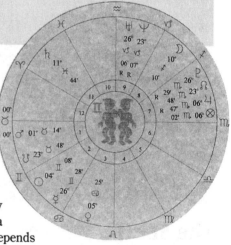

Catstars, $19.95 + $3 S&H

Dr. Gary Miller
3033 E. Thunderbird Rd., #2023
Phoenix, AZ 85032
(602) 992-2193

Surround Yourself with Warmth

There's nothing like a warm afghan on a cool night. A pretty tapestry design featuring cats and kittens makes this throw especially nice when you need a little warmth: 100% cotton, machine-washable, 46″×67″.

Tapestry Afghan, $45 + $5.95 S&H (Tex. res. add 7.25% sales tax)

Accessory Pet
5836 Pathfinder Trail
Plano, TX 75093
(800) 558-7387

Kitty on Your Pillow

Jeff Thorssell—"Head Sewer, Head Designer, Mail Boy, and Custodian" at Our Cats—makes your gift-giving easier with these high-quality stuffed and dressed cats. They're a hoot! The cats stand 15″ tall and have jointed arms, legs, and head. The fur is a top-quality synthetic imported from Germany. All four paw pads and inner ears are made of UltraSuede. Bare cats meet with U.S. Consumer Product Safety Division standards for all ages, but are labeled "not for children under three years" when dressed with accessories. Sample outfits include the Aerobics Cat, Country Dress, Ballerina, and Rain Slicker. Many other styles available, including custom-made kitties. Gift card sent with your order. One belongs on *your* pillow!

Stuffed Kitties, $51–$70 + $7 UPS S&H (Md. res. add 5% sales tax)

Our Cats
8167 Pleasant Plains Rd.
Baltimore, MD 21286
(800) 808-MEOW (6369)

The Beauty of Time

This amusing cat tea-party desk clock looks expensive, but it isn't. Soft pastel watercolors feel like a picnic—in a meadow with wildflowers, under a tree—on a warm summer day. Runs on one AA battery; 6″ h. × 5″ w.

Cat Tea-Party Desk Clock, $18 + $4.95 S&H (Tex. res. add 7.25% sales tax)

Accessory Pet
5836 Pathfinder Trail
Plano, TX 75093
(800) 558-7387

Red Cat, White Cat ®

Cats live it up in this wonderfully illustrated hardcover, meant to be read to young children. Just two words on each page ("Short Cat; Tall Cat; Farm Cat; Town Cat"). Great for kids with cats!

By Peter Mandel, 1994, 26 pp., $14.95

Henry Holt & Company
115 W. 18th St.
New York, NY 10011
(800) 488-5233

Dress Up in Cats, It's BBQ Time!

Why not get Dad some fun barbecue or chef's accessories with a humorous cat design? All decked out, he'll keep food off his clothes while cooking. Those oven mitts provide great protection against heat. Fun fashion for the joyful cook. Set includes apron, two mitts, chef's hat, and pot holder.

Matching Chef Set, $39 + $5.95 S&H (Tex. res. add 7.25% sales tax)

Accessory Pet
5836 Pathfinder Trail
Plano, TX 75093
(800) 558-7387

Sam, Bangs & Moonshine ®

How does a young child separate imagination from reality? Some children live so much in their heads that they have trouble distinguishing between the two, which can be charming when it's creative, and unsettling when it takes the form of lying. This is a book about imagination and lying, and how a young girl named Sam—with the help of her wise cat, Bangs—begins to see the difference between the two. Impressionistic pen-and-ink and charcoal illustrations contribute to the book's message and tone. A helpful book for parents whose children seem stuck in this stage. Don't worry—they'll move on.

By Evaline Ness, 1966, 40 pp., $5.95

Henry Holt & Company
115 W. 18th St.
New York, NY 10011
(800) 488-5233

Sticky Face!

You know your pet is beautiful. Show her off with these peel-off stickers to share, swap, or place on correspondence. Send in a kitty picture (5″ × 7″ or smaller) along with a photocopy of the picture cropped the way you want the sticker to look. Presto! Three weeks later, 56 1″ × 1³⁄₁₆″ full-color stickers arrive at your door.

Photo-Pets Stickers, $16
(Ohio res. add 6.25% sales tax)

Photo-Pets
2747 Crawfis Blvd.
Suite 105167
Fairlawn, OH 44333
(330) 864-5793

A New Ferrari 348 tb/ts Spider "Gato" Luxe SX Convertible, for You and Kitty!

Why not have some decent wheels for you and the cat? Picture you and Kitty purring down the road to cat shows. Dropping by the fish market. Humoring yourselves with a visit to see the mice and birds at the pet store. This will get you there in a hurry, racing from 0 to 60 mph in 5.3 seconds, covering your first quarter-mile in 13.75 seconds on your way to a top speed of 171 miler per hour! A masterpiece of Italian design!

Serious transportation for the discriminating cat. (Just kidding, of course!)

Ferrari 348 tb/ts Spider "Gato" Luxe SX Convertible, $122,000

Information:
Ferrari of San Francisco
595 Redwood Highway
Mill Valley, CA 94941
(415) 380-9700

Special Appointments for the Proud Owner and Cat

- *Five-point Cat Restraint System:* adjustable black-leather passenger-side harness straps attach to each leg and the tail. A smart investment for cat owners with convertibles.
- *Festiva Italia:* the world's largest "on-the-go" automotive litter box. Measures an impressive 4½′ l., 3′ w., and 1½′ deep (capacity 130 lbs. cat litter) for those long road trips.
- *Glove Box* holds 12 qts. of engine oil (not supplied) and 40 road flares (who knows if you'll need them) *or* 80 10-oz. cans of cat food (not supplied) and can opener *or* one 40 lb. bag of kitty kibble (not supplied) plus one large jar of stuffed Italian green olives (supplied).
- Cat in a bad mood? Relax with Ferrari's scratch-resistant, hand-tooled leather seats. Matching *Pride of Italy Feline Crash Suit and Helmet.*

TRUE CAT FACT

The Hairless Cat

The beauty of the hairless Sphynx cat is all in the eye of the beholder. Warm to the touch (they've been called the hot-water-bottle cat), light gray or brown in color, the Sphynx provokes an immediate reaction in people, whether they're attracted or repelled. Covered with a very fine layer of downlike fur, they have a regal bearing, an easy personality, and great loyalty to their owners.

Glorious Cats I, Boxed Notecards ®

Self-taught artist Susan Powers offers some of her finest cat art in this collection of blank notecards. Includes *A Tabby Cat, Two Colorpoints, An Orange Tabby,* and *Amanda.* Perennial favorites of cat-loving, card-writing friends, Susan Powers's art can be found in the permanent collections of many museums. Five each of four subjects, with 20 envelopes.

Glorious Cats I, Boxed Notecards, from the Jay Johnson Gallery, $12.95 Add $3.95 S&H (N.Y. res. add sales tax) when ordering direct.

Galison Books
36 W. 44th St.
New York, NY 10036
(212) 354-8840

The
COMPLETE CAT BOOK

Expert advice on every phase of cat ownership

Official standards for every breed

Written by an international all-breed judge

RICHARD H. GEBHARDT
Former President, CAT FANCIERS' ASSOCIATION, INC.

The Complete Cat Book ®

This is *the* resource book you'll need to own if you want to show your cat or have a serious interest in the technicalities of the "cat fancy." Written by a highly respected all-breed cat judge, it includes must-know information, like the Official Standards for every breed and photographs to show those standards. The scoring to evaluate cat breeds is complex, and you'll need to know the rules if you intend to show your kitty. Great hardcover guide, perfect for both the beginner and the seasoned pro.

By Richard H. Gebhardt, 1991, 224 pp., $19.95

Macmillan Publishing USA
Howell Book House
201 W. 103d St.
Indianapolis, IN 46290
(800) 858-7674

See-Through Spaceship Carrier! ®

Two-in-one kitty carrier buckles in with your seat belt when you and Kitty are in the car. Or take off the door and use it as a classy, comfy pet bed. Measures 29½" h., 19" dia., takes up the space of one person in your car. User-friendly handle on top. Cats love the see-through look, spacious interior, and thick cushion!

Three colors: travel-safer smoky gray, ultra-ride blue, ultra-ride rose. Vet-approved for cats under 30 lbs.

The Alyssa Transporter, $59.95.

Information:
Alyssa Industries
P.O. Box 4533
Elkhart, IN 46514
(219) 522-2518

Good Owners, Great Cats ®

A wonderful, warm book by one of America's best-known animal trainers. Many of us would love to do more with our cats, but we labor under some misconceptions. The most common is that cats can't or won't learn any-thing. Not true. This master trainer and feline lover has a million good ideas for eliciting feline cooperation, from the simple commands "sit" and "come" to correcting undesirable behavior through deterrents, alternative outlets, and positive reinforcement. Nicely illustrated paperback with 100 black-and-white photographs. A sensitive book that shows you how to get into your cat's head and heart.

By Brian Kilcommons and Sarah Wilson, 1995, 224 pp., $19.95

Warner Books
1271 Avenue of the Americas
New York, NY 10020
(212) 522-7200

Strolling with Kitty

Your cat might like to take a walk with you sometime. This kitty jacket curls under her body for comfort and support. Leash hooks above the shoulders, and three adjust-able straps buckle on the same side. No pulling on Kitty's neck. Easy to put on and take off. With the collar adjusted correctly, your cat is safely on a lead. Detailed usage instructions are included. Available in royal blue or red with ⅝″ black webbing. One size fits most adolescent and adult cats.

Walking Jacket for Cats, $15 + UPS shipping (Calif. res. add 7.75% sales tax)

Metropolitan Pet
354 Oaktree Dr.
Mountain View, CA 94040
(800) 966-1819

Al Dente Spaghetti Puzzle?

This 500-piece jigsaw puzzle offers your brain a rainy-weekend workout. It's a 20″ dia. picture of two cats slurping one long noodle off a plate. Is this puzzle so tough because it's al dente? You'll find out.

Italian Evening Jigsaw Puzzle, $9 + $4.95 S&H (Tex. res. add 7.25% sales tax)

Accessory Pet
5836 Pathfinder Trail
Plano, TX 75093
(800) 558-7387

Hang It Here

This charming hook rack is both decorative and functional. Use it in any room of your home. Sturdy construction—14-gauge steel finished with attractive black enamel—makes it perfect for hanging coats, sweaters, or umbrellas by the front door or the back porch. Use the fishy hooks in the bathroom or kitchen for hanging towels or an apron. Crafted in the USA for indoor or outdoor use, measures 20″ l. × 10″ h. × 2″ dia. A consistent favorite with cat lovers.

Cat with Four Fish Hooks, $30 + $4.50 S&H (Calif. res. add 7.75% sales tax)

Just-Cats
P.O. Box 60028
Santa Barbara, CA 93160
(800) 805-CATS

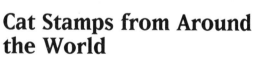

Cat Stamps from Around the World

If there is something you can hold in your hand to prove that cats are loved the world over, this is it. This wonderful color booklet and price list is absolutely what you need if you collect, or would like to collect, cat stamps from around the world. The beauty of these stamps is amazing. Ladd Publications sells a collection of 100 different stamps for just $7.50. Ask to be put on their mailing list.

Illustrated Cat Stamp Checklist (Domestic Cats, 1930–1993), $8.95 (includes shipping to U.S. & Canada). Overseas, add $1 for airmail postage.
100 Cat Stamps from Around the World, $7.50

Ladd Publications
P.O. Box 137
Jacksonville, FL 62651
(217) 245-2598

In the Company of Cats: A Tribute to the Feline ®

Put together unusually good cat photography, a few choice words here and there, and the result is an illustrated book you will enjoy again and again. Photographs of many different breeds, great for learning about all the different kinds of cats.

Edited by Linda Sunshine, 1991, 96 pp., $15 + $2 S&H

Andrews and McMeel
4520 Main St.
Kansas City, MO 64112
(816) 932-6700
(800) 826-4216

A Kitty for Your Mouse

Gail Columbo and her six cats seem to be having lots of fun putting out her catalog. Inside there's a picture of Gail with a big smile, reading *Vogue,* and pictures of all her six cats hanging around her office or standing on the keyboard, staring at cat pictures on her computer screen. This is a nice mouse pad with a friendly, smiling face to keep you company during the quiet hours of early morning.

"This cat won't eat your mouse, or shed fur on your keyboard! Adorable brown-and-black cat will enchant any cyber person or cyber cat. Soft cloth surface is machine-washable, and imprint is guaranteed for the life of the pad, which measures 10″ w. × 7″ h."—Gail Columbo

Cat Shape Computer Mouse Pad, $13.95 + $4.50 S&H (Calif. res. add 8.5% sales tax)

Cat Faeries
260 Hazelwood St.
San Francisco, CA 94127
(415) 585-6400

It's a Cat's Life ®

What better way to understand the lives of all cats than to explore the experiences and stories of six individual cats, from kittenhood to old age? Each cat's story is different, and among these heartwarming tales is practical advice on your cat's diet, the giving of medications and nutritional supplements, and an appendix of information on holistic healing. By the authors of the best-selling *The Natural Cat.*

By Anitra Frazier with Noram Eckroate, 1990, 164 pp., $7.50

The Berkley Publishing Group
200 Madison Ave.
New York, NY 10016
(800) 223-0510

Training Tips: Climbing the Drapes

Some cats love to scale the drapes, shredding as they go. You need to "outthink" the cat. Here's one simple method. Attach the drapes loosely to the rod on top, just enough to hold them. Next time the cat decides to go for a climb, the drapes will come tumbling down on his head. Make sure there's nothing sharp to poke him when they fall. Keep doing this until the cat gives up. He will. Vertical blinds are also a good choice. They can't be climbed, are easy to spread apart for the cat to look through, and they don't collect hair.

The Many Moods of Kitty

We all have favorite photos of our cats doing neat stuff. This 8″ × 16″ wooden frame has openings for you to include nine of your favorite pictures in a colorful printed mat. Here's your chance to show Kitty in all sorts of poses . . . catnapping, leaping through the air, playing around, doing the fun stuff that makes cats such good companions.

Cat Photo Frame, $20 + $4.95 S&H (Tex. res. add 7.25% sales tax)

Accessory Pet
5836 Pathfinder Trail
Plano, TX 75093
(800) 558-7387

Pet-Sitting v. Boarding Your Cat

The last time I boarded our two flealess cats, they came home hopping with the critters. This was no fleabag joint either; it was clean, reputable, expensive ($20 a day for both). They spent their stay in a cage. They were fed about a dollar's worth of dry food and water. When I picked them up from boarding, they were in shock. I brought them home and they walked around in a daze. Must have been like being locked up in jail; it took them a week or so to get back to their normal fun-loving selves. So why do it? The explosive growth of independent pet-sitters is a direct result of the trauma that pets undergo when they're carted off to boarding-jail. A pet-sitter will come to your house, feed and water the cats, pet them, say a few kind words, make sure they're healthy and happy—for half the cost ($10 or less per day). The cats are relaxed when you return home. They do not have fleas. They have not been exposed to cat diseases that potentially can be transmitted by being near the cage of a sick cat.

When you consider a pet-sitter, expect at least three local references and see how he or she gets along with your pets before you leave: Lots of animal lovers are bonded pet-sitters. Pet Sitters International will recommend one in your area. Or look under *Pets* in your yellow pages. It's so much better.

Free Pet-Sitting Brochure

Pet Sitters International
418 E. King St.
King, NC 27021
(800) 268-SITS

Looking for a Pet Sitter?

You *Can* Tell Me. Having a Good Day?

Many cat owners know, in their hearts, that they communicate on an intuitive level with their companions, but there's something else brewing on the horizon. It's a new humanity, a sensibility growing out of the fact that all animals have intelligence and *feelings*. Beatrice Lydecker is the animal psychologist to the stars, from Elizabeth Taylor to Jay Leno. Perhaps you've seen her on TV talk shows. She's also been in *People* magazine and the *Wall Street Journal.* She really knows her stuff. In this two-part tape, she sits you down with a group of pet lovers and explains the world of animal communication and feelings. Remarkable, compassionate presentation by a gifted speaker, with nary a boring minute.

Bea Lydecker's Animal Communication Seminar and Workshop, 2 Vols., 2½ hours, VHS, $39.95 + $6.95 S&H (Va. res. add sales tax)

Wave Communications
P.O. Box 296
Alexandria, VA 22313
(800) PET-HUGS

Cat Nap ®

Most parents have heard the refrain "I don't *want* to take a nap" many more times than once. For very young children, here's a reassuring look at naps by many different animals who *do* want to take them. Sweet.

By Elizabeth Greenaway, 1994, 14 pp., $2.99

Random House
400 Hahn Rd.
Westminster, MD 21157
(800) 733-3000

CAT NAP

Elizabeth Greenaway

The Wildest-Looking Domestic Cat

That distinction goes to the ocicat, with its spotted leopard coat. Looking very much like a "wild" cat, the ocicat is a man-made creation combined from American Shorthair, Siamese, and Abyssinian breeds. Black leopard spots are scattered randomly throughout its light gray/brown coat, and this interesting hybrid (now a fully recognized breed) is known for its intelligence and warmth.

Let's Choose Life

Reality can be tough, and the statistics are terrible. Last year 15 million pets were euthanized at U.S. animal shelters. It's mind-boggling. There are exceptional circumstances — lethal injuries, mortal illness—where euthanasia is the only humane alternative. But the mass slaughter of so many millions of animals—each with a personality, most of whom just need good homes—makes you wonder about the humanity of humans. Fortunately, some people are doing something about it. This annual directory published by the nonprofit group Doing Things For Animals lists 180 pro-

NO-KILL DIRECTORY

HUMANE ORGANIZATIONS THAT PROVIDE RESCUE, SANCTUARY AND REHABILITATION TO ANIMALS IN NEED.

Compiled & Edited by Lynda J. Foro

© Doing Things For Animals, Inc.

grams in 38 states where animals are not killed, and another hundred or so that provide sanctuary and life to animals without homes. All life is precious.

The No-Kill Directory, $15

Doing Things For Animals
P.O. Box 2165
Sun City, AZ 85372
(602) 977-5793

Holiday Craziness Hat ®

Break out the champagne— here's a scream for your next Christmas party! Dress up the cat in this one-size-fits-all red felt Santa hat with a white pom-pom and adjustable Velcro closure under the chin. Made for parties. Your friends will never forget this.

Santa's Hat, $7.95

Information:
Weazer Wear
P.O. Box 2849
Stamford, CT 06906
(203) 967-4624
Contact: Kaki Mack

Take Your Pet USA: A Guide of Accommodations for Pets and Their Owners

There's tons of information in this paperback on traveling with your cat. It contains detailed alphabetical listings by state and city of about 4,000 hotels across the country that admit four-legged guests, with notations about on-site exercise areas, local vets, and outdoorsy attractions of interest to both man and pet. Don't forget: Hawaii has a 120-day quarantine waiting period on all arriving pets. Size and species restrictions are also included. I know you're all cat loving, but, for your information, the Marriott Long Wharf hotel absolutely cannot stand snakes, so don't try to check in with one curled around your neck!

1995, 280 pp., $11.95 (add $2.50 for S&H)

Artco Publishing
12 Channel St.
Boston, MA 02210
(800) 255-8038

Smiles Awake You . . .

Each day presents you with the gift of life. Start it out right with a smiling kitty-face mug (10 oz.), bowl, and tumbler (6 oz.) as you nibble on breakfast and prepare for the new day. Hand-thrown by John Walker. His entire family pitches in, helping bring the kitty pottery to completion in a kiln firing to nearly 2400°. Each is available in creamy beige stoneware accented with your choice of country blue or green stripes.

Kitty Mug, $14.50 + $3.50 S&H
Kitty Bowl, $12.50 + $3.50 S&H
Tumbler, $7.50 + $3.50 S&H
(Ind. res. add 5% sales tax)

Walker Art Pottery
12 E. Roszell Dr.
Nineveh, IN 46164
(317) 933-2931

Cat in Search of a Friend ®

Who's the best friend for a cat—or a young child? Is it really the one who's biggest and strongest? Or should we depend on our own sense of self and pride? This is an instructive, brilliantly illustrated, easy-to-read book for young children about developing a sense of pride and self-reliance and putting the need for friends in perspective. First published in Austria, this is one in a series of children's books by Kane/Miller.

By Meschack Asare, 1986, 30 pp., $10.95

Kane/Miller Book Publishers
P.O. Box 8515
La Jolla, CA
92038
(619) 456-0540

Meshack Asare

CAT
IN SEARCH OF A FRIEND

Paw Prints Where You Least Expect Them

Perhaps you won't use it every day. But for the right occasion, this is crazy enough to be fun. What's wrong with creative fringe behavior for cat fanatics? We all know we're crazy—about cats, that is. Why not show it off? Great for parties. Black paw prints on white paper.

Paw-Print Toilet Paper, $6.49 per roll; 2 for $6 each + S&H (N.Y. res. add sales tax)

Pedigrees
1989 Transit Way
Brockport, NY 14420
(800) 548-4786

Counting on Calico ®

A big fun counting book—all the way up to 20! Calico the rambunctious kitten races around doing all that cool kitten stuff—jumping and spinning and turning and playing—that's so impressive to very young children. Large format, well-illustrated paperback for children ages 3 to 8.

By Phyllis Limbacher Tildes, 1995, 32 pp., $6.95

Charlesbridge Publishing
85 Main St.
Watertown, MA 02172
(800) 225-3214

Disposable Luxury ®

Traveling in a Cadillac today? Kitty can, with this foldable, disposable cardboard cat carrier. Clean white interior includes an absorbent pad. Quick setup, folds down for storage, reinforced handle. Fast and easy.

Cat-A-Lac, $6.10

Information:
Designer Products, Inc.
P.O. Box 201177
Arlington, TX 76006
(817) 469-9416

Celebrate Your Cat's Birthday!

Something like 50% of all cat people buy their cats a birthday or Christmas present. Amazing, huh? I'm sure you're not one of those *creeps* who forgets your cat is important. I certainly hope you're holding up your end of things and not being a disappointment to your one and only cat who loves you deeply and for whom you can *never do enough.* If you've forgotten the holidays, or your child's cat has a birthday coming up and you're out of ideas, call for a basket of kitty treats and toys. Looks nice, very little effort, smart idea as a gift.

Gift Baskets for Cats, $15 (small wicker); $18 (large wicker); $15 (bowl)
Add $8 S&H (Ga. res. add sales tax)

- The Pet Pantry
P.O. Box 723814
Atlanta, GA 31139
(404) 443-0346

TRUE CAT FACT

Training Tips: Biting

It's not ever okay for the cat to bite you (some normally pleasant cats become tigers when bath time rolls around, but that's an exceptional, frightening situation that can be worked on over time). When a cat bites you out of anger, you must do something instantly, not 10 seconds later. Immediately let out a loud yowl like an animal that's been bitten, and put a toy in front of your cat, substituting that as something to bite instead of your hand. You can combine the yowl with sharp hissing to discourage the cat. Warfare between you and the cat does not make for a pleasant household. If necessary, consult an animal behaviorist to resolve the problem.

A Keepsake of Cats ®

A delightful compendium of wonderful prose from the world's most admired writers about one, and only one, subject: cats! From Mark Twain to Rudyard Kipling, Susan Coolidge to Lewis Carroll, writers have been fawning over cats for centuries. Here's the best of the best in a small gift book containing prose and full-color illustrations.

"A home without a cat, and a well-fed, well-petted and properly revered cat, may be a perfect home, perhaps, but how can it prove its title?" —Mark Twain

Edited by Kate James, 1992, 52 pp., $5.99

Random House Value Publishing
Gramercy Books
40 Engelhard Ave.
Avenel, NJ 07001
(800) 733-3000

Big-Fish-Dinner Screen Saver

Here's a cute deep-sea plastic screen saver of fish bubbling around on the sea bottom, with a colorful plastic screen frame of very interested cats awaiting a seafood dinner. Fits 14″ and 15″ monitors. Frame attaches easily with Velcro (included). Screen saver is for IBM compatible PCs. Attractive and practical.

Cat Screenie & Saver, $20 + $4.95 S&H (Tex. res. add 7.25% sales tax)

Accessory Pet
5836 Pathfinder Trail
Plano, TX 75093
(800) 558-7387

The Worldwide Home of Pedigreed Cats

The Cat Fanciers' Association is the world's largest registry of pedigreed cats. First begun in 1906, CFA has no individual memberships: Breeders and exhibitors are members of local cat clubs affiliated with the association. As of 1994, there were 653 clubs worldwide. CFA produces two publications: the *Almanac* and the *Yearbook.* A separate organization, the Robert H. Winn Foundation, supports studies of the medical problems affecting cats. CFA has many books and videos you can order. If you have a serious interest in purebred cats, or would like to register your cat, these are the people to talk to.

The Cat Fanciers' Association
1805 Atlantic Ave.
Manasquan, NJ 08736
(908) 528-9797

The
Cat Fanciers'
Association, Inc.
World's Largest Registry
of Pedigreed Cats

CFA

1805 Atlantic Avenue
PO Box 1005
Manasquan NJ 08736-0805
908-528-9797

Pretty Kitty Wastebaskets

We all need to have a circular file, and these attractive baskets with kitten prints are as good as any you'll find. Clear lacquer finish protects the surface. They have a soft, feminine look in muted pinks and blues that's very pleasing. 13″ tall.

Siamese Kitten Wastebasket, $20 + $4.95 S&H
Playful Kittens Wastebasket, $20 + $4.95 S&H
(Tex. res. add 7.25% sales tax)

Accessory Pet
5836 Pathfinder Trail
Plano, TX 75093
(800) 558-7387

The Cat Postcard Book ®

Instant art history in a postcard book of 30 full-color cat portraits from famous artists of centuries past. Choose the one you like, remove it from the book, write a few dear words, kiss it good-bye, and mail it off.

Compiled by Running Press, 1987, 60 pp., $7.95 (+ $2.50 S&H)

Running Press
125 S. 22nd St.
Philadelphia, PA 19103
(800) 345-5359

TRUE CAT FACT

Training Tips: Counter Jumping

Most people don't want the cat on the kitchen counter. For all you know, he just walked out of the litter box! Discourage cats from roaming the countertop by leaving out light pans or aluminum soda cans where the cat will knock them over when he jumps up. Cats hate loud noises, and when all that metal crashes to the floor, he'll bolt. You can also leave dishwashing detergent on the counter so he steps in it (nasty but nontoxic to lick off paws) or two-sided sticky masking tape that isn't fun to walk on. Until the cat is trained, consider defrosting meat and other foods in a sealed space like the oven or microwave or refrigerator.

Christmas—Or Shall We Call It Catmas? ®

This cassette tape and booklet of favorite Christmas songs is an irreverent goof on cats and Christmas, with cat-oriented lyrics to the Christmas music we've heard for years. The sound quality, orchestration, and singing are very good, and the lyrics clever. Teenagers, the "Christmas-weary," and cat lovers with attitude will find this amusing.

Catmas Carols Audio Tape with Book, $12.95

Chronicle Books
275 Fifth St.
San Francisco, CA 94103
(800) 722-6657

TRUE CAT FACT

The Blue Cat

The remarkable Chartreux cat of France has a long history, dating back to the 16th century when they were bred by Carthusian-Chartreux monks (known for the Chartreuse liqueur they produce). A strong, sensitive, loving cat with great tolerance for almost any situation, they have a silver/blue coat and copper eyes, and a small upper lip that makes them appear to have an amused smile. Rare in the U.S.

Professional Help for Troubled Cats

Some cat behavior is very tough to explain. And hard to live with. You've asked your vet, read endless books, watched cat-behavior videotapes—all that, and nothing's working. It's time for a good feline behaviorist to look at the problem.

Kate Gamble is an experienced behaviorist who's helped hundreds of cat owners. She's known nationwide from her TV and radio appearances, newspaper articles, and, most important, successful results. She conducts monthly seminars and volunteers generously to animal shelters and humane groups.

She works by phone nationally and internationally (or pays a personal visit when necessary) using case-history forms, interviews, and an astounding depth of knowledge about why cats do what they do. What you'll spend on a phone consultation is cheap compared with having your $1,000 sofa shredded.

WHY DOES MY CAT DO THAT?

KATE GAMBLE, PROFESSIONAL FELINE BEHAVIORIST

Cat Behavior by Kate, $50 an hour

Kate Gamble
P.O. Box 16025
San Francisco, CA 94116
(415) 564-5555

Whisker Knuckle Keys

A key ring that looks good— glossy red, black, silver, purple, pink, or blue enamel over sturdy lightweight aluminum. Your index and middle finger fit in the holes while the cat-whisker part fits in your palm. Kitty brass knuckles? Not really. Carried that way—with the two points sticking out—it could be a useful psychological companion on a dark, lonely street. Solid, very well-made, and smart.

Pet Patrol Kitty Key Ring, $6 + $1 S&H (Calif. res. add 8.25% sales tax)

Pet Patrol
2401 South Santa Fe Ave.
Los Angeles, CA 90058
(213) 583-7970

Yarn Cat

Cats love chasing a ball of yarn. Here's a frame that'll let you surround your kitty's beautiful face with yarn. Braided deep green frame holds a 3″ × 5″ picture.

Decorative "Yarn" Picture Frame, $14.99 + $5.29 S&H (N.Y. res. add sales tax)

Pedigrees
1989 Transit Way
Brockport, NY 14420
(800) 548-4786

The Kama Sutra for Cats ®

Do your cats sleep in your bed? If so, they might have to deal with human bedroom activities. This manual helps cats navigate the bedroom, with amusing illustrations of them holding on for dear life as human occupants twist and turn in bed. The positions of the cats on the bed are carefully arranged to keep the cats at a nice, even temperature when the humans under the sheets are boiling. Life in bed, on a "sea" of covers. Nutty fun.

By Burton Silver, 1993, 71 pp. $9.95

Ten Speed Press
P.O. Box 7123
Berkeley, CA 94707
(800) 841-2665

Cat Air Conditioner

Back in the old, old days before there was refrigeration, liquids used to be kept cool by evaporation. You'd wet the outside of a canvas bag that held a liquid, keep it in the cellar or the shade, and the natural evaporation of the water would keep the liquid inside the bag cool. Now this technique is available for cats. If you're in a hot spot, your cat isn't going to like it. They hate to be hot, and it's actually dangerous for them if the temperature is too extreme. This little bandanna can provide quick cooling action for a hot cat on a boiling summer day; it makes good sense to take it along on a car trip in hot weather. Simple to use, good idea.

Pet Affairs Wet Tie, $7.99 + $3.80 S&H (Ariz. res. add 7% sales tax)

Pet Affairs, Inc.
691 East 20th St., Bldg. III
Tucson, AZ 85719
(520) 623-4275

The Easy Cat-Flap Door ®

This lockable cat flap features clear Lucite material wrapped in weather stripping to keep drafts and dirt out of the house. Simple to assemble. Comes complete with trim and finish panels, and template and mounting screws. Virtually silent open-and-closing action.

Cat Mate Lockable Cat Flap, $27.85

Information:
Classic Products
1451 Vanguard Dr.
Oxnard, CA 93033
(805) 487-6227

Cajun Capers

Cajun is a 16-pound neutered male cat who was abandoned at an apartment complex three years ago. He now resides comfortably at the Cat Care Society in Lakewood, Colorado, where he's something of a character, making his debut as Visiting Cat with their Humane Education program. Okay, he's actually just adorable, with the personality to match. And every time you make a purchase of these full-color "Cajun Capers" cards (blank inside for you to write your message), you'll be helping this wonderful group of folks who care for so many animals. It's a fund-raiser for them, and you won't be disappointed.

Cajun Capers, 12 cards, $12 + $2 S&H (Colo. res. add 7% sales tax)

Cat Care Society
5985 West 11th Ave.
Lakewood, CO 80214
(303) 239-9690

The Cat's Meow ®

This pleasant collection of cat quotes, quips, history, and legend captures the allure of our favorite companion. Includes History of the Cat, Cat Culture, Cat Fancy and Cats Not-So-Fancy, Cat Talk, and Cat Tales. More insight into the world of cats.

Edited by Kevin Osborne, 1994, 40 pp., $6.95

Andrews & McMeel
Ariel Books
4520 Main St.
Kansas City, MO
64112
(816) 932-6700
(800) 826-4216

Classy Beaded Collars

Looking for something unusual in a kitty collar? Shari Tucker makes glass bead collars in a variety of colors. Clasp is jewelry-quality, and it's designed to stretch—and break if necessary—if Kitty gets caught in something. Handmade, looks great. Very lightweight. Cats that won't wear a regular collar sometimes tolerate beaded collars. Shari also makes customized velvet and rhinestone cat collars.

Beaded Cat Necklace, $12.95 + $2 S&H
(Calif. res. add 8.5% sales tax)

Feline Frenzy
5337 College Ave.
Oakland, CA 94618
(510) 444-0250

The Complete Persian ®

Saying the Persian is popular is an understatement. It is by far the most popular breed in the United States—the number of registered Persians exceeds the number of registrations for all other breeds of cats combined. A big part of their popularity is due to their gentle and affectionate natures. Persians can be mellow, intelligent, loving companions. Their visual beauty only adds to the beauty of their personality. Persians like people.

By Will Thompson and Eric Wickham-Ruffle, 1993, 224 pp., $24.95

Macmillan Publishing USA 201 W. 103d St. Indianapolis, IN 46290 (800) 858-7674

Upscale Kitty Gifts

Count on Baxter & Charming for quality cat goodies. Shown, clockwise from left: hand-painted, stain-finished and sealed hardwood frames (in three sizes, including a solid brass medallion in a pewter casting—with your choice of jewels, to match the color of the frame, in carnelian, black onyx, or emerald); herbal quilts and sachets of blended botanicals and scented oils to create a fresh scent in your pet's bedding while discouraging fleas; porcelain kitty bowl made from the finest domestic porcelain, measuring 5¼" dia., and including gold accents (two designs, each inscribed with a proverb and illustration depicting feline characteristics); and Miss Charming's catnip pillows (3" × 1" dia.), handsewn from exquisite fabrics, detailed with satin cording and filled with an ounce of premium catnip.

Picture Frames, from $38
Herbal Quilts & Sachets, from $16
Porcelain Kitty Bowls, $31
Catnip Pillows, from $4
Add $4.50 S&H
(Ill. res. add sales tax)

Baxter & Charming, Ltd.
11 W. Main St., Suite 300
Carpentersville, IL 60110
(847) 426-5900
Email: baxterpets.@aol

Driving with Miss Kitty

Now you can learn about cats while you drive, with this two-cassette-tape program for cat lovers. All sorts of information—from how to select a kitten to extrasensory cats who find their way home over great distances, why some cats don't kill mice, why cats behave the way they do. Recommended by *Library Journal* and other publications.

Cat Lovers Only, $14.95 + $3.50 S&H
(Conn. res. add $1.50 sales tax)

BFI AudioBooks
1397 Hope St.
Stamford, CT 06907
(800) 260-7717

Hawaiian Beach Cat

There's nothing like a visit to Hawaii to liven up your spirits. Whimsical kitty tote bag evokes this island paradise. The people who make these bags live part of the time in New York, part of the time in Hawaii.

Tropicats Tote Bag, $19.95 + $2.50 S&H
(N.Y. res. add $1.70 sales tax)

Tropicats
98-151 Pali-Momi St., #195
Aica, Hawaii 96701
(888) 876-7228

Cat on a Wall

How'd you like a huge photo of your cat on your wall? It's simple. Just send in your best crisp, well-focused photo to these folks, and they'll blow it up to any size you want . . . 16″ × 20″, 24″ × 36″. They'll even make you a wall mural! Imagine a whole wall with your beautiful cat's smiling face. It gets better and better.

Larger Than Life Paw Prints, prices starting at $35

Dynamic Photo Imaging
4210 227th Ave.
Buckley, WA 98321
(800) 464-7226

Japanese Cat Carrier

Strange, but true. This space-age handheld cat carrier has a cool high-tech appearance and detailed practicality. Streamlined design includes armor-type windows to protect against direct rays from the sun.

Light- and dustproof with a unique ventilation system. Transparent smoked twin doors, front and back, make for easy cat entrance and exit. Large doorknob with a one-touch locking system, plus a detachable carpet floor.

Measures $10\frac{5}{8}$″ w. × $19\frac{11}{16}$″ l. × $15\frac{3}{8}$″ h. Available in red, pink, green, and white. Patented. Holds one cat comfortably.

Hello Pet Carrier, $49.99 + $5.99 S&H (Kan. res. add sales tax)

Doggie & Kitty
NYT Worldwide Corporation
5145 NW Topeka Blvd.
Topeka, KS 66617
(913) 246-0177

Choosing a Kitten

You will have your cat for many years, so choosing the right kitten to begin with is an important step. There in front of you is an adorable litter of kittens. Which should you choose? Watch the kittens for a while. Sit down, take your time. Make sure the kitten is lively and active. A kitten that walks up to you, unafraid, tends to be dominant and self-assertive—the polar opposite of a shy, sensitive cat that might not take well to kids and a busy household. The eyes should be clear and bright, ears clean with no smell, milk teeth nicely arrayed in her mouth. The kitty should be fully weaned and eating food, with no evidence of diarrhea. Ask for a vaccination certificate.

If you think two kitties would be even better than one, choose two from the same litter (they grew up together, and know each other), and have them both spayed/neutered. The cost of your kitten is related to the time of year. Christmas is the most expensive time (high demand = high prices); late spring and early summer the least expensive. Consider going to a local cat show to check out the various breeds and breeders, or look for that most enticing of signs by the road or a bulletin board: FREE KITTENS!

Animals . . . Our Return to Wholeness ®

The field of animal communications has exploded during the past several years, and this paperback is a real eye-opener. Penelope Smith, animal-communication specialist, reveals the thoughts and stories of animals who have communicated with her telepathically, revealing their spiritual understanding of the world, their purpose, and their symbiotic relationship with humans. This is a fairly new phenomenon, heading east across America from California. Smith actually communicates with animals, and knows their thoughts and feelings. It's not as fringe as you might think. By my way of thinking, anything that contributes to compassion for and understanding of animals can only help.

By Penelope Smith, 1993, 355 pp., $19.95

Pegasus Press
P.O. Box 1060
Pt. Reyes Station, CA 94956
(415) 663-1247

Kitty Bandannas from the Old West ®

Rustle up that western look with kitty bandannas for wearing around the house. Tie loosely so Kitty doesn't get stuck on anything, rent yourself a John Wayne movie, and have a Western Party.

Kitty Bandannas, $1.99 to $2.99

Omega Products, Inc.
292 Old Dover Rd.
Rochester, NH 03867
(800) 258-7148

Just About Everything on Earth for Pets and Livestock

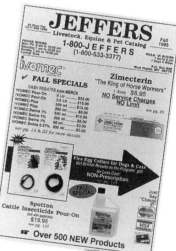

Get ready to roll up your sleeves. This monster, 168-page catalog from the folks at Jeffers in West Plains, Missouri, contains basic cat products from toys to vaccines—like the kind of hands-on stuff you'd find in a country farmhouse or barn. Not what you'd call a fancy presentation—it's printed on newspaper—but there's plenty of content for your horse, dog, sheep, goat, pig, poultry, reptile, or cow in addition to your cat.

In the words of Keith Jeffers, Ph.D. and chief executive officer, "We don't go home until every order is out!"

Jeffers Livestock, Equine, and Pet Catalog

P.O. Box 948
West Plains, MO 65775
(800) JEFFERS

You Want Me to Sit Where?

Cats like a spot that smells like home, and that's true for beds, baskets, and all favorite spots. This cute cat towel helps define Kitty's personal space, and protects your furniture against clawing and shedding. Remember how much you loved *your* security blanket? Machine-washable 16″ × 25″ white terrycloth towel with a playful design of a cat toying with a ball of yarn. It might keep some fur off your sofa.

Cat's Towel, $10 + $4.95 S&H
(Tex. res. add 7.25% sales tax)

Accessory Pet
5836 Pathfinder Trail
Plano, TX 75093
(800) 558-7387

Hands and Whiskers of Clay

As evening rolls around, consider lighting one of these hand-thrown stoneware Kitty Candlesticks for a soothing atmosphere. Or brighten things up with the soft glow of a Kitty Face Oil Lamp. Made by John Walker and family of Walker Art Pottery in Ninevah, Indiana, they're both available in creamy beige with country blue or green stripes. Nice quality, made one at a time.

Kitty Candlestick, $16
+ $3.50 S&H
Kitty Face Oil Lamp, $24
+ $5.50 S&H
(Ind. res. add 5% sales tax)

Walker Art Pottery
12 East Roszell Road
Nineveh, IN 46164
(317) 933-2931

Dribbles ®

Siamese kittens Benny and Bing are rather curious about the old cat who has just come to live in their house. This handsomely illustrated hardcover tells a story of compassion that reflects on life and old age. It's helpful in explaining a difficult concept to children: the inevitable end of all life. Parents will find this invaluable when talking to their young children about a pet soon to pass away.

By Connie Heckert, 1993, 32 pp., $14.95

Houghton Mifflin
Clarion Books
222 Berkeley St.
Boston, MA 02116
(800) 225-3362

Messages from the House Cat . . .

Since the cat rules the house—it is *his* house, after all—you might just as well accept it and hang one of these hand-painted 5″ × 7″ porcelain plaques in your kitchen. This clues your guests in to the fact that they must pass the stringent approval of the house kitty. Magic Earth has other cat goodies, including chimes and T-shirts. Ask for their brochure from either

Michael or Jana Gray, deep in the mountains of Colorado.

Houseguests Plaque or **Spoiled Rotten Cat,** $16.95 each + $6.95 S&H & Insurance (Colo. res. add 7% sales tax)

Magic Earth
P.O. Box 67
Paonia, CO 81428

Moving Day

Can't find your cat on moving day? It's a common experience. She's already upset by all the packing and bustling about, and cats also have a strong attachment to territory. You can make it easier by keeping her in one room for several days as you finish packing, or even boarding her and then bringing her to the new home, where you'll have ready all the familiar items she loves: food and water bowls, toys, bed, scratching post, litter box. Keep the old stuff because it's reassuring to cats, who don't like change. Comfort her with extra attention and petting, walk through the new house with her, give her time to get used to things. Close off extra rooms and gradually allow her to enter new rooms over a period of a week or so. If you're going to let her outside in a fenced yard eventually in a fenced yard, first keep her indoors in the new house for three to four days. Easy does it! Finally, remember to catproof the place; fix any potential cat dangers (equipment, furnace openings, anywhere the cat can get stuck).

Notes to Yourself ®

Your thoughts and hopes and dreams have found a place to live in this blank-page journal. It awaits your hand.

The Notable Cat, $19.95 + $2.50 S&H

Running Press
125 S. 22nd St.
Philadelphia, PA 19103
(800) 345-5359

Stamp on Cats!

People collect rubber stamps just like they collect postage stamps. The Rubber Stamp Ranch down in Albuquerque sells all kinds of rubber stamps, including 44 cat stamps. Big free catalog.

Cat Rubber Stamps, $3.50 to $7.00 + $3.20 S&H per order

Rubber Stamp Ranch
3400 Anderson Ave., SE
Albuquerque, NM 87106
(800) 728-9762

Beat-the-Heat Screen Door

When the summer sun beats down, and the thermometer's rising, you'll be wanting to use the screen door. This nifty device helps prevent the cat from shredding the screen, and keeps you from having to let him in and out. Made of durable lightweight plastic that snaps right into any metal or fiber screen, it also has magnets to keep it from swinging open in a strong breeze, keeping out the bugs and mosquitoes. You can lock it securely from the inside, and the 8″ × 10″ opening easily accommodates cats up to 30 pounds. Fully guaranteed.

Pet Screen Door, $25.95 + $3.00 S&H
(Calif. res. add $2.01 sales tax)

Borwick Pet Screen Door
P.O. Box 30345
Santa Barbara, CA 93130
(800) 365-5657

Cat in the Night

These ethereal glowing cats are miniature works of night-light art. Choice of four (from top): Cat Over the World, Muffy with a Heart, Longhair Cat, and Shorthair Cat. Very attractive, crafted from a thin, translucent porcelain using the old art of lithophane carving.

Porcelain Lithophane Cat Night-lights, $15 each + $4 S&H (Iowa res. add 5% sales tax)

Schirmer Designs
501 E. Kirkwood
Fairfield, IA 52556
(515) 472-6801

Terry Brown's Cats

Terry has an instantly recognizable illustrating style. Clean lines; happy, friendly cat faces; humorous ideas. Her greeting cards, rubber stamps, ceramic tiles, Christmas ornaments, and mugs are available with a variety of clever illustrations. Great gifts.

Greeting Cards, $11.95 per dozen
Rubber Stamps, $6.95 each
Ceramic Tiles, $11.95 each (includes gift box and bio card) + $3.50 S&H
Christmas Cat Ornaments, $7.95 (includes gift box)
Terry Brown's Cats Mugs, $8.95 each (includes gift box)

Terry Brown's Cats
91698 Burton Dr.
McKenzie Bridge, OR 97413
(541) 822-3785

The Worst Witch at Sea ®

Jill Murphy is well known for her Worst Witch books. In this story, the tabby cat of Mildred Hubble—a student at Miss Cackle's Academy for Witches—is banished to the kitchen, so Mildred devises a plan to bring her along to class each day. Unfortunately, Tabby has been lost at sea, and disaster looms. But all is well in the end as Mildred solves many mysteries and winds up feeling like the luckiest girl in the world, instead of the worst witch in school. Preteen readers. Hardcover.

By Jill Murphy, 1995,
222 pp., $16.95

Candlewick Press
2067 Massachusetts Ave.
Cambridge, MA 02140
(617) 661-3330

"Buckle Up Your Kitty Cat, When the Wind Is Free . . ."

If you start early, you can train your cat to walk on a leash. Walking a cat is interesting because they are so wary. Dogs plunge on ahead, while a cat tends to be tentative and contemplative. This soft embossed leather harness and leash comes in glamorous gold. It buckles on top (away from teeth and claws) and it's been thoughtfully designed with a flap under the buckle to protect skin and hair. Guaranteed for life and fully adjustable for perfect fit and comfort. One size fits all cats unless you have an absolute behemoth (in which case a diet makes more sense than a harness).

E-Z Comfort Harness, $9 + $2 S&H

Vee Enterprises
1066 S. Ogden Dr.
Los Angeles, CA 90019
(800) 733-1903

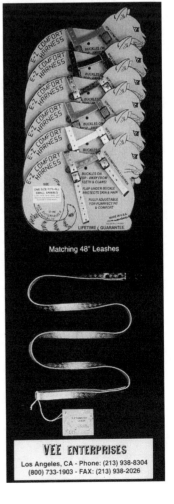

Matching 48" Leashes

So Many Cats ®

Cats are scooting all over the house in this cheery rhyming book for very young children. At first there was one, and now there are 12. Easy counting book and lots of fun!

By Beatrice Schenk de Regniers, 1985, 32 pp., $5.95

Houghton Mifflin
Clarion Books
200 Berkeley St.
Boston, MA 02116
(800) 225-3362

Your Cat's Life Story

Finally—a baby book for your four-legged babies! My Cat's Story is the original whole-life baby book/scrapbook for your cat. Keep all your special memories, favorite photos, and important records—from adoption to the golden years—in one beautiful album. A first-class book, as good as anything made for human babies. Full-sized (9″ × 12″) hardcover with gold-embossed linen endpapers. Lovely artwork on each page. A nice treasury of your life with your cat.

My Cat's Story, $20.95 + $4 S&H

Deertracks
14415 Hawthorne West
Lake Forest, IL 60045
(847) 362-2125
E-mail: deertracks@aol.com

Vicky's Crazy Cat Stuff

Vicky Grady of Anacortes, Washington, has a line of quality cat T-shirts with fun cat and animal art, and more than a dozen cat greeting cards—called Foto-Notes—that reflect her wry sense of humor. When you request her catalog, you'll get a color photocopy of the shirts and cards. She's a one-person operation; everything's handmade.

I'm the Cat's Meow T-Shirt, $16.95 + $3 S&H (Wash. res. add $1.32 sales tax)

Vicky Grady
461A Gibralter Rd.
Anacortes, WA 98221

New Arrival Gift Set!

Here's the perfect gift for a friend with a new kitty. Beautiful basics—including a pretty cat-shaped food dish and matching paws place mat, a mouse toy and crunchy cat treats—all in one clever package!

Four-Piece Cat Gift Set, $16.95 + $3.95 S&H (Wash. res. add 8.2% sales tax)

Keller Design, Inc.
P.O. Box 3854
Seattle, WA 98124
(800) 683-1227

Cats by the Yard!

Like to sew? Looking for some great kitty fabric? Giselle Blythe has yards and yards of cat-print material. Constantly changing selection—new fabrics every month. Wonderful service. Write her a note asking for Cat Fabrics information and include a stamped, self-addressed #10 envelope. She'll tell you about the latest fabrics and current prices, and also send swatches. You'll have cats all over the house!

Cat Fabrics

Blythe Designs
P.O. Box 17506
Seattle, WA 98107
(206) 789-6772

Nutty Rubber Cats

Here's a great catalog of cat (and other) rubber stamps that's amusing to browse through, especially if you're into rubber stamps. Personalized pet stamps available, too! Everything about this company screams *fun*. Purchase of catalog is fully refundable with a $12 order.

Alley Cat Stamps

Catalog: $1
5232 Beechwood Rd.
Milford, Ohio 45150
(513) 831-0004

For the Love of All Animals

The U.S. Humane Society has great information for both new and experienced cat owners. *Cat Care Facts* ($1.95 + $3 S&H) is a brochure with thorough hands-on information about taking care of cats. *Facts About Cat Fables* (50¢ + $3 S&H) is an illustrated brochure about common cat misbeliefs. *Facts About Cat Law* ($1.50 + $3 S&H) is a 20-page booklet on legislation that protects cats. *Shelter Sense* is a ten-issue-a-year publication ($8). If you join the USHS Global Humane Family, your membership dues will help protect animals and their environments all around the world.

The Humane Society of the United States
Global Humane Family
Memberships: $10 individual, $18 family

2100 L St., NW
Washington, DC 20037
(202) 452-1100

Training Tips: Toilet-Paper Stories

Toilet-paper rolls are a natural toy for cats. They swat the roll, paper comes off, and it *keeps* coming off. That huge pile of paper on the floor is fun to play in. Your cat thinks it's very thoughtful of you to keep replacing the toy! Here are a few tips to cut down on your paper bills. Try balancing a plastic cup with pennies or water on the top of the roll. It will rain down harmlessly on Kitty's head next time he plays. Or have the roll unroll out the back, toward the wall, instead of in front so that it will keep from flying off when swatted by Kitty's paw. You can mold aluminum foil to cover the roll and remove when necessary. Or you can peel apart an empty cardboard roll core and stretch it over the new paper roll as a covering device. Nothing works? Invent and patent a foolproof toilet-roll-cat-protection device and make a fortune. Or keep the door closed.

A Miscellany of Cat Owners' Wisdom

Eclectic mixed bag of practical cat facts, hints, valuable knowledge, and amusing tales that help you better understand how the small, active brain between those two fuzzy ears works. There is always more to learn about your cat. Hardcover.

By Kay White, 1992, 96 pp., $14.95 (+ $2.50 S&H)

Running Press
125 S. 22nd St.
Philadelphia, PA 19103
(800) 345-5359

The World of Cats, on Your TV

Ann Childers, noted animal behaviorist and founder of the Animal School, Inc., is the engaging host on this A-to-Z video about the stages of a cat's life. Most of the filming was done in real homes with families and children. A substantial, warm introduction to the world of cats. Perfect for new or prospective cat owners.

Kittens to Cats, 60 minutes, VHS, $19.98 (includes S&H)

PetAvision, Inc.
P.O. Box 102
Morgantown, WV 26507
(800) 521-7898

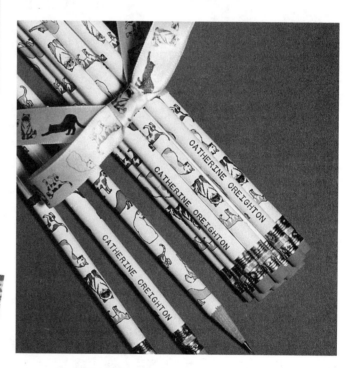

Writing with Style

Twelve perfect pencils for cat enthusiasts of any age. Pencils feature striped, solid, and spotted cats doing what cats do—stretching, observing, sleeping. Each is personalized with the name or message of your choice (up to 30 characters and spaces). Quality #2 pencils made in the U.S.A. Don't forget to order a personalized Cat Note Pad—50 pages personalized with your name (up to 30 characters and spaces) on a white pad, printed with cats on top and bottom. Perfect gifts.

Penny's Pencils, $7.50 + $1.50 S&H
Personalized Cat Note Pads, $7.95 + $1.50 S&H
(Conn. res. add 6% sales tax)

The Nipper Group, Ltd.
P.O. Box 4028
Old Lyme, CT 06371
(203) 434-0470

Captivating Cats ®

A paperback celebration of cats in loving quotes from poets and feline aficionados. Includes heartwarming stories about cats and their personalities. Written as an act of love.

By James Armstrong, 1995, 88 pp., $16.95 (Calif. res. add 7.25% sales tax)

Information:
Cedco Publishing Company
2955 Kerner Blvd.
San Rafael, CA 94901
(415) 457-3893

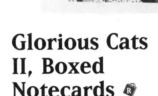

Glorious Cats II, Boxed Notecards ®

The realistic art of Susan Powers seems to jump right off the paper in this exceptional collection of blank-inside notecards featuring five each of four images. Includes *Cat on a Blue*

Quilt, Cat with a View, A Somali (my favorite, of a cat on a library shelf), and *Randolph.*

Glorious Cats II, Boxed Notecards, $12.95

Add $3.95 S&H (N.Y. res. add sales tax)

Galison Books
36 W. 44th St.
New York, NY 10036
(212) 354-8840

Cat on Your Lap & Kitten Surprise Package

This handsome lap-desk will make your writing, reading, or snacking more convenient. Accessories include cat stationery, notecards, a journal, coffee mug, and gourmet coffee and cookies. Items are attractively arranged on the desk and then shrink-wrapped for shipping. Thoughtful gift. Gail also makes a terrific kitty gift basket (shown) if you're expecting a new arrival. A new kitten in the house is always cause for celebration! A bountiful

basket is filled with purr-fect items to welcome a new little one. Includes toys and treats, a designer food bowl, and a large journal to keep records of important dates, photographs, and memories. Fun for Kitty's birthday, too.

The Cat's Meow Lap-Desk & Accessories, $49.95 + $5.95 S&H
New Arrival Kitten Basket, $52 + $7.95 S&H (Ill. res. add 7.25% sales tax)

Gail's Gifts and Baskets
11447 14th St.
Pekin, IL 61554
(309) 348-3345

Tropical Kitty Mug

First it was sunbathing. Now Kitty is scuba diving and having big fun with fish in the warm waters off Hawaii. Relive the memory over coffee, or just dream you're there.

Tropicats Hawaiian Kitty Mug, $6.95 + $2.50 S&H (N.Y. res. add 59¢ sales tax)

Tropicats
98-151 Pali-Momi St., #195
Aica, Hawaii 96701
(888) 876-7228

The Cat Hat

This very amusing children's story is about a woman who loses her cat and suspects— among other things—that her neighbor is wearing the cat, as a hat, on his head. Her imagination runs wild. The illustrations are crazy fun. Enough suspense to last for a two-night bedtime read. There's a happy ending, of course! Hardcover.

By Eva Lindstrom, 1989, 32 pp., $6.95

Kane/Miller Book Publishers
P.O. Box 8515
La Jolla, CA 92038
(619) 456-0540

Smooth Rolling Kitty

Try carrying a 20-pound Himalayan cat through miles of airport corridors, and you'll begin to get the idea behind this clever Japanese import.

The streamlined body includes one body grip, plus two built-in handles at both ends for one or two people to use for carrying. Twin doors allow easy entrance or exit for kitty, while the smoked doors allow a view without harsh sunlight. Carrier has wheels and a folding lever so that you can pull Kitty rather than carry her (smart, huh?) as you make your way through the terminal. An all-around bumper helps avoid shocks. Carrier is 16½" w. × 29⅛" l. × 20 1/16" h. Available in pink, dark green, light green, and wine red. Big— you could probably hold two or three cats in this thing

without too much crowding.

Hello Pet Limousine, $169.99 + $11.99 S&H (Kan. res. add sales tax)

Doggie & Kitty NYT Worldwide Corporation
5145 NW Topeka Blvd.
Topeka, KS 66617
(913) 246-0177

The Cat's Mind: Understanding Your Cat's Behavior

Getting inside a cat's head takes some doing. You could sit in a nice fat stuffed armchair and attempt a conversation with Kitty, but that's not going to do it unless you've got telepathic abilities that would land you on the TV talk shows. Understanding a cat's mind is like putting together the pieces of a jigsaw puzzle. You start with understanding a cat's senses and how they influence behavior. You learn how cats communicate with each other and how they develop—based upon the influence of their parents, litter mates, and humans—and then, and only then, do you have even a glimmer of hope of changing behavior. This hardcover includes an excellent treatment summary after a discussion of various behavioral problems, and a concise scientific approach to what does and doesn't work. Understanding your cat takes patience and time, and nothing you do will make it happen overnight. Hang in there, read the book, you'll catch on.

By Bruce Fogle, D.V.M., 1995, 204 pp., $14.95

Macmillan Publishing USA
Howell Book House
201 W. 103d St.
Indianapolis, IN 46290
(800) 858-7674

Minou

Minou Illustrations ©1987 Itoko Maeno

Minou has the perfect life. Her owner, Madame Violette, sees to her every need. She is fed, bathed, and brushed, and her only responsibility is to be cute and cuddly. But things change, as they do in real life, and that's the lesson of this hardcover for children ages 8–10. Tragedy strikes, and Minou finds herself on her own, unskilled and unable to take care of her herself. Illustrated with beautiful images of Paris, *Minou* is a gentle story about one of the harder realities of life: the need to be self-sufficient. Minou's tale will have real meaning to many children.

By Mindy Bingham, 1987, 64 pp., $14.95

MarshMedia
Advocacy Press
P.O. Box 8082
Shawnee Mission, KS 66208
(800) 821-3303

Kitty Cards from Fresno

Robin Senter sells her cat cards two ways: direct to folks and through pet stores nationwide. She also has two color brochures—a green brochure featuring photos of wild animals, and a white brochure, primarily of domestic pets, including lots of cats in great poses. They're nice color cards worth asking for.

Robin's Nest Greeting Cards, $1 per card

Two-Color Catalogs: $1
Robin's Nest
1343 W. San Ramon
Fresno, CA 93711
(209) 438-NEST (6378)

Catnip Sleeping Mats!

This is new! After your cat has rolled around and played with the mat—which is filled with the finest organic catnip—you place it in this wicker cat basket, handmade by the folks at Kitchen Table Crafts in Freeport, Maine. What was once a toy is now a cozy bed. Contemporary kitty design is silk-screened in brilliant blues, greens, and yellows. Unzip the mat when it gets dirty, pour out the old catnip, wash and dry, then refill with fresh catnip. Catnip paradise!

Catnip Sleeping Mat with Cat Basket, $31 + $3.50 S&H (Maine sales tax included)

Pleasant Hill Products
P.O. Box 392
Freeport, Maine 04032
(207) 865-1447

Ceramic Kitty Smiles

Nicole Chapman is busy making porcelain cat faces for earrings, pins, and Christmas tree ornaments. Her lifelike kitties come in a staggering variety of sizes and colors, in bisque white, blaze white, natural color, 24k gold, luster pearl, silver with white gold, yellow gold, and pearl. She also makes unusual cat-face magnets, necklaces, ornaments, pendants, pins, and tie tacks. Seventeen total varieties of cat faces. Pin on your favorite.

Nicole's Creations, various prices, catalog: $1

Nicole's Creations
P.O. Box 2453
Darien, CT 06820
(203) 357-0275

Home-Study Course Teaches You How to Say "Meow"

Understanding that mysterious, marvelous cat in your life just got easier. Pop these cat videos into your VCR, get comfortable, and you'll find yourself laughing out loud as you watch feline behaviorist Kate Gamble explain the inexplicable. Tape 1: *What Makes Tabby Tick?* (20 minutes) explores why territory is of utmost importance to cats, and why changes and threats to territory are the biggest source of cat-behavior problems. Tape 2: *Home Introductions* (20 minutes) explains how to establish a new cat in your home, how to introduce a new cat to resident cats or other pets, and solutions for dealing with a cat's aggressive behavior toward you or toward or other cats. Tape 3: *Correcting Bad Habits* (30 minutes) helps you discover why cats scratch, spray, and stop using the litter box—and you'll learn how to correct these misbehaviors via easy-to-follow step-by-step instructions. Proceeds from your purchase are used to save cat lives at the "no-kill" nonprofit San Francisco SPCA, founded in 1868. Excellent, TV-quality tapes with down-to-earth infor-

mation. A pleasant way to gain insight into your cat's sometimes mysterious behavior.

Cat Behavior 101 (3 Tape Series), $34.95 + $4 S&H (Calif. res. add 8.5% sales tax)

The San Francisco SPCA
2500 16th St.
San Francisco, CA 94103
(800) 211-7722
(415) 554-3050

Cats and Carols ®

Such a lovely idea for a book. Lesley Anne Ivory's award-wining cat paintings illustrate the words of favorite Christmas carols. A fabulous hardcover for adults and children as they celebrate the spirit of Christmas. Instead of people, we have cats frolicking in the snow next to a cat snowman, kittens in the manger, a gorgeous kitty peering out the window for "It Came Upon a Midnight Clear," and much more. Magical.

By Lesley Anne Ivory, 1995, 32 pp., $14.95

Little, Brown and Company
Bullfinch Press
34 Beacon St.
Boston, MA 02108
(617) 227-0730

Kitty Baking Kit & Victorian Kitty Celebration!

Baking friends will appreciate this gift of a kitty cutting board with baking accessories. Includes the *Animaland Cookbook* (with recipes from superstars and tales of their pets), a ceramic cookie mold, cookie cutters, whisk, gourmet cat-treat mix, spoon rest, and recipe cards. In a Victorian mood? Gail's attractive book basket features *Parlor Cats,* based on that period's love affair with the feline, and filled with full-color photographs, dazzling collages, and quotes from popular authors. Also included is a cat mug, coaster, gourmet coffee, and cookies. Everything you need to make someone's day!

Kitty Cutting Board with Baking Accessories, $69.95 + $7.95 S&H
Parlor Cats Basket, $45 + $5.95 S&H
(Ill. res. add 7.25% sales tax)

Gail's Gifts and Baskets
11447 14th St.
Pekin, IL 61554
(309) 348-3345

Litter-Box Manicure System

Alan Kacic has a 2½-year-old blue Malaysian cat that wrestles with him. That, in itself, is impressive. But Alan would head out the door in the morning with all these *scratch marks* on his arms and people would . . . you know . . . wonder. Being a resourceful guy, he came up with the Kitty-Cure Automatic Feline Self-Manicure System. How's it work? He'll send you this amazing stuff that has the texture of sandpaper. You measure the bottom and sides of your litter box. Cut out the special material, paste it down, and the next time Kitty uses the litter box, his claws will be trimmed as he pushes the litter around! A manicure every day. Might even eliminate the need for declawing. What will they think of next?

Kitty-Cure, $9.95 + $4.75 S&H (Ariz. res. add 7% sales tax)

KC Innovations
6119 North Black Bear Loop
Tucson, AZ 85750
(800) 548-8928

Cat Goody Assortment

More goodies from those smart folks at Keller Design and their Pet Buddies collection. Cat serving spoon in pink and gray is made of easy-care melamine, completely dishwasher-safe. Cat Bristle brush is just right—not too hard or soft—for maintaining a pretty kitty coat!

Cat Serving Spoon, $4.49 + S&H
Cat Brush, $5.49 + S&H (Wash. res. add 8.2% sales tax)

Keller Design, Inc.
P.O. Box 3854
Seattle, WA 98124
(800) 683-1227

Where We Going Today? ®

Traveling with Kitty just got easier, and the view has definitely improved. Nylon mesh open sides provide plenty of ventilation and visibility, and Kitty can enter through either the top or side. Includes zippered side pocket for storage, removable (nonabsorbent) coated floor, clear window for easy identification, and a strong web handle (or use the shoulder strap with pad) for support as you travel together.

Soft-Sided Pet Carrier, $30.72

Information:
Designer Products, Inc.
P.O. Box 201177
Arlington, TX 76006
(817) 469-9416

Glorious Cats Journal with Calico Cat ®

With a Calico Cat cover illustration by artist Susan Powers and a sturdy green binding to help hold your thoughts, this lined journal has 128 blank pages for you to record or capture your musings on the wonders of life. Ribbon marker conveniently marks your pages so you can easily resume your writing as your thoughts resume.

Calico Cat Journal, 1995, $9.95
+ $3.95 S&H (N.Y. res. add sales tax)

Galison Books
36 W. 44th St.
New York, NY 10036
(212) 354-8840

Cats That Love Water

Too beautiful to use? These lovely cat soaps belong in your bathroom. Order the Feline Threesome of three sleepy kitties (pink, blue, and white), which includes a cat-shaped soap dish, or go for the full effect with a whole family of two adult cats and three kittens in the Feline Deluxe (shown).

Pretty, colorful, with a mild fragrance.

Feline Threesome, $11.25
+ $3 S&H
Feline Deluxe, $11.95
+ $3 S&H
(Calif. res. add 8.25% sales tax)

World House Company
115 Alto Loma
Millbrae, CA 94030
(800) 206-9152

Where's Kitty? ®

Where is Kitty, indeed? You'll find her hidden all over in this chunky book meant to be read to young children. Includes fun flip-open doors—each with a new surprise—that are perfect for curious little fingers.

By Mercer Mayer, 1991, 12 pp., $3.99

Random House
Green Frog Publishers, Inc.
J.R. Sansevere Book
400 Hahn Rd.
Westminster, MD 21157
(800) 733-3000

The Quotable Cat: A Collection of Quotes, Facts, and Lore for Feline Fanciers ®

A literary celebration in hardcover by hundreds of writers, poets, and philosophers on living with cats, the differences between cats and dogs, the naming of cats, and much more. Asking anyone "What is a cat?" is bound to provoke wildly different responses—these are some of the best.

Compiled by C. E. Crimmins, 1992, 148 pp., $12.95 (+ $2.50 S&H)

Running Press
125 S. 22nd St.
Philadelphia, PA 19103
(800) 345-5359

Turning on the Lights

These are very nice cat switch-plate covers. From the top, Classic Cats, Virginia Miller, Favorite Felines, and Lesley Anne Ivory. Designs are colorful, practical additions to your house. Pipsqueak also has an extensive line of cat clothing, a cardboard playhouse, greeting and notecards, and lots of cat goodies. Ask for their color catalog.

Cat Lightswitch Covers, $9.95 each + $3.95 S&H (Pa. res. add 6% sales tax)

Pipsqueak Productions
P.O. Box 1005
Honesdale, PA 18431
(717) 253-4330

Room-to-Room Door

Perhaps you've moved the litter box out of the bathroom and into the utility room or basement—somewhere out of sight. Sounds like a good idea, but how will the cat get to it? Here's a great solution— an easy-to-install wooden door (pine, oak, or walnut) with solid brass hinges. It can be inserted in solid-core or hollow-core (luan) doors. Opening measures 8″ × 10″ for small or medium pets. Custom sizes and finishes upon request. Quantity discounts available. With one or more doors, the cat can walk anywhere in the house, through doors you keep closed.

Wooden Kitty Passage, $40 + S&H

CaitCour, Inc.
P.O. Box 565
McHenry, IL 60050
(815) 363-8930

Everything's Coming Up Felix

Felix—the one and only Felix—has been around a long time. And he's not going away. This catalog offers new and antique Felix the Cat products from all over the world. Felix socks, shirts, glasses, towels, 3-D pillows, boxer shorts, china, coffee mugs, tote bags, purses, pocket watches, underwear, floating pens, wind chimes, hair bands, book bags, neckties, teapots, cat-food bank, needlepoint, cross-stitch, dolls, vests, posters, coin purses, barbecue aprons, stationery, magnets, rubber stamps, calendars, very cool clocks with moving Felix heads, suspenders, pails, puzzles . . . you name it.

Felix, like Elvis, is forever. A "must have" for true fanatics. You know who you are.

Felix Old and New,
catalog: $2

Felix Old and New
316 Mid Valley Center, Suite 115
Carmel, CA 93923
(800) JW-FELIX

How Much Is That Kitty in the Window?

Sitting at work? Feeling a little homesick for the furry one? Just send a crisp photo or slide to these folks and they'll make a personalized screen saver of your very own kitty. Requires Windows 3.1 or higher and display capable of a minimum of 256 colors. Your photos will be returned along with the screen-saver software and the digitally processed color images, in both 8- and 24-bit formats. Great price!

Kitty Screen Saver, $19.95
(Calif. res. add 7% sales tax)

Sirius Software
P.O. Box 84463
San Diego, CA 92138
(619) 456-0109
E-mail: 70366.1264@
compuserve.com

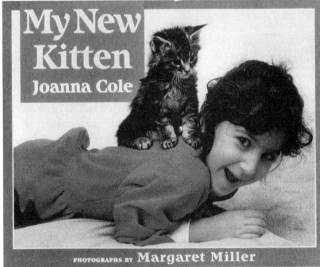

My New Kitten ®

Mama Kitty has a big tummy, and kittens are on the way. This delightful story of a young girl, her Aunt Bonnie, and her new kitten Dusty is a lovely introduction for a young child about to receive his first kitten. Sweet color photographs depict Dusty growing to the age of eight weeks, then leaving to live

happily ever after with the little girl. What could be nicer?

By Joanna Cole, 1995,
38 pp., $15

William Morrow and Company
Morrow Junior Books
1350 Avenue of the Americas
New York, NY 10019
(212) 261-6500

Cat Game Fun!

Rainy day, lazy night? Bring out the Cats at Play game and get those dice rolling as you try to be the first cat to pounce on a catnip mouse. Easy rules— just three small pages of instructions—and lots of fun twists and turns. Be warned: There are dogs in the bushes, and if you don't have an ID tag, or you get fleas, you're headed straight —nonstop—to somewhere else! Great fun for you and the kids.

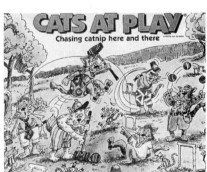

Cats at Play, $24.90
+ $4.90 S&H

Just So Games
1356 Boca Raton Dr.
Lake Oswego, OR 97034
(503) 636-0318

Who's in Charge Here? The Kitty Supervisors.

Cari Summer's got her sewing machine humming again. She makes these cool cat visors that poker-playing, party-hopping felines may wear to their favorite hot spots. Also ask for her unusual catalog of recycled cat toys. Nice products that will give you ideas about recycling stuff around the house to make your own cat toys.

Kitty Supervisors, $8
Recycled Cat Toys, $5
+ 75¢ S&H per item (Calif. res. add 7.25% sales tax)

Cari Summer
P.O. Box 61205
Santa Barbara, CA 93160
(805) 964-5950

Flying with You

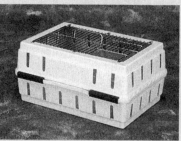

Approved by airlines as carry-on pet transportation, this Cabin Kennel slides easily under an airplane seated to provide a convenient way for Kitty to travel with you. Made from high-density luggage-grade plastic. Comes equipped with a hinge pin opening system for long-lasting service. Wire top lets you stick your fingers in and rub Kitty's head as you zap through the air. Measures 8" h. × 12¼" w. × 17" l.

Always remember to call ahead and inform the airline that you are bringing your feline friend into the cabin as carry-on baggage. Never check your pet as baggage into the hold of any plane. Too many horror stories.

Cabin Kennel, $14.98 + $4.75 S&H (Ohio res. add 6% sales tax)

Pet Warehouse
P.O. Box 310
Xenia, OH 45385
(800) 443-1160

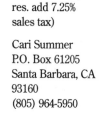

The Cat Notebook ®

Simulated parchment gives this notebook a nice feel. Plenty of room on each page for your thoughts, drawings, whatever. An occasional piece of lively cat art and a pithy cat quote on each page make for casual observation as you work your way through its blank pages. Nice price.

$5.95 + $2.50 S&H

Running Press
125 S. 22nd St.
Philadelphia, PA 19103
(800) 345-5359

The View from Here ®

To most cats, a window is their opening to the world. The house cat reclines in the sun, watching the world go by. The indoor/outdoor cat pauses to check things out before jumping through an open window to the outside world. This charming collection of blank notecards shows photographs of four cats —two from France, two from Spain—observing the world from windows in their centuries-old homes. A reassuring, timeless scene that has been repeated since man began living in houses. Twenty notecards, five each of four subjects, and twenty white envelopes.

Cats in Windows, $12.95 + $3.95 S&H (N.Y. res. add sales tax)

Galison Books
36 W. 44th St.
New York, NY 10036
(212) 354-8840

A Message for Hubby

This just about says it all. Post prominently for daily reading. Framed in light pine, and ready to nail to the wall.

Husband and Cat Missing Poster, $12.95 + $5 S&H

The Cat House
110 Crowchild Trail, NW
Calgary, Alberta
T2N 4R9
Canada
(800) MEOW-CAT

A New Look for Your Room

This colorful Kittens & Flowerpots Border is a lively way to dress up a room. Prepasted, strippable border is 20½" h. for a super decorator look. Specify your choice of flower color, either pink or violet, on each 15 ft. roll. Very pretty, and a dramatic change of decor.

Kittens & Flowerpots Border, $24.95 + 4.95 S&H (Ark. res. add 6.5% sales tax)

Cat Claws, Inc.
1004 W. Broadway
Morrilton, AR 72110
(800) 783-0977

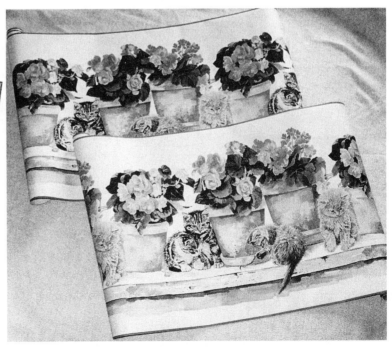

Warm Cat with Attitude

What have we here? T-shirts? For people? No, for cats! Actual miniature-size T-shirts in cool colors with great artwork and fun words. This is a real product, sort of like a kitty coat, only not as heavy. Front paws fit through the sleeves, head pokes through the neck opening, and the tail and back paws stick out of the bottom of the shirt. Expressions include: "I Eat Dogs for Lunch," "I Love Sushi," "Party Animal," "Have a Mice Day," "Cool Cat," "I Love My Vet," "Meowy Christmas," and many more. Minishirt actually makes sense when the cold weather hits. Big fun, super cute, many choices, holiday and party favorite.

Cat Knits, $9.99 + $2 S&H (Ga. res. add 6% sales tax)

Tawn Chi & Associates, Inc.
123 Fifth St., NE
Atlanta, GA 30308
(404) 872-8811

Fashion Stretch Collars

"My cat has a boring collar," you've probably muttered to yourself innumerable times. Liven things up with this stretch collar with sequins and feathers. Easily pulls off if cat gets caught; not for use with a leash or lead. Include your cat's neck size and choice of colors.

Sequin Stretch Fashion Kitty Collar, $6 + 50¢ S&H (Ohio res. add 5.5% sales tax)

The Barking Lot
10925 State Rt. 235
Findlay, OH 45840
(419) 859-BARK

TRUE CAT FACT

Controlling Hunting

Many owners don't like their cats to kill birds. Here are some simple solutions:

1. Put a bell or two on his collar, so the noise alerts birds.
2. Move your bird feeder out into the open, where there is no cover for the cat to hide in.
3. Replace the feeder on the ground with a hanging feeder you can view through your window.
4. Control the amount of spilled bird seed on the ground, which is where many birds meet their demise.
5. Develop an association between hunting and an unpleasant surprise. Buy a powerful water pistol with a long shooting range. Wait out of sight while the cat stalks a bird, and squirt him as he's about to charge.
6. Fence off your yard in such a way that the cat cannot get out. Fencing systems also exist for you to place around tree trunks to keep him out of bird nests.
7. Be patient. It takes time to change innate behavior.

Kitty ID Pouch

Far more cats than dogs have permanent stays in animal shelters. Why? Many people don't ID their cats, though they sorely miss them when they're gone.

Lots of ID options exist, including this Pet Pocket Jr., which features a water-resistant metal-snap pouch that slides onto your cat's collar. Inside is a waterproof ID card you complete, then put back into the pouch. You can also get a cool photo ID of your cat from this company. Available in six colors. Great idea. Isn't your cat worth six dollars?

Pet Pocket Jr., $4.75 + $1.25 S&H (Colo. res. add 3.8% sales tax)

Diverse Designs, Inc.
139 Harper St.
Louisville, CO 80027
(800) 786-9981

A Cat's Christmas

Experience the uplifting magic of your favorite Christmas music—sung by cats and dogs! These crazy, hilarious versions of 20 holiday classics set to witty instrumentals are sure to liven up any Christmas party.

Jingle Cats Meowy X-mas CD, $15.95 + $4.95 S&H (Minn. res. add 6.5% sales tax)

Wireless Catalog
Rivertown Trading Company
P.O. Box 64422
Saint Paul, MN 55164
(800) 663-9994
http://www.giftcatalog.com

Jean-Luc and Babe in the Mail

The card arrives from you. A colored pencil portrait of Jean-Luc, Babe, or Spumoni. Inside, a few choice words, some of your thoughts. Mail these lovely cat portraits to anyone in the world.

Jean-Luc and Friends Notecards (box of 8), $10 + $3.50 S&H (Ohio res. add 6% sales tax)

Elite Cats
825 S. Tecumseh Rd.
Springfield, OH 45506

Classy Kitty Carriers

These are some great-looking cat carriers. Each includes an interior leash and a moisture-control tray and moisture-control pad with a spare. Double-locking zipper sides. Guaranteed against breakage of supports and tearing; approved by most major airlines as carry-on luggage. There's also a glamorous gold-and-silver-trimmed pet carrier and a huge variety of other styles from which you can choose. Can you keep a secret? They also have clever coverlets for the times you or your pet desire privacy. With the coverlet in place, the pet carrier appears to be a very nice duffel bag. You can take your cat anywhere, as long as he doesn't announce his presence. No muffled meows, puleeze.

Pompous Pet Carriers
Small: $65 + $7 S&H (Calif. res. add $5.04 sales tax)
Medium: $75 + $7 S&H (Calif. res. add $5.81 sales tax)
Large: $85 & $8 S&H (Calif. res. add $7.86 S&H)

Pompous Pet Carriers & Accessories
225 N. Euclid Way
Anaheim, CA 92801
(800) 400-7789
E-mail:
sappier.@ix.net-com.com

Bavarian Kitty Angels

Here's something great for your holiday tree. Standing upright (with two golden wings) or flying (with one golden wing), each angel holds a gray mouse, and both kitty and mouse have halos. Kitty's eyes are turned up toward heaven, and the nose and tongue are pink. Available in Siamese, black, black/white, cream, red/orange, or blue/gray. Frosted balls have a dia. of 2⅝″. Beautiful colors, nice conversation pieces.

Bavarian Glass Kitty Angels,
$6.95 each + $3 S&H
(Fla. res. add 6% sales tax)

Cats 'N More
781 Aspen Dr.
South Daytona, FL 32113
(904) 322-9116

Delightful Ceramic Kitty Companions

What a group of characters! The ceramic "flat cat" vase (left) is perfect for your favorite floral creation; measures 9½″ l. × 2¾″ w. × 7¾″ h. The center figurine is pleasing to the eye. To its right, Kitty holds a picture frame (4″ w. × 5½″ h.) for your favorite 2½″ × 2¾″ photo. In front of the photo frame is a cute bank, meant for

holding those loose coins that turn into big money over time. Great for the kids. In front are salt and pepper shakers, measuring 2⅝″ h. and 2⅛″ l., and just behind the shakers is a cute ceramic bell to ring when Kitty's dinnertime rolls around.

Ceramic "Flat Cat" Vase, $12.99

Figurine, $10.99
Photo Frame, $6.99
Bank, $8.25
Salt & Pepper Shakers, $6.59 (set)
Bell, $5.25
S&H: $3.95 ($20 or less), $4.95 ($20.01 to $30), $5.95 ($30.01 to $40) (N.J. res. add 6% sales tax)

Kittytowne, USA
308 Duff Ave.
Wenonah, NJ 08090
(609) 468-3183

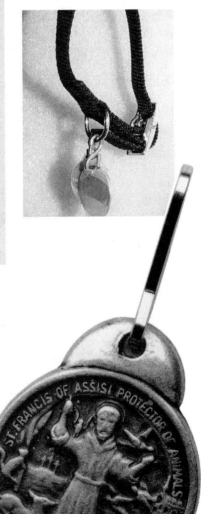

St. Francis of Assisi Tag

St. Francis of Assisi (1181–1226) is the patron saint of animals, ecology, and the nation of Italy. Born the son of a wealthy cloth merchant, he experienced a spiritual awakening after recovering from a grave illness. Unhappy with their son's new outlook on life, Francis's parents rebuked him and demanded that he give back all of the material luxuries they had provided him. Francis stripped himself naked and took a simple

brown robe tied at the waist with a rope to cover himself. Thus began the Franciscan Order, dedicated to helping the poor and spreading the message of peace. These beautiful 1″ brass tags from the loving people at Pine Tree House are an invocation of kindness and protection, as exemplified by the life of Assisi, "protector of animals." Both my cats have one, and you can too, with your cat's name, area code, and phone number

engraved on the back. No kindness goes unrewarded.

St. Francis of Assisi Pet Tag, $8 (1 tag); $15 (2 tags); $22.50 (3 tags)
S&H: 1–2 tags add 75¢, 3 or more tags add 25¢ per tag (Ariz. res. add 5% sales tax)

Pine Tree House
P.O. Box 31233
Flagstaff, AZ 86003
(520) 773-8073

The Paw ®

When night comes, Leonie, a seemingly ordinary little girl, assumes her secret identity as the Paw—cat burglar extraordinaire and heroine of the underdog. Like her idol, Robin Hood, the Paw takes from the "haves" and gives to the "have-nots." She steals caviar to give to starving cats, slips $50 bills under orphans' pillows, and after a night of adventure, climbs through her window back into her bedroom, all unbeknownst to her father. Super color illustrations, plus a *female* adventure story, for a change! Leonie's bravery and independence make her an excellent role model for little girls and a unique heroine for any child. Winner of the Honor Book Award by the Children's Book Council of Australia.

By Natalie Jane Prior, published by Allen & Unwin, Australia, 1993, 32 pp., $14

Independent Publishers Group
814 N. Franklin St.
Chicago, IL 60610
(312) 337-0747

Where Is Your Cat?

For almost 20 years, John Keane has been reuniting people with their pets. As Sherlock Bones, Tracer of Lost Pets, he's an expert when you don't have the time or resources. Sherlock consults on finding your pet, most of the time by phone, though on-site searches can be arranged anywhere in the world. His other nationwide services include personalized two-color posters (shipped to you the next day), mailing lists to people in your neighborhood, vet hospitals, groomers, pet stores, you name it. You can

Sherlock Bones ®

find out more at his Internet address, or call.

Sherlock Bones, Tracer of Lost Pets
1925 Fages Ct.
Walnut Creek, CA 94595
(800) 942-6637
http://www.sherlock.com/home/sherlock

Cat Tech Specs ®

Hilarious color poster reviews all aspects of the typical cat, much like a product description of a new car or computer. Heavy on the sales pitch and promo language; perfect framable poster for a techie who likes cats and details. Very cool.

Computa-Cat, $6

Information:
Pomegranate Calendars and Books
210 Classic Ct.
Rohnert Park, CA 94928
(800) 227-1428

Her Pillow

This decorative pillow in cat paisley design has accent cording and a gusseted cover to maintain shape. Even the most finicky cat will enjoy resting on this bed, which is completely washable. Big—22″ dia.

Cat Pillow, $27.50

Information:
Caddis Manufacturing, Inc.
3120 N. Highway 99W
McMinnville, OR 97128
(503) 472-3111

TRUE CAT FACT

Abandonment

You go to work. You come home. The drapes are shredded, the furniture is torn, the cat has chewed up your favorite plant. What's going on here? Abandonment frustration. Some cats hate to be alone. They also get intensely bored if there's nothing to do but sleep. There are many solutions, the best of which is a good view. Get one of those cat hammocks and place it next to a sunny window facing the street. Your cat will spend hours being entertained by the birds, dogs, cats, and the mailman—life, coming and going. You can also obtain a companion cat for your kitty, which is sweet when they get along. Try leaving your radio on a soothing classical-music station, not too loud. What's the objective? Between catnaps they need to be occupied! Cats are intelligent. They miss your company.

Cookies & Tea

A thoroughly incredible Cat Teapot (5″ h.) includes both the cup and the pot, with a beaming kitty holding a golden yellow fish. Absolutely great! Cat Racer Collectible Cookie Jar— driving a light green fish with red lips—stands an impressive 9¾″ h., enough to hold 112 oz.

Clay Art Cat Teapot/Cat Racer Collectible Cookie Jar, $19.99 to $25 each

Information:
Clay Art
239 Utah Ave.
San Francisco, CA 94080
(415) 244-4970

Matched Dining Set

Black-and-white cats on this high-impact fiberglass tray (12″ × 16¼″) with bright, cheery flowers make this a natural for any cat lover. Include the matching dishwasher-safe 5″ × 2″ ceramic bowl and there couldn't be a nicer way to start your day!

Happy Trails Tray, $19.95
Happy Trails Bowl, $14.95
+ $6 S&H (up to $35) (Tex. res. add 8.25% sales tax)

Happy Trails Gourmet Accessories
P.O. Box 25316
Dallas, TX 75225
(214) 696-3722

Ttouch for Cats & Kittens

What's Ttouch? It's a physical technique designed to calm and train your cat or kitten and improve or correct behavior problems, including scratching, nervousness, fear of people, biting, timidity, aloofness, fear of visits to the vet, fear of loud noises, and fighting. The package contains a video with Linda Tellington-Jones demonstrating Ttouch; a 48-page A–Z Tipbook; a 40-page Guidebook; and Flashcards as quick-reference guides to Ttouch. Linda is nationally known for her remarkable abilities with animals, which you may now learn through this video, and share with friends. Amazing package!

Ttouch Cats & Kittens, $39.95 + $5.95 S&H
(Calif. res. add 7.75% sales tax)

Thane Marketing International
78080 Calle Estado, 2nd Floor
La Quinta, CA 92253
(619) 777-0217

Natural Healing for Dogs & Cats ®

"Natural" is the key word here. Almost every conceivable natural and alternative therapy for your cat's health is explored, from massage to herbal remedies, acupressure, nutrition, vitamins and minerals, psychic healing, homeopathy, acupuncture, flower essences, and muscle testing. One of the wonderful things about living in this day and age is that you have so many choices when it comes to health care for your kitty. This is a virtual encyclopedia of alternative remedies that are moving—each and every day—into mainstream health practice. Sensitive, loving, highly informed, recommended for open-minded feline fanciers with an interest in holistic healing methods.

By Diane Stein, 1993, 186 pp., $16.95

The Crossing Press
P.O. Box 1048
Freedom, CA 95019
(800) 777-1048

Pet Fire Safety

Here's an in-home fire-detection system that takes your pet into account. When the smoke alarm senses smoke, it sounds an alarm and sends a signal to your master desktop unit, which communicates to Safe Pet's Central Station. The Central Station operator calls your house to see if it's a false alarm. If there is no answer, the operator will immediately call your local fire department. The operator tells the fire department that there's a fire and that *your pet is inside the house*. He gives them your address and tells them the type of pet you have and your pet's name, then contacts you and/or a neighbor. For an initial fee plus a monthly monitoring cost of $18 (lower if you pay by the year), you get a master system desktop unit, a wireless smoke detector, and one or more decals to place in your window. Check it out.

Safe Pet Smoke Alarm System, $299.99 + shipping
Safe Pet Decals, $4 for one + $1 S&H
(N.J. res. add 6% sales tax)

Information:
Safe Pet
91 Rockaway Dr.
Boonton, NJ 07005
(201) 335-SAFE

IN CASE OF FIRE
PLEASE SAVE MY
PET

DECALS SUPPLIED by SAFE PET (201)335-SAFE

Party Surprises!

These are a scream. Cats look great in bow ties! Each of the Classy Cat "safety stretch" bow-tie collars comes in sizes 10″–12⅜″ (small) and 12″–14⅜″ (large) in fabulous patterns, including a classy red with white dots, a wild leopard pattern, stars and stripes for the Fourth of July, blue with white dots, black, black-and-white plaid, green, red with paisley (for that distinguished hippy look), red Scotch plaid (for that "Scottish" look), pink (perfect for the feline lady of the house), royal blue, and gorgeous red to accommodate your kitty's personality. Super quality. They might even do in a pinch for a very skinny man of the house!

Classy Cat Bow Tie Collars,
$8.99 + $1 S&H
(N.J. res. add 6% sales tax)

Little Giant Products
P.O. Box 51
Bogota, NJ 07603
(201) 833-2555
E-mail: 103224.2700@compuserve.com

The Little Old Woman and the Hungry Cat

BY NANCY POLETTE
PICTURES BY FRANK MODELL

The Little Old Woman and the Hungry Cat

What if your cat ruled your life? This rather insufferable feline lives with a pleasant old lady. He proceeds to eat not only all her cupcakes, but everything else that comes his way. In the end he's put in his place, but it's a struggle of wills. Who wants a tyrant—either two-or four-legged—in the house?

By Nancy Polette, 1989, 22 pp., $12.95

William Morrow & Co.
Greenwillow Books
1350 Avenue of the Americas
New York, NY 10019
(212) 261-6500

Cat Mailbox Flag

Bright red kitty with south-western motif will bring a smile each day to your mail-man and neighbors. Solid steel with durable baked-on finish; complies with postal regulation. Universal mount-ing bracket and hardware included. Easy to install.

Cat Mailbox Flag, $16.90 + $3.50 S&H (Mass. res. add 5% sales tax)

The Catnip Trading Company
P.O. Box 451
Lexington, MA 02173
(800) 822-8647

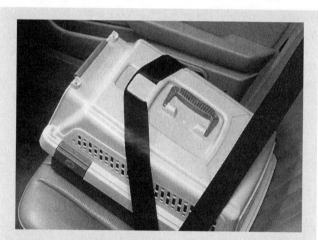

Furrarri on Wheels! ®

The Lil' Furrari Pet Carrier is one of the best for safe automobile trans-portation of your kitty. Designed to work with seat-belt-compatible clips, it's available in opaque or translucent models, two sizes for each. Features four-sided ventilation, quick-release latches, dual door lock, a heavy-duty front door, smooth grateless interior, and it meets all airline safety regulations. Take it from the car to the plane. Limited five-year warranty.

Lil' Furrari Pet Carrier, $20 (small); $40 (large)

Information:
Dogloo, Inc.
1241 Old Temescal
Corona, CA 91719
(909) 279-9500
E-mail: dogloo1@aol.com

Inscrutable Kitty Vase

Elegant in style and design, this hand-painted lac-quered porcelain vase features the lovely vis-age of a rather inscrutable cat, which to all appear-ances has a smile like that of the Mona Lisa. Green-checked border; 11″ h.; black-and-white cat; pleasing rich green patina. It awaits your bouquet.

Cat Porcelain Vase, $69.95 + $7.95 S&H (N.J. res. add 6% sales tax)

Kittytowne, USA
308 Duff Ave.
Wenonah, NJ 08090
(609) 468-3183

TRUE CAT FACT

Always Starved

You know the scenario. The cat comes up to you, makes eye contact, and demands more food. Most people either serve Kitty two meals a day, like clockwork, or play it by ear and leave food out all day. I recommend the all-day method, provided Kitty has a little self-restraint. Yacking up at night on the carpet? Remove the food before you go to bed. Turning up his nose at food from the fridge? Warm it. Cats like food served warm, not hot. Cat eating the dog's food? Okay in small amounts, but he won't get all the nutrients he needs from dog food. Always famished? Have the vet check him for tapeworms (from fleas), diabetes, or a thyroid condition. Be careful of feeding him too much liver, which can build up vitamin A to toxic body levels. A cat cannot live on a vegetarian diet (he could go blind), nor can he live solely on meat (bad for bones and growth). You must intelligently decide what's good for your cat, even if he's a fussy epicure or hung up on junk food.

Trouble-Free ®

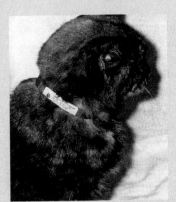

Tabby Tags include information about your kitty directly on the collar. They're suspended from a red expandable collar with a Velcro closure, so there's less chance Kitty will get in trouble by snagging his collar or tags. Makes sense.

Tabby Tags, $6.99
(Calif. res. add 7% sales tax)

Information:
Winterburn Enterprises, Inc.
4546 El Camino Real
B-10, Suite 340
Los Altos, CA 94022
(408) 735-7526

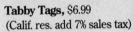

Dollhouse Toys & Furniture!

Now your dollhouse can include lovingly crafted super-realistic cat toys and furniture. Created by Joan Mrazik on a scale of 1 ft. = 1 in., these tiny, colorful toys belong in every dollhouse in America. Now your doll's cat can have it all.

Cat Teepee, $7
Play Tunnel, $7
Single Condo, $7.50
Double Condo, $9
Tall Post, $12
Birdie Bopper, $5
Doorknob Scratcher, $2

Carpeted Post, $6
Sisal Scratching Post, $7.50
(N.J. res. add 6% sales tax)

Daffodil Dolls
484 Sylvan St.
Saddle Brook, NJ 07663
(201) 843-8372

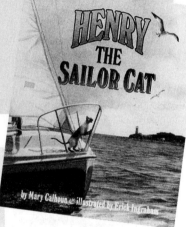

Henry the Sailor Cat ®

Henry the cat wants to go sailing with his owners, a father and son, and the only way to do it is to stow away onboard ship. Henry is soon at the top of the mast, enjoying the view, watching dolphins and whales cruise by. But it's not a smooth cruise for long. Henry saves the day when Dad falls overboard.

By Mary Calhoun, 1994, 40 pp., $15

William Morrow & Co.
Morrow Junior Books
1350 Avenue of the Americas
New York, NY 10019
(212) 261-6500

Kitty Banks for Kids

Kids can watch their savings mount up with these two see-through cat coin banks. Both feature movable eyes, and a heart-shaped stopper that's easily removed for inserting coins and bills. Handcrafted in the USA. Choose from either the Reclining Cat (left, measures 10″ l. × 6¼″ h. × 1½″ w.) or Sitting Pretty (11″ h. × 6½″ l.) banks. Great gift idea for kids!

Reclining Cat Bank or **Sitting Pretty Bank,** $19.95 each + $3.95 S&H (N.J. res. add 6% sales tax)

Kittytowne, USA
308 Duff Ave.
Wenonah,
NJ 08090
(609) 468-3183

More Trips with Kitty

Though they can look alike, all cat carriers are not created equal. Many offer combinations of zippers, windows, and easy ways to get the cat in and out. The Prime Pet Designer Carrying Bag is durable, featuring strong handles and shoulder straps. It includes mesh panels on two sides for ventilation and visibility. Available in Tunnel Green and Tunnel Red.

Prime Pet Designer Carrying Bag, $59 + $5 S&H (Calif. res. add 8.25% sales tax)

Prime Pet Products
260 S. Beverly Dr., Suite 301
Beverly Hills, CA 90212
(310) 273-5364

Rhinestone Collar ®

The UltraSuede Kitty Collar is a decorative collar for the cat with class. Easily snipped to fit your kitty's neck, it features wonderful, soft UltraSuede fabric dotted with genuine rhinestones for that glittery, upscale look. You know she deserves this!

UltraSuede Rhinestone Kitty Collar, $6.50

Information:
UltraMouse, Ltd.
123 Assembly Ct.
Cary, NC 27511
(800) 573-8869

Gleaming Kitty Key Holder

The shining brass of this key holder includes hooks for five sets of keys. Measures 6½" l. Includes two mounting screws for easy installation on the wall, near the door. Attractive, smooth feline.

Brass Cat Key Holder, $9 + $5 S&H

The Cat House
110 Crowchild Trail, NW
Calgary, Alberta T2N 4R9
Canada
(800) MEOW-CAT

All About Himalayan Cats ®

I love the personalities of my Himalayans, Rollo and Bella. They're affectionate, love to play, and the moment you sit down, they join you. Great cats. Naturally, I read this hardcover with particular interest: It provides interesting details on Himalayan history, grand champions, basic care, and personality. Thorough book with more than 90 photos on just about everything you'll need to know to enjoy your furry friends.

By Joan McDonald Brearley, 1976, 160 pp., $17.95

Information:
TFH Publications, Inc.
One TFH Plaza
Third and Union Ave.
Neptune City, NJ 07753
(908) 988-8400

Cup Cats

Keep your coffee warm in these white ceramic cat cups, complete with paw lids. Cats are gray-and-black twins, with rosy noses and green eyes. Holds 10 oz. of your favorite beverage. Comes as a set of two cups; lids also work as coasters.

Ceramic Cat Mugs, $14.95 (pair) + $2 S&H (Minn. res. add 6.5% sales tax)

Chandler Enterprises
Suite 2904 Galtier Plaza
168 E. Sixth St.
St. Paul, MN 55101
(612) 291-0498

Pewter Kitty Tags ®

Who said cat tags have to be boring? These decorative, whimsical tags are fashioned from cast pewter and plated in silver or gold. Ten styles for you to choose from. Double O-ring is easily attached to Kitty's collar.

Kitty Fashion Tags, $6 + $1 S&H (Calif. res. add 8.5% sales tax)

Laid Back Enterprises
4020 Will Rogers Pkwy.
Oklahoma City, OK 73108
(800) 764-9552

LID ACTS AS A COASTER
10 OZ. CAPACITY

Personalized Cat Signs

These heavy-duty weatherproof cat signs are personalized with your kitty's name. Put one up, inside or outside the house, to let folks know who's really the owner of the place. Nice catalog of designs for your cat's special personality.

Personalized Cat Signs, yellow or white, $12.95 (N.Y. res. add 8% sales tax)

FunCraft Designs
P.O. Box 750
Rensselaer, NY 12144
(518) 432-8550

My Gr-r-reat Uncle Tiger

When Marmaduke the tabby cat discovers a picture of a tiger, he decides they must be related—after all, they both have yellow eyes and stripes. Off he and his friends go to the

zoo, where they meet his "uncle" Tiger with unexpected results. There is a subtle lesson here that encourages very young children (ages 2–6) to think before they speak. Humorous text; big splashy illustrations.

By James Riordan (illustrated by Alex Ayliffe), 1995, 32 pp., $14.95

Peachtree Publishers, Inc.
494 Armour Circle, NE
Atlanta, GA 30324
(404) 876-8761

Good Products, Good Cause

Felines, Inc., is a nonprofit group that runs a shelter for abandoned cats in Chicago. Volunteers do most of the work. They have an adoption program, a spay/neuter program, pet counseling, and a sponsorship program, where, for a tax-deductible $10 a month, you can help with food and medical expenses for one special cat, whose photo and background information you'll receive. These are nice people, and they sell products to help

pay for the shelter. Scrappy Kitty is a very cute patchwork kitten with a big red ribbon. The Cross-Stitch Kitty has blue eyes, a pink nose and mouth, and green-and-black shadings. The Kitty Christmas Stocking (shown) is green with a red-and-white cat and a lace-trimmed top with a red ribbon loop for hanging. The Cat Sweatshirt has nice white line art on a long-sleeved black sweatshirt. Ask your local shel-

ter about cat products they might sell. Many do.

Scrappy Kitty, $12 + $2 S&H
Cross-Stitch Kitty, $10 + $2 S&H
Kitty Christmas Stocking, $10 + $2 S&H
Cat Sweatshirt, $20 + $3 S&H
(Ill. res. add 7.25% sales tax)

Felines, Inc.
The Shelter for Abandoned Cats
P.O. Box 60616
Chicago, IL 60660
(312) 465-4132

Annoying Stray Cats

Stray cats can be pests, using your garden as a litter box and upsetting your indoor cats. Here are some tips for safely keeping away strays:

1. If a stray cat "marks" (sprays) on the walls of your house, pour on some inexpensive distilled vinegar and rinse off with the hose. Vinegar eliminates the marking odor, and cats hate the smell.
2. Mark the outside territory of your yard with feces from your cat's litter box.
3. Orange and lemon rinds are offensive to cats. Sprinkle those around the outside of your yard, or wherever the stray enters and hangs out. Replace these deterrents each week. (Incidentally, lightly rubbing an orange peel on furniture will discourage your cat from using it as a scratching post.)
4. If nothing else works, make some noise. Take an empty soda can, add some pennies, tape it closed, and next time you see the stray in your yard, toss it his way. Don't try to *hit* the cat, just frighten him to discourage him from entering your, and your kitty's, territory.

Kitty Mirrors

These handcrafted mirrors, made of solid oak with an early American molding, showcase handsome felines while reflecting your rooms' decor. You can choose from the Smokey Cat with a hand-gilded frame (left) or the Tabby Cat with a maple-stain finish

Overall size is 10″ w. × 18″ h. Solid Yankee quality.

Cat Mirrors, $75 + $8 S&H (Mass. res. add 5% sales tax)

Kensington Cat Company
162 Main St., Suite E
Wenham, MA 01984
(800) 772-6615
E-mail: kenscat@aol.com

Kitty Celebration Songs

Garrison Keillor joins German opera superstar Frederica Von Stade and noted conductor Philip Brunelle on this all-new recording of 16 songs that celebrate cats. Enchanting recording; 70 minutes on one cassette or CD.

Songs of the Cat, $11 (cassette); $13.95 (CD); + $2.95 S&H (Minn. res. add 6.5% sales tax)

Highbridge Audio Catalog
P.O. Box 64541
St. Paul, MN 55164
(800) 755-8532

Colorful Kitty Wastebasket

Finally, a use for those plastic grocery bags with handles. They slip perfectly over the heart-carved arms of this really nice wastebasket, serving as liners. Colorful cat paintings in a variety of designs on select hardwood makes this an exceptional and amusing wastebasket. Call for the design of your choice.

Kitty Hardwood Wastebasket, $35 + S&H

Cats 'N More
781 Aspen Dr.
South Daytona, FL 32113
(904) 322-9116

The Cat's Meow: Purr-fect Quilts for Cat Lovers ®

The love that people put into their quilts—incredible colors, gorgeous patterns—never ceases to amaze me. The sheer time and commitment speak volumes about their dedication to the creative process. This excellent book includes 19 original cat-quilt patterns, including clever designs like a one-eyed cat peeping into a seafood store. The author is an avid quilter who teaches and lectures in the Pacific Northwest about quilt making.

By Janet Kime, 1994, 96 pp., $19.95
Add $4 S&H (Wash. res. add 8.2% sales tax)

That Patchwork Place
P.O. Box 118
Bothell, WA 98041
(800) 426-3126

Christmas Kitty Tree

Elizabeth B. Doss of McClellanville, South Carolina, has been making her hand-painted kitty ornaments for years. Each is from an original design, they're unbreakable (good idea for an ornament), and each is suspended from an attached gold or silver cord. Angel Cat (center) is a sizable 5″ in dia., while the Silver Cat (top) and Black Cat (bottom) each measure 4″ in dia. Handcrafted originals you'll cherish for many holidays to come.

Silver Cat, Black Cat, $15 each; **Angel Cat,** $21 + $2.50 S&H (S.C. res. add 5% sales tax)

Christmas Cats & Details
9977 Alert Rd.
McClellanville, SC 29458
(803) 887-3965

Kitty Shoulder Tote

Take a stroll around town—or to the vet—with this acrylic-coated nylon bag on your shoulder. You can also remove the convenient padded strap, and use the adjustable handles. Two screened windows with flaps. Available in navy or red.

Le Pet Bag, $19.29 (S) + $5.95 S&H; $21.98 (M) and $24.18 (L) + $6.95 S&H (Pa. res. add 6% sales tax)

Discount Master Animal Care Catalog
P.O. Box 3333
Mountaintop, PA 18707
(800) 346-0749

101 Reasons Why a Cat Is Better than a Man Ⓡ

Do we detect a note of cynicism here? Anybody who can come up with 101 reasons is definitely sold on the idea that cats make better companions. Naturally, most of the reasons make complete sense!

By Allia Zobel, 1994, 74 pp., $5.95

Bob Adams, Inc.
260 Center St.
Holbrook, MA 02343
(800) 872-5627

Cat on a Hot Beach

Who says the cat gets to use this great towel? Perfect for the beach, the heavy white Cool Cat Towel measures a big 35″ × 60″ and is printed in aqua, magenta, California yellow, and black. Cool Cat T-shirt of 100% cotton comes in all the usual sizes and match-es the towel.

Cool Cat Beach Towel, $19.95 + $3.95 S&H
Cool Cat T-Shirt, $14.95 + $3.95 S&H (Calif. res. add sales tax)

Rabbit Foot, Inc.
23247 Oxnard St.
Woodland Hills, CA 91367
(800) 228-6902

The Cat's Towel ™

The Good-Luck Cat

Dating from at least the 13th century and known for its silver-blue coat and green eyes, the Korat is known as Si-Sawat in Thailand: *Si* meaning "color" and *Sawat* meaning "prosperity." A gift of this cat bestows prosperity and good luck on the recipient. Intelligent, loving cats, they are held in high esteem and often given as very special gifts.

Glorious Cat Teapot

Your favorite cup of Earl Grey or jasmine tea tumbles into your cup from the raised paw of this very attractive and affordable Kitty Teapot. Carefully detailed, hand-painted, ready to greet you each morning or evening by the fireplace. Measures 5″ l. × 5½″ h.

Raised Paw Kitty Teapot, $4.99 + $3.95 S&H (N.J. res. add 6% sales tax)

Kittytowne, USA
308 Duff Ave.
Wenonah, NJ 08090
(609) 468-3183

Kids' Kitty Sled

When was the last time you saw a hand-painted sled? It's a great children's gift for winter, available in either small (approx. 20″ l.) or large (approx. 30″). Hand-crafted; wooden runners; a variety of kitty designs; finished with multiple coats of varnish and hand-rubbed with paste wax for a durable finish.

If you ask, they can customize the sled with the name of your choice.

Children's Decorative Sled, $30 to $75

Cats 'N More
781 Aspen Dr.
South Daytona, FL 32113
(904) 322-9116

TV Cats from Dr. Jim

Dr. Jim Humphries is a nationally recognized veterinarian and radio and TV host and columnist. He's a nice guy who knows what he's talking about, and his video will fill you in on just about everything you need to know to select a cat, and feed and train her for a long, happy life. From obesity and exercise to the five most common behavior problems —plus entertainment and toys—this is a 90-minute gem for cat fanciers. He's the best, with a heart.

Current Cat Care, $19.95 + $3.50 S&H (Tex. res. add 8.25% sales tax)

St. Francis Productions, Inc.
4444 Westgrove Dr.
Suite 300
Dallas, TX 75248
(214) 380-6500
http://rampages.onramp.net/~drjim

Smooth Tile Cats

Ceramic tiles look great as a display, but they look even better on a countertop or embedded in a wall. Marracini makes nice stuff: good-quality tiles with pleasing cat designs. You can purchase one tile or a hundred. The Cat & Hearts 4″ × 4″ tile is $5.95 or $11.95 mounted on a wood heart. The Persian is a 6″ × 6″ trivet, or tile picture for hanging, $9.95 with a cork backing. You can also have it mounted on a heart frame. The

orange Sleeping Kitty or black-and-white Sitting Kitty (above) each measure 12″ × 12″. Many more in their catalog; custom work (below) available.

Marracini Studios
1010 E. Gaucho Circle
Deltona, FL 32725
(407) 321-8897

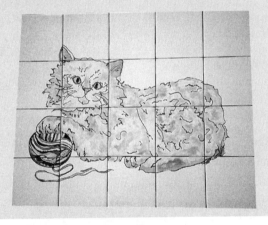

Don't Eat the Bird That Sings for You

Gloria Mulder from Santa Maria, California, makes these fun, dishwasher-safe tiles and mugs. Tile is 6″ square. Both have the same pithy saying, which, if you think about it, makes sense. She also makes ceramic cat

ornaments, cat notecards, and other kitty goodies.

Ceramic Kitty Tile and Mug, $20 each (includes S&H)

Charis
4298 Eastwood Dr.
Santa Maria, CA 93455
(805) 937-2002

Old-World Christmas

Heinz Mueller-Blech of Inge-Glass in Bavaria is the thirteenth generation of his family to produce Old World Christmas glass ornaments, many from molds not used since the 1930s. Cats Who Come for Christmas offers Heinz's work, as well as traditional handmade European glass ornaments from Whitehurst, Kurt S. Adler, and other importers. These are among the very best designs, from vintage molds passed through many generations of artisans. Mad Hatter's Tea Party—an antique store with a year-round display of these superior objects—offers an ever-changing catalog of fabulous ornaments, including collectible cat ornaments. Among the very best in the world.

Cats Who Come for Christmas Ornaments
Catalog: $3 (refundable with purchase)

Mad Hatter's Tea Party
46 Central St.
Ipswich, MA 01938
(508) 356-9444

Where Are You Going, Little Mouse? ®

Little Mouse thinks nobody loves him. Not his mother, nor his father nor his sister, nor his brother. What to do? Well . . . thankfully he doesn't go too far, and we're all relieved when he realizes things aren't nearly as bad as he imagines. In fact, life is good. Featuring Little Mouse's imaginary adventures with a six-eyed cat, this helpful little illustrated book is for when a child fears "nobody loves me."

By Robert Kraus, 1986, 32 pp., $16

Greenwillow Books 1350 Avenue of the Americas New York, NY 10019 (212) 261-6500

Slightly Bent Kitty

Actually, *very* bent. This heirloom-quality steam-bent wooden box has a faux burl finish on the inside, painted sides and bottom, and different kitty designs on top. Each piece is finished with multiple layers of varnish and hand-rubbed with paste wax for lasting beauty. Boxes come in a variety of sizes, shapes, and detail.

Bentwood Box with Cat, $25 to $120

Cats 'N More 781 Aspen Dr. South Daytona, FL 32113 (904) 322-9116

Les Chats Writing Tools

The Steinlen Cats Stationery includes 25 each of the following: 10″ × 7½″ writing paper, second sheets, envelopes, and self-adhesive stickers. The stationery is die-cut at the top, silhouetting cats in their various poses. From the collection of the Museum of Fine Arts, in Boston.

Steinlen Cats Stationery, $19.90 + $4 S&H (Mass. res. add 5% sales tax)

The Catnip Trading Company P.O. Box 451 Lexington, MA 02173 (800) 822-8647

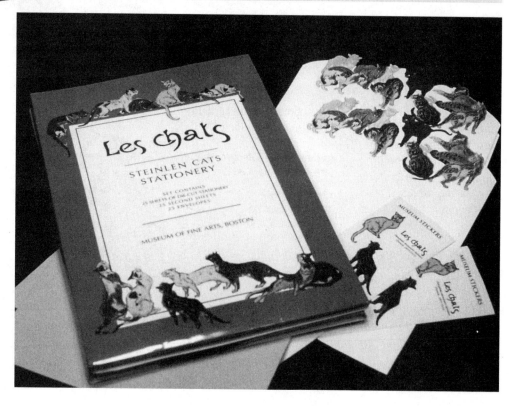

Seven Kitties on a Wall

Where'd I leave the keys? That's a common refrain around most households, but now cats can help keep you organized. This amusing and practical 7″ brass key holder is just right for keeping keys in one place.

Sitting Cats Wall Key Holder, $14.95 + $3.95 S&H (N.J. res. add 6% sales tax)

Kittytowne, USA
308 Duff Ave.
Wenonah, NJ 08090
(609) 468-3183

Come Out and Play, Little Mouse ®

The huge orange house kitty keeps asking the house mouse to play. Wisely, the mouse stalls, but eventually he runs out of excuses. What was supposed to be play turns into something else, but I'm not going to reveal the happy ending. Beautifully illustrated, lively book for young children!

By Robert Kraus, 1987, 32 pp., $16

William Morrow & Co.
Greenwillow Books
1350 Avenue of the Americas
New York, NY 10019
(212) 261-6500

The Senior Cat

A senior cat has special needs. Rich foods, such as red meat, need to be decreased in favor of smaller, more frequent meals, which put less of a strain on the digestive system. Try more chicken and fish, and consider vitamin and mineral supplements, which can put a new strut in his step. Keep fluid consumption up, so the kidneys excrete properly. If constipation is a problem, reduce dry food and try bran in his meals. Kitty laxatives are also available. Have your cat checked by the vet every half year or so. Common senior kitty conditions—largely treatable—include arthritis, kidney disease, mouth and teeth problems (don't forget to brush), and heart problems. Bonding and grooming go together. Your senior cat will appreciate the extra attention.

Bright Kitty Collars ®

Beastie Bands for cats come in lightweight nylon-laminated neoprene with lots of fun designs, including this bright yellow fish on a teal blue collar. Trim-to-fit design; Velcro closure. Fun collars.

Beastie Bands for Cats, $5

Information:
Derbographx
502 W. Seacliff Dr.
Aptos, CA 95003
(408) 662-0866

Kitty Angels Everywhere

The glorious illustrations of Julie Ticota Davis look exceptional on her T-shirts, sweatshirts, zipper/grocery tote bags, notecards, and postcards. I've been carrying one of her heavy-duty 100% cotton canvas (12″ w. × 17″ h.) grocery tote bags to the beach for the past year or so, and it's held up just fine. Cats with wings, cats sitting on a crescent moon, cats as glorious angels, cats lovingly rendered on everything she makes. If you love cats, and mystery, and angels, check out her catalog.

Grocery Tote Bag, $17.95 (Mo. res. add 6.45% sales tax)

Angels Afoot
P.O. Box 3002
Joplin, MO 64803
(417) 781-7190
E-mail: angelsaft@aol.com

Ceramic Kitty Switches

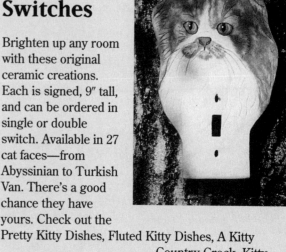

Brighten up any room with these original ceramic creations. Each is signed, 9″ tall, and can be ordered in single or double switch. Available in 27 cat faces—from Abyssinian to Turkish Van. There's a good chance they have yours. Check out the Pretty Kitty Dishes, Fluted Kitty Dishes, A Kitty Country Crock, Kitty Spoon Rest, and Kitty trivets in their free catalog. And make sure you specify the cat face of your choice prior to ordering!

Kitty Light Switch Plates, $14.95 + $4.95 S&H (Fla. res. add 6% sales tax)

Marracini Studios
1010 E. Gaucho Circle
Daytona, FL 32725
(407) 321-8897

CD Cats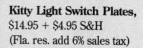

Multimedia Cats is the first interactive CD of the world's cats—large and small, domestic and wild, adult and kitten. Use the Cat-Scan feature to search for your cat, or browse the many breeds, enjoying the full-motion video, CD-quality audio, and stunning photography. Available at many software outlets, or buy it direct.

Multimedia Cats
Interactive CD-ROM for
Mac/Win $29.95 + $5.95 S&H
(Colo. res. add 7% sales tax)

Inroads Interactive
Affiliated label of: Broderbund
1050 Walnut St., Suite 301
Boulder, CO 80302
(303) 444-0632
E-mail: inroadsint@aol.com

Outrageous Cat Mailbox

U.S. mail being handled by animals? Looks like it, with this delightful cat mailbox. Made in the USA, postmaster-approved, rust-resistant, hand-crafted and -painted quality, can be personalized just for you. Ran over your mailbox recently? They'll replace it free with "mailbox insurance." Just about the *coolest* mail-boxes on Earth.

Cat Mailbox, $59 + $7.90 S&H (Calif. res. add $4.58 sales tax)

More Than a Mailbox, Inc.
The Foundry Wharf
617 B 2nd St.
Petaluma, CA 94952
(800) 331-3252

Monkey Cat on the Table

Let's liven things up a little bit. This light-colored natural-wood cutout will playfully hold your napkins on the table day and night, never tiring, and he's always in a good mood. Measures about 5″ × 5″, nicely crafted.

Wooden Cat Napkin Holder, $15 + $5 S&H

The Cat House
110 Crowchild Trail, NW
Calgary, Alberta T2N 4R9
Canada
(800) MEOW-CAT

Along Came Toto

Percy the dog loves to be alone. Toto the kitten loves to be with Percy. All the time. Every-where. Never a moment alone. Can they work this out and still be friends? Big, splashy art. For very young children, ages 2 and up.

By Annie Axworthy, 1995, 30 pp., $4.99

Candlewick Press
2067 Massachusetts Ave.
Cambridge, MA 02140
(617) 661-3330

TRUE CAT FACT

Contagious Anxiety

Do people make their cats uptight? It's widely accepted by veterinarians that stressed-out humans often have stressed-out cats. Cats under stress will obsessively lick their legs and stomach, frequently pulling out the fur and becoming bald in those areas. Cats feel, on a conscious level, the anxiety of their own-ers. People worried about their jobs or other issues transmit anxiety to their cats, who act it out.

World's Toughest Cat?

The Norwegian forest cat is at home in the freezing temperatures of Scandinavia, and prefers it that way. The breed has existed naturally in the wild for thousands of years, but due to declining numbers, a serious effort to breed routinely this wonderful cat was undertaken in the 1970s. They're big—as large as or larger than the Maine coon cat—and are available in the U.S. in limited numbers. Persian-like in appearance, longhaired, strong, and highly intelligent, they have an affable personality and enjoy nothing better than being with people. A perfect cat for a country home in a cold climate.

All About Siamese Cats ®

Breeder and fancier Barbara Burns has written a very thorough book on the Siamese, one of the most popular breeds. Printed on super-laminated pages, the color photos seem to pop off the page. The content justifies this extra effort: There's a thorough review of the Siamese as a breed; information on how to buy a kitten; training and care; grooming; nutrition; health; injuries; how to decide whether to breed your cat; CFA show standards; and more. A well-written addition to your Siamese library.

By Barbara S. Burns, 1993, 160 pp., $23.95

Information:
TFH Publications
One TFH Plaza
Third and Union Aves.
Neptune City, NJ 07753
(908) 988-8400

Kitty Music Culture

Providing culture, enrichment, and education for your kitty should be one of your life goals—I know it's high on my list. *Classical Cats* is 60-plus minutes of retitled classical works, e.g., George Bizet's "Danse Boheme" from *Carmen* becomes "The Great Mouse Hunt." Recordings are introduced with the orchestra tuning up, complete with authentic cat meows. Includes a small sample of catnip for listening pleasure.

Classical Cats, $9.98 (cassette) + $3.95 S&H; $15.98 (CD) + $3.95 S&H (N.Y. res. add sales tax)

Zanicorn Entertainment
355 W. 52nd St., 6th Floor
New York, NY 10019
(800) 760-MEOW

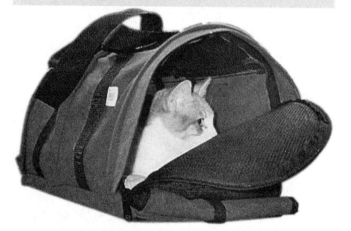

On the Road, Again

Moving Kitty around requires a good carrier. Something comfortable, soft-sided, with plenty of ventilation and windows so he can check out the scene around him. The Sturdi-Bag is Scotchgarded to keep Kitty dry, and includes a washable pillow for comfort. Add in the cedar baseboard —which keeps the floor sturdy while repelling nasty fleas—and the removable fiberglass rods that help the carrier keep its shape, and you're both ready to hit the road. Many attractive color choices.

Sturdi-Bag, $85 (S); $90 (M); $100 (L); + $6.95 S&H

Sturdi-Bag, Inc.
P.O. Box 3546
Everett, WA 98203
(206) 347-1690

Spectacular Cat Prints

Greenwich Workshop publishes some of the finest gallery-quality prints anywhere. Clockwise from top left: *Basket Cases* and *Bag Ladies,* by Braldt Bralds; *Pavane in Gold* (reclining cat), by John Simpkins; and *Big Gray's Barn and Bistro,* by Bonnie Marris are just a sampling of their extraordinary collection. All are colorful limited editions, available at art galleries and authorized Greenwich Workshop dealers in the U.S., Canada, and the U.K.

Basket Cases, $150
Bag Ladies, $150
Pavane in Gold, $175
Big Gray's Barn & Bistro, $150

The Greenwich Workshop, Inc.
One Greenwich Pl.
Shelton, CT 06484
(800) 577-0666

The Allure of the Cat ®

Quite possibly the most beautiful book of cat photography you will ever see. Accompanying text provides an interesting history of cat breeds and the early domestication of cats in Egypt, along with additional information on feline hair types, coat colors and patterns, eye color, and domestic cat classification. First and foremost, though, the great appeal of this book is the extraordinary cat photography by Tetsu Yamazaki. Expect plenty of oohs and aahs when you give this stunning hardcover.

By Richard H. Gebhardt and John Bannon, photography by

Tetsu Yamazaki, 1992, 304 pp., $79.95

TFH Publications, Inc.
One TFH Plaza
Third and Union Aves.
Neptune City, NJ 07753
(908) 988-8400

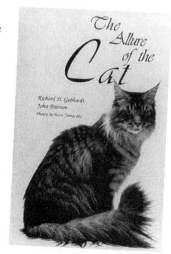

The Circle of Hearts

Sometimes my cats wear bow ties around the house. Sometimes they wear this very sweet, pink Circle of Hearts collar. It's superlightweight, adjustable (fits 6″ to 12″ kitty necks), and has a Velcro tab closure. My cats wear one for a few days; then we try something else.

Circle of Hearts Cat Collar, $3 + $1 S&H (Ill. res. add sales tax)

FoxStone Creations
P.O. Box 205
Mount Prospect, IL 60056
(708) 427-8384

Dream Litter Box

No more scooping? No more odors? No more gagging? As much as we love our cats, we all face the same problems with the litter box. This amazing machine electronically senses, using an infrared electric eye, when your cat has used the litter box. Ten minutes later, a computer chip instructs a comb to sift through the litter box, dragging away all clumped litter and waste and dumping it into an airtight waste container. The comb then returns to its original position, waiting for the next visit. When the waste container is full, just empty and reuse, or replace with a new one. Plugs into any wall outlet but can also operate on eight D batteries in the event of a power failure or when electricity isn't available. Many cats will choose the carpet over a dirty litter box. Now the box is always clean.

Comtrad Industries
2820 Waterford Lake Drive
Suite 102
Midlothian, VA 23113
(800) 992-2966

Littermaid System, $199
+ $16 S&H
Waste Container Refills (4), $11 + $4 S&H

Embroidered Just for You

Karin Rylander embroiders aprons, tea towels, and personalized cat collars. Aprons come in a variety of materials, one size, with two pockets. Tea towels with trim include various cat sayings ("Home Is Where the Cat Is"); Cat Collars are embroidered with your cat's name and phone number in your choice of red, royal blue, black, white, yellow, pink, and bright orange. Everything embroidered!

Embroidered Aprons, $16
+ $3 S&H
Tea Towels, $8 each,
$15 for two
Personalized Cat Collars,
$12.95 + $2.50 S&H
(Ontario res. add sales tax)

Embroider Anything
125 Rue du Comte
Plantagenet, Ontario
Canada K0B-1L0
(613) 673-2980

National Cat Associations

American Cat Association
8101 Katherine
Panorama City, CA 91402

American Cat Fancier's
Association
P.O. Box 203
Point Lookout, MO 65726

Canadian Cat Association
52 Dean St.
Brampton, Ontario
Canada L6W 1M6

Cat Fanciers Association
P.O. Box 1005
Manasquan, NJ 08738
http://www. cfainc.org/cfa/

Cat Fanciers Federation
9509 Montgomery Rd.
Cincinnati, OH 45242

The International Cat
Association
P.O. Box 2684
Harlingen, TX 78551
http://www.alaka.net/
~denalimc/tica.html

The Traditional Cat
Association
1000 Pegasus Farms La.
Alpharetta, GA 30201
http://www.covestoft.com/
tca/

United Cat Federation
5510 Ptolemy Way
Mira Loma, CA 91752

Cat Breed Clubs

Western Abyssinian Cat Club
http://www.taysntufts.com/
wacc/

American Curl Cat Club
100 Westmont Rd.
Syracuse, NY 13218

National American
Shorthair Club
1331 N. Wingra Dr.
Madison, WI 53715

National Birman Fanciers
P.O. Box 1830
Stephenville, TX 76401

International Bombay Society
5782 Dalton Dr.
Farmington, NY 14426

United Burmese Cat Fanciers
2395 NE 185th St.
N. Miami Beach, FL 33180

Calico Cats Registry
P.O. Box 944
Morongo Valley, CA 92256

Cameo Cat Club of America
1800 W. Ardel
Kuna, ID 83635

Chartreux East
305 Aylee Ave., NW
Leesburg, VA 22075

Les Amis des Chartreux (USA)
202 Scott Ave.
Nashville, TN 37206

Club du Chat des Chartreux
(Europe)
M. Simonnet
66 rue de Ponthieu
75008 Paris
France

Cornish Rex Society
720 Fisherville Rd.
Fisherville, KY 40023

Cymric Cat Club
1307 W. 134th St., #25
Gardenia, CA 90246

Egyptian Mau Club
52 Gregory Rd.
Framingham, MA 01701

Feral Cat Coalition
http://www.electriciti.com/
~rsavage/fcc.html

Happy Household Pet Cat Club
Membership Dept.
8862 Sharkey Ave.
Elk Grove, CA 95624
http://www.best.com/~slewis
/HHPCC/

Havana Brown Fanciers
893 Lincoln Ct.
San Jose, CA 95125

The Himalayan Society
P.O. Box 17343
Anaheim, CA 92817

Internet Cat Club
http://www.taylsntufts.com/
~icc/

Japanese Bobtail Breeders
Society
1272 Hillwood La.
Vineland, NJ 08360

Maine Coon Breeders and
Fanciers Association
http://www.mcooncat.com/
gentle-giants/mcbfa.html

Maine Coon Club
7452 N. Pt. Washington Rd.
Fox Point, WI 53217

Norwegian Forest Cat
Fancier's Association
2507 Ocean Drive South
Jacksonville Beach, FL 32250
http://users @ aol.com/
nfcfa/nfcfa.html

Ocicats International
8 Turnberry
Arden, NC 28704

Online Feline Fanciers
2407 South Vineyard
#B 150
Ontario, CA 91761
E-mail: 71620.1455@
compuserve.com

United Persian Fanciers
663 N. Dayton Lakeview Rd.
New Carlisle, OH 45344

Ragdoll Fanciers Club
7041 67th Street, NW
Gig Harbor, WA 98335

Rag Breeders United
446 Itasca Ct., NW
Rochester, MN 55901

Russian Blue Society
1602 Southbrook Dr.
Wadena, MN 56482

Scottish Fold Breed Club
49 Hancock St.
Salem, MA 01921

Siamese Cat Society of
America
304 SW 13th St.
Ft. Lauderdale, FL 33315

International Singapura
Alliance
P.O. Box 32218
Oakland, CA 94604

Snowshoe Cat Fanciers of
America
P.O. Box 121
Watkins, CO 80143

The Great Somali Society
238 Church St.
Poughkeepsie, NY 12601

Somali Cat Club of America
5027 Armstrong
Wichita, KS 67204

International Sphynx Breeders
and Fanciers Association
Rt. 1, Box 190
Benton, MS 39039

Tonkinese Breed Association
6427 Singing Creek La.
Spring, TX 77379

Tonkinese Breed Club
17 Ashwood Rd.
Trenton, NJ 08610

Tonk's West
9875 Gloucester Dr.
Beverly Hills, CA 90201

Turkish Van Club of North
America
1302 Exchange
Emporia, KS 66801

A Kitty Newsletter and Club from the Author

John Avalon Reed, author of *The Whole Kitty CATalog,* and his sidekicks Rollo and Bella publish a kitty newsletter. We review just-published books, share heartwarming cat stories, and review the latest cool stuff for cat owners and their furry companions. What's new? We'll tell you in each issue!

Your subscription to six issues of *What's New, KittyCAT!* gives you the following:

- **Wonderful cat stories**—Heartwarming, fascinating cat stories that explore the magic of our feline companions.

- **Reviews of new, cool stuff for cats** and the people who love them . . . all available to you as a subscriber, direct from the company.

- **Reviews of new cat books** for adults and children. Whimsical, practical books for you and your pet.

- **Savings on the best cat products, books, and services.** Toys, clothes, furniture, grooming supplies, gifts, gourmet cat food—many products reviewed are specially priced so you can buy them at a discount from the suggested retail price.

- Advice from our **Cat Shrink™**. Cat acting a little nuts? Behavior getting out of line? Cat driving *you* crazy? Practical tips on "cat parenting" from this country's one and only real **Cat Shrink™**. Expert advice from the best cat behaviorists: people who know and love cats.

Just the Best For a King or Queen!™

Good for You and Kitty!

There are many wonderful books, helpful services, and great goodies for your cat, and you. Your subscription brings everything to make your life with Kitty even better. We do the research and testing to find Just the Best™.

Yes! I'm a cat lover. I want to receive news and reviews on Just the Best™ for me and my cat. Please send me six issues of *What's New, KittyCAT!*

- ❏ 1 year, $25 (U.S.A. and Canada)   ❏ 1 year foreign, $50
- ❏ This is a gift for:

Name _____

Address _____ City _____

State _____ Zip _____

Your Name _____

Address _____ City _____

State _____ Zip _____ Daytime Telephone _____

Please make your check payable to *What's New, KittyCAT!* and mail it to P.O. Box 515, Mill Valley, CA 94942. © 1996 Providence Publishing